THE ETERNAL FEMININE

Henri de Lubac, S.J.

THE ETERNAL FEMININE

A Study on the Poem
by Teilhard de Chardin

followed by

TEILHARD AND THE PROBLEMS OF TODAY

Translated by
RENÉ HAGUE

COLLINS
ST JAMES'S PLACE, LONDON
1971

William Collins Sons & Co Ltd

London · Glasgow · Sydney · Auckland

Toronto · Johannesburg

152.4
L96e
86918
Feb. 1974

L'Éternel Féminin was first published in France
by Aubier-Montaigne, Paris, in 1968

© 1968 by Éditions Montaigne
English translation © 1971 by William Collins
Sons & Co Ltd, London, and
Harper & Row, Publishers Inc, New York

ISBN 0 00 215462 5

Set in Monotype Bembo

Made and Printed in Great Britain by
William Collins Sons & Co Ltd Glasgow

Contents

*

PART ONE

The Eternal Feminine

CONTENTS

PART TWO

Teilhard and the Problems of Today

THE ETERNAL FEMININE

*

'Igneus est illis vigor et caelestis origo'
(Motto of the Teilhard de Chardin family)

Preparation

*

I. 'IN HONOUR OF OUR LADY'

Hardly a month after finishing the first important essay of his
that we have, 'Cosmic Life',[1] we find Pierre Teilhard de
Chardin, then a corporal stretcher-bearer in the First Company, 4th Mixed Zouave and Light Infantry Regiment,
promising himself to get down to a study of a subject in which
he was deeply interested: virginity. At that time he was nearly
thirty years of age; he had been born on 1 May 1881, and had
been a Jesuit for nineteen years and a priest for seven. There is
an entry in his notebook, under the date 29 April 1916:[2]
'Virginity: an undoubted invasion of the cosmos by the
Revealed.' It is true, of course, that 'virginity is, in one aspect,
a natural efflorescence', but what Teilhard had more particularly
in mind was 'Christian virginity'. On 1 May, he decided to
undertake this study 'in honour of Our Lady'; and during the
following days, and again in June and July, his thoughts began
to take shape. He was trying in the first place to define the
cosmic nature of virginity: 'All the great and pure loves, love
of God, of speculative inquiry, of the cosmos, are they not
transformations of the fundamental, cosmic (=sexual) love,
which the individual diverts towards particular objects?' Thus
a 'liberation' or 'detachment' is effected, which he forthwith
generalizes in a bold hypothesis: 'It is perhaps in order to
detach itself as one whole in this way that mankind labours.
Since the time taken in coming to maturity is very long, the
phenomenon of virginity cannot affect all souls immediately'
(4 May).

On 8 May 1916 he sketched out a first plan. This was to include three dialectically linked 'visions': in a first vision 'the struggle against the flesh' would be seen as opposed to 'involvement in the flesh'. Conversely, a second vision would concentrate on 'the parasitism of spirit', in opposition to which stands 'fruitfulness, which is the justification of the individual's existence'. The third would be the vision of the Virgin Mother in whom the opposites are united. There 'the Feminine' would be seen in its supreme realization, in 'Our Lady'. On the next day, 9 May, he wrote:

What attracts me in this subject is the conjunction of a completely certain revealed fact (the excellence of virginity) with a human instinct (the sexual and maternal instinct) which is at one and the same time, (1) the most clearly recognizable evidence we have (experientially speaking) of the way in which individuals are dominated by a tremendous vital current, (2) the source, we might say, of our whole affective potential, and finally, (3) an energy which is eminently endowed with the power to develop itself, to enrich itself with countless ever more spiritualized refinements, and to direct itself to a great variety of objects, and particularly to God.

Is the 'touch of the helm' given by Our Lord to this profound instinct when he elevated virginity above motherhood – is it an indication that natural life has reached a final and permanent ceiling, so that henceforth continuation of the race yields precedence to refinement of individuals? Is it simply a new 'component' destined to exist side by side with the sexual instinct and designed, without in any way proscribing it, to correct it? Is it an essential task which natural life has still to accomplish? This is the question that worries me: a particular case of the opposition Kingdom of God/progress, detachment/conviction-based human work – but a particular typical case in which there is opposition

between extremely certain, vital and exact facts. – I pray
that Our Lady may keep me from going off the rails in a
matter which bears equally on two of her most eminent
prerogatives (of being Virgin and Mother). And she, I am
quite sure, is *the living solution of the problem.*[3]

A few further entries appear in the notebook, on 27 June,
24 and 30 July; but his thought was making no real progress.[4]
At the same time Pierre Teilhard was realizing that he could
form a correct view of virginity only by widening the problem
to include a treatment of the Feminine in general – in doing
which he was again to relate it to the Virgin Mary. Thus, on 2
September 1916, we read:[5]

> The true, pure, Feminine is pre-eminently a luminous and
> chaste Energy, compact of courage, ideality and goodness=
> the blessed Virgin Mary. Woman is, rightfully, the great
> source which radiates purity – that is the seemingly con-
> tradictory fact, insufficiently noted, which emerged with
> Christian Virginity. Purity is above all a feminine virtue,
> because it shines eminently in woman, it is most readily
> communicated by her, and has as its effect in some way to
> make feminine (in a most beautiful and mysterious sense of
> the word). Why is that so? . . . By what strange association
> of extremes? By what new application of the principle *vita ex
> morte*?

Here again, it will be noted, Pierre Teilhard's thoughts end
with a question. The inquiry he had been engaged on since the
end of April was making little progress, and it was to be some
time before it was completed. Nevertheless, there is more than
one indication that he did not lose sight of his target during the
intervening period. On 20 September of the same year, in his
'Mastery of the World and the Kingdom of God', he notes
incidentally that reason alone, once it has denied God, cannot
'impress on men the eminent value of virginity, nor convince

implies effort

productive: inventive. imaginativ...

them of the duty of fecundity', nor even find a basis for morality; and in consequence it cannot prevent man's auto- nomy from abandoning itself 'to enjoyment and the line of least effort'.[6] He keeps firmly in view an ideal of perfect purity. 'May Our Lord', he writes to Marguerite Teillard on 1 February 1917, 'make of each of us a purifying leaven . . .'[7] At about the same time (February–March), when engaged on 'The Struggle Against the Multitude', he wrote a couple of pages on purity considered side by side with charity as one of the chief Christian virtues: what the latter effects 'within the collectivity of souls' the former brings about 'within the individual being'; it cures the evil of dissociation at the deepest interior level: its 'specific act (what the scholastics would call its formal effect) is thus to unite the inner powers of the soul in the act of a single passion of extraordinary richness and intensity'. Like charity, it is founded upon renunciation and mortification. The pure soul 'tempers its unity . . . in the red-hot fires of God's simplicity'.[8] We find some similar features again in 'The Mystical Milieu' (June–August 1917),[9] and later in 'Creative Union' (October–November), which brings out 'the direction in which love should seek expression, and explains its too frequent lapses from grace', and once again emphasizes the 'two fundamental virtues' of Christian moral- ity, chastity and charity, of which the former 'unifies the monad in its own self', while the latter 'unifies the monads among one another'.

Earth

> Love . . . cannot and must not dispense with matter, any more than can the soul. Just as Spirit is never so enfranchised from matter as to be able to reject it, so every union of love must begin on the material basis of sensible confrontation and knowledge. It is a fundamental law of creative union that the fusion of spiritual apexes presupposes a coincidence of their bases.[10]

Particularly noteworthy is a letter dated 10 June 1917 which refers to the working out of 'The Eternal Feminine'. Pierre Teilhard writes to his cousin: 'In one issue [of *Études*], I saw that . . . there's a translation of Dante's *Vita Nuova* by Henry Cochin. Noticing this reminded me that one of the most interesting mystics to study from my point of view would, in fact, be Dante, so possessed by and passionately interested in the real. In any case I believe that there are few better examples than Beatrice to make one understand what is meant by the scaling-up (to the level of the universe) of the feeling nourished by a particular object (and of the object itself).'[11]

This last sentence is worth remembering. It has its exact counterpart – and written at exactly the same time – in 'The Circle of Presence', the first of the circles which (as in St Teresa's *Interior Castle*) make up the 'mystical milieu';[12] it is still an outer circle, the first of the doors that lead within.

> Through the sharp tips of the three arrows which had pierced me,[13] the world itself had invaded my being . . . And, under the glance that fell upon me, the shell in which my heart slumbered, burst open. With pure and generous love, a new energy penetrated into me – or emerged from me, which, I cannot say – that made me feel that I was as vast and as loaded with richness as the universe.
>
> Thus, while the pursuit of an essential fulfilment of our nature gathers us in upon ourselves, and forces us into the limitations and isolation of individuation, each one of our emotions, *the more it is aesthetic*, the more it tends to break up our autonomy. The Real incessantly reawakens us to an impassioned awareness of a wider expansion and an all-embracing unity.[14]

In such a passage there is an obvious personal allusion, as Mme Barthélemy-Madaule and M. André-A. Devaux have noticed. The encounter to which reference is made (already well in the past) – and which Père Teilhard himself recalled more openly – produced an emotional shock which is still

reflected in the vibrant style of the writing.[15] Nevertheless, it
neither 'diverted' nor 'dissipated' the energies of the young
priest,[16] who overcame the temptation of the flesh and of
self-centred introversion, to extract from his discovery a new
vision and a new ardour.[17] Or rather, he realized that it was
the Lord who effected this transformation in him:

> Lord, it is you who, through the imperceptible goadings of
> sense-beauty, penetrated my heart in order to make its life
> flow out into yourself. You came down into me by means of
> a tiny scrap of created reality; and then, suddenly, you
> unfurled your immensity before my eyes, and displayed
> yourself to me as Universal Being . . .
>
> Underlying the medley of inessential detail and surface
> charms, the Presence that spreads through all things is the
> only source that gives me light and the only air that I can
> ever breathe.[18]

Here we have no more than a starting-point, a first stage in
the process which culminates in mystical initiation; it is the
first of the experiences, the whole series of which does not
claim to represent anything more than 'an introduction to
mysticism'. The term of the process is indicated in a short
conclusion, the equivalent of which was later to reappear in
'The Eternal Feminine'. At the moment we are concerned
with tracking down the slow gestation of that poem. Two
passages in the Journal can help us here. Once again they
witness the continuity of Teilhard's thought.

First, there is a paragraph from the detailed scheme he drew
up on 10 November 1917 for his essay on 'Creative Union'.

> Love is consciousness of the need for unification – the
> intoxication of sexual encounter, for example, derives from
> the fact that the union effects a very special form of contact.
> We are tempted to look in increased physical contact for an
> increase in union and happiness. A mistake: matter repels

matter=disappointment, satiety, impotence. True contact,
love that unifies indefinitely=spiritual love. This is something we must really understand: that *spirit* is never so
released from the multitude which it synthesizes as to be able
to dispense with it. Every union must begin on the material
plane, from the multiple: but it must progress in the
direction of spirit, and to every higher degree of spiritualization there is a corresponding specific contact.[19]

This passage is interesting for two reasons. In the first place
it shows the close connexion between his line of thought on
'creative union' and what was soon to be the subject-matter of
'The Eternal Feminine'. We can already recognize the intimate
kinship of the two Teilhardian themes of creation and love:
'for union is the creation-process',[20] 'to create is to unite',[21] and
the more there is real union, within the being or between
beings, the more also there is differentiation: 'union differentiates', 'union personalizes'.[22] 'Love', Teilhard was to say in
1937, 'is only the concrete expression of this metaphysical
principle';[23] and again, on 13 March 1954: 'The problem of
love can be solved only by starting from a general theory of
being-through-union – of which it is in fact simply a direct
corollary.'[24] Starting at a certain level, 'union differentiates'
can therefore be translated as 'love personalizes'.[25] Secondly,
we can see in this passage from the Journal the unifying role
which Teilhard attributes to chastity in the moral formation
of the person. It is a role that, as we saw earlier, was noted in
'The Struggle Against the Multitude', and which is brought
out still more explicitly in 'Creative Union' itself. 'By fighting
against the powers in the being that cause it to disintegrate,
chastity maintains the elements of Spirit in their state of hard-
won coherence, and carries them farther.'[26]

Another entry in the Journal, dated 12 January 1918,[27]
foreshadows our poem even more closely:

I am occupied once again by my plan to write something

about chastity: it represents a concrete reality of the first value in life, suggestive, illuminating, critical; in connexion with chastity you meet the great problems of the Good, of progress,[28] of union. – Chastity is still treated in a completely irreflective and empirical way . . . It is the nature of love that should be clarified, its dangers, its function as a motive force – how one can use it without killing it – the road it opens to beatitude (=*unitive contact* with the world).

So we find Teilhard drawing up a number of 'possible plans' with the intention of studying 'love and evil – and the Good – and the better', 'love and initiation, power – and progress – and detachment (an extension of chastity=total chastity)', and contact with the universe, 'love's (cosmic) lessons', and finally, the 'breaks'. As in 1916, it is still an ambitious programme: chastity points to an orientation and an ideal, but what is envisaged is the whole problem of love in its cosmic dimensions. And in the event there was to be no narrowing of his aim.

Meanwhile the symbol of Beatrice, which had suggested itself to him six or seven months earlier, continued to be at work in Pierre Teilhard's subconscious. It was to prove a source of inspiration and serve as a catalyst for his thought, just as did a little earlier the symbol of the moon (to which we owe 'The Great Monad'), and, shortly afterwards, the symbol of Elias, which gave concrete expression to his views on 'The Spiritual Power of Matter'. 'The Eternal Feminine' was finished on 25 March 1918, at Verzy (Marne), a village not far from Rheims, and it bore an enigmatic dedication (the explanation of which we shall soon meet), 'To Béatrix'.

2. THE THREE WEEKS OF COMPOSITION

In spite of the preparatory reflection we have been tracing since April 1916, when Père Teilhard took the subject up again at the beginning of March 1918, neither the title, the plan, nor even the exact subject or literary form had been decided upon. For two long weeks, from the 2nd to the 18th March, he was feeling his way. A third week was then sufficient for the final draft of the poem in the form in which it can be read in *Writings in Time of War*.[29]

The beginning of the entry in the Journal, under the date of 2 March, echoes those of 1 May and 2 September 1916: 'I ought to write something about chastity, e.g.: "Before a Veiled Virgin".' It shows his continuing concern to treat such a subject – such a mystery, he calls it – as though under the compelling influence of the Virgin Mary. The form he first had in mind would appear to have been simply an essay, even though it could not fail to contain a certain element of the lyrical (which is constantly present in all these wartime writings).[30] The aim would be to bring out 'the mystery of chastity, its specific qualities, the problems it raises', and at the same time 'the dynamism of the Feminine, which chastity preserves and transposes'. The attempt at analysis is concentrated first on 'passion', this force which is 'disturbing' on more than one count. 'It seems to bring to the surface in us something of the Other (whose origination is outside our control); it seems to be an ungovernable force suddenly unleashed; we feel that it is dragging us down into the mud; and finally it unites, to produce a *tertium quid*': from this are derived the problems of progress in its relation to morality (can evil in some way be fruitful?),[31] of the individual in relation to the race, of freedom in relation to cosmic forces, etc. Should one fall back on a timorous virtue, or purify the dynamism of passion?[32] Is there not danger in plunging into the sources of life? Is it not the temptation of 'natural pantheism' which is notoriously 'the great danger of Art'?

On the very next day, 3 March, Pierre Teilhard notes that he cannot make up his mind between two subjects; the first is 'the puzzle of life (the problem of the appearance of life and its assumption of a moral character)'; the other, 'chastity, or the Feminine'. In fact, the new provisional plan he drew up combined the two. What he proposes to do is to consider chastity in its relation to the cosmos. On two occasions, we already find him using the expression 'the eternal Feminine'. On 4 March, he seems to have decided on 'the puzzle of life', which he intends to deal with in dialogue form, or rather in the form of a 'triple monologue': the scientist, the artist, and the believer will put forward their point of view, each in turn. We are to see how spirit is nurtured and released 'from among the crude and complex elements, the violent and undisciplined attractions', to be moulded into the image of God and by contact with him. Reference will be made to the 'harmony' which reigned 'in the Earthly Paradise'. And then once again we meet the mysterious allusion to the 'veiled virgin', 'virgin and yet woman', the living and perfect symbol of 'feminine dynamism'.

By 5 March his choice had been made: the whole poem was to centre on 'the Feminine', 'the absolute Feminine', 'the universal Feminine', 'the absolute feminine element', or 'the transcendental Feminine', and finally 'the eternal Feminine' – all expressions which in fact designate the same reality, but seen from different points of view, and from different situations, as yet imperfectly arranged in order of importance. By the last expression, 'the eternal Feminine', Teilhard means the eternal element, the element of union, of fecundation and spiritualization – ultimately of 'virginization' – which subsists throughout the various transformations of the feminine principle. This principle is 'a cosmic element of attractive force', but one which can operate in opposite directions. 'Enigmatic, attractive, maternal, purifying' – such are woman's characteristics, and they run through the whole universe. The attraction exercised by the Feminine properly so called, in its human incarnation, is the concentrated form (which at the same time is destined to spread itself more widely) of the attraction exercised by the cosmos.

The Christian, however, goes further. For him, the Feminine is not a neutral principle. Its perfection is realized in a personal being, and that being is the Virgin Mary. 'Without any doubt Our Lady has an essential role.' The idea had already appeared in 'Cosmic Life', in which Teilhard saluted 'the Pearl of the Cosmos, . . . the Blessed Virgin Mary, . . . the true Demeter'.[33] Now he notes that in order to determine Our Lady's role more exactly and to ensure that it shall not encroach on the sovereign role of Christ, he will have to examine in turn the relationship of the Virgin to Christ ('the Child held by the Virgin, *mulier amicta sole*'), Christ's relationship to the Church, and finally, within the Church, sacramental marriage and chastity, which is 'adherence to the pure feminine or spiritual'. The poem will accordingly be a meditation 'before the veiled Virgin; *Who* is she? *Where* is she leading us?'

The draft plan is still imprecise; but on the 7th the whole thing assumes a structure and settles down. The aim of the study will be 'to discover Our Lady's place in the cosmos'. If the Feminine is 'the attractive element of the cosmos', then 'it comes into flower (it is transformed) in the Virgin'. 'Christ appears to us through you, Mary.' It is from this point of view, accordingly, that he will have to consider chastity, whose function will henceforth be extended in a new way. 'In consequence, the only function of chastity would not now be, perhaps, to concentrate the individual mind upon itself, but to foster a special sort of union with things – one different from the union produced by charity . . . Charity=attraction refracted by the monads; chastity=direct cosmic attraction?' Teilhard is still, we can see, trying to pin down the idea, or rather the idea is trying to reach further afield – in a direction which, in spite of the very great difference of context and language, makes one think of Francis of Assisi.[34]

Nevertheless, the plan is becoming clearer: after the 'birth of the Feminine (the universal Feminine)' is to come the analysis of its 'attractive power', then that of its 'spiritualizing function: the eternal Feminine'. The whole will be preceded by a 'Prologue', devoted to 'the mystery of woman'.

The title of the projected prologue will be 'Before a Veiled Virgin: to Béatrix'. The meaning of the last two words is now self-evident. Béatrix is the veiled Virgin. She is not yet explicitly Our Lady, since the Virgin is still veiled, but she is already a symbol for her: Père Teilhard did not spell the name 'Beatrice', and this was undoubtedly by design: for he has not chosen, as Dante did, the love of a young girl. It is not, as in Dante's case, a particular person who is made into a symbol for Teilhard (or who, in her persisting reality, becomes equally a symbol);[35] whatever may have been the conflation of a personal memory with the Beatrice of *The Divine Comedy*, it is a universal principle – 'the Feminine' – which becomes the symbol of a concrete person, in whom it attains its highest realization.[36] Teilhard's reflections on 8 March, which complete those of the 7th, confirm this interpretation; Béatrix is 'the Feminine', and the Feminine is 'the Virgin', because the Virgin, 'who appears to destroy the Feminine, brings about its growth'. 'As a centre of congruence and unruffled power in the midst of the storm and the ungoverned currents', the Virgin solves the riddle of the universal Feminine, by answering the question: 'Is it the world or a person, is it matter or spirit, that speaks to us through Woman?'

The notes dated 9 and 10 March 1918 introduce a new element. We can see from them that if the subject makes so strong an appeal to Teilhard the reason lies in the approach of his final vows. He was to take advantage of his next leave for making his religious profession. This was to take place on 26 May at Sainte-Foy-lès-Lyon, in the chapel of the novitiate of his province. The study he was engaged on was a preparation for his vow of perpetual chastity.[37] 'Before my vows', he notes on 9 March; and the title he then had in mind was

'Before a Virgin, a Pre-vow Meditation'. Then, on the 10th,
we read: 'In order to obey you, Lord, I am about to pledge
myself to your virtue; but I wish to do so with my full consciousness as a man.' He then asks himself, 'Is the Feminine to
vanish entirely for me? . . . Is it not the Feminine that gives my
being its sensitivity and ardour?' He resolves 'to fight against
this feeling that the vow is a separation (=non-transformation)
– a restriction from the world (as though one cut oneself off
from a cosmic force and shut oneself up inside an impoverished
universe.' He is looking, accordingly, for a principle that 'will
introduce order into *his* nature, into the world and Christ'.
There is nothing abstract about this principle; he is still
meditating 'before the Virgin'. He hints at a parallel (though
he did not follow it up) between Eve and Mary. As to the
literary form, he now sees it as a 'dialogue with virginity' in
order to rediscover in virginity 'the universal axis'.

Two days later, Teilhard is again undecided; or rather he is
trying to widen the scope of his theme, to include an explanation not only of the vow of chastity but of all three of the
religious vows he is preparing to take. 'I am hesitating about
treating the Feminine by itself. It might perhaps be better to
try to deal with the whole matter in general terms, under the
title "Transformation" (in particular of wealth, woman,
freedom – blessed matter – zest for the cosmos – material,
dynamic consistence). – To show that the strength, the zest, of
every lower reality pass into God, in mysticism' (12 March).
There, indeed, he expresses one of the key categories of his
thought, to which we shall have to return later. And the idea
of the threefold transformation effected by the three vows will
soon reappear in a passage in 'The Priest' (8 July 1918). 'The
Priest' is part of the same pattern as 'The Eternal Feminine'. It
was written after his profession, and was an attempt to bring
out its meaning. Profession should consist in salvaging 'through
self-denial all the heavenly fire imprisoned within the threefold
concupiscence . . . to hallow, through chastity, poverty and

obedience, the power enclosed in love, in gold, and in in-dependence'.[38] The same idea was to come up again in the lectures Père Teilhard gave in 1930 to a university group meeting during the autumn at Chadefaud (Puy-de-Dôme) under the chairmanship of Marcel Légaut.[39]

However, during this same month, March 1918, he soon abandoned both so wide a plan and the dialogue form. By the 15th, he had returned to his original scheme and had finally decided on the title: 'The Eternal Feminine'. He proposed to treat the subject 'in the form of a very free paraphrase of the Book of Wisdom'. It was to consist of two parts, each corresponding to one of the two words of the title, and also to one half of the text he had taken from the Bible: '*Ab initio creata sum, et usque ad futurum saeculum non desinam*' – 'From the beginning was I created, and unto the world to come I shall not cease to be.' The quotation entailed the choice of a mono-logue form. As in the Book of Wisdom in Holy Scripture, it was to be the eternal Feminine who spoke, telling her story, describing her origin, her nature, the different forms in which she appeared, her permanence. First he would have to bring out how 'man is at a loss when faced by the Feminine', then 'the spiritualizing function (which makes itself manifest in virginity)', and finally 'the continuity of passion in virginity'. He would have to make it clear that beneath the diversity of its successive forms, the Feminine – the magnetic and unitive force – must lead to God, and that the supreme realization of the Feminine is none other than 'the transparition of Christ in the Virgin'.

The notes made that day are already a complete outline, with a strongly poetic tinge. And in the final transformation of what initially appeared solely as a principle of cosmic fecundity (that is, the unitive and magnetic aspect of beings), can finally be seen the countenance of the enigmatic Béatrix. 'I am the translucent medium between God and men. It is I who drew the Word down to earth, and it is I whose charm draws the

earth to me, that I may give it to God. In me – and not in the
flesh – are consummated the nuptials of world and Creator. I
am Mary the Virgin – the Church.' The governing idea, the
plan, the literary form, the spiritual context, the doctrinal
development, are now clear; and with the successsive stages
fixed, the conclusion up to which the whole leads is also clear.
'Gradually, the spiritualizing beam of my charm shifts – the
rainbow turns . . . It has almost emerged from the flesh –
where its most fully refracted rays fall, it still illuminates the
beauty of the arts and science . . . Gradually *haec omnia evacua-
buntur*. And ere long nothing will be left but "the Eternal
Feminine"=the unitive charm of the total Christ.'

On 17 March, in a series of reflections of a more technical
cast, his sole aim is to focus his thought more accurately:
'Man's fundamental error has been to deny mobility to the
Feminine . . . It is only by becoming the Virgin that the
Feminine avoids sterility and retains its intensity.' A detailed
new plan explains the phenomenon of 'the segregation[40] of the
Feminine', describing 'its growth and pursuit up to Omega'.
This is in fact the same plan as that drawn up two days earlier,
but it is fuller and more precise. It again includes the assertion,
at once twofold and simple, 'I am the Church, I am Mary the
Virgin', with the Scriptural quotation '*Mulier amicta sole*'. The
form is still a monologue. It ends with the words, more
explicit than in the earlier plan, 'If you are to attain me, you
must follow me into Christ. Arrived in Christ, I steal away, I
vanish=the logic of renunciation (of renouncing the inter-
mediate stages that have been left behind). – But even then,
invisible though I am, I am in some way living, the medium
quo)[41] through which unity is knit together, through which
magnetic power is concentrated=I, the Eternal Feminine.'

A few slight alterations were finally made to the plan on
18 March. Teilhard wished to explain more clearly how the
Feminine is 'doubly illuminated': in extension, in the Cosmos;
and in idealization, in Christ.[42] He was concerned also to

introduce the 'imbalance' brought in by sin, and to show that if man's driving force comes from the transformation of the sexual instinct, then to 'reject the transformation is to produce the worst (an inhuman) disorder'. Finally, 'the notion of fruitfulness' needed to be given more weight; virginity is fruitful. In virginity, in its 'Prototype', God reveals himself and shines through with ever greater clarity . . . God was drawn down by virginity, was born of the virgin; she is *amicta sole*. 'I am Mary the Virgin, the Church. (End on that.)'

After 18 March there are no further indications in the notebook of this exploratory preparation. The time had come for producing the final version. The numerous corrections in the manuscript affect only shades of meaning, changes in the wording and stylistic details. The poem was finished on 25 March, the feast of the Annunciation.

CHAPTER 2

The Poem of Love

*

I. SUMMARY OF THE POEM

As Wisdom speaks in Holy Scripture, so here it is Béatrix, the eternal Feminine, who speaks. In telling her story, she unfolds, as Claudel would say, 'the vast octave of creation'; for she, the first to issue from the hand of God, is the great hidden force by which everything exists and is made one, bears fruit, moves, is raised up, and is coordinated. We follow her through the different degrees of being, from atomic attraction to love of God, by way of the successive phases of human love. 'I am', she tells us, 'the magnetic force of the universal presence and the ceaseless ripple of its smile. I open the door to the whole heart of creation . . . He who takes me, gives himself to me, and is himself taken by the universe.' Here, however, we soon meet her ambivalence. There is a disturbing side to that universal force. Béatrix now speaks in theological terms and points out the temptation for man which lies in that force, followed by the Fall.

> In the knowledge of me, alas, there is both good and evil.
> Man's initiation has proved too strong meat for him.
> When he saw that I was for him the universe, he thought to encompass me in his arms. . . .
> At that very moment, I fell apart in his hands.
>
> For a long time man, lacking the skill to distinguish between the mirage and the truth, has not known whether he should fear me or worship me.

He loved me for the magic of my charm and my sovereign power; he feared me as a force alien to himself, and for the bewildering riddle I presented.

I was at once his strength and his weakness – his hope and his trial. It was in relation to me that the good were divided from the wicked.

Indeed, had Christ not come, man might well have placed me in the camp of evil.

The whole of the second part of the poem then consists in Béatrix's glorifying the wonder of Christ's work, who re-created her as virgin, more beautiful than in her first manifestation and to bear more exalted fruit.

Henceforth my name is Virginity.

The Virgin is still woman and mother: in that we may read the sign of the new age.

She celebrates, as we shall be noting again later, the transformation of love which she inspires; she sings of the 'tender compassion' and the 'hallowed charm' which, as she approaches, sets men 'ablaze'. Finally, she will disclose herself, in her perfected, exemplary form, both twofold and single:

I am the Church, the bride of Christ.

I am Mary the Virgin, mother of all human kind.

It is thus that, having issued from God and being co-extensive with the whole history of the cosmos and the whole adventure of man, she leads all God's creation back to him in a reversal of the movement. 'The centre of my attraction is imperceptibly shifting towards the pole upon which all the avenues of Spirit converge. . . . It is God who awaits you in me!'

As we shall shortly see more clearly, the poem has a very Platonic flavour, a very biblical cast; its teaching and its spirit are completely Christian. It has not been sufficiently realized, for example, that although the word is never used it contains the doctrine of original sin (considered from the particular angle suggested to the author by the choice of subject) and also that of the Redemption.[1] In this poem, Père Teilhard returns, taking up a slightly different point of view, to the themes he had treated in May 1917, in 'The Struggle Against the Multitude'. He shows how powerless man is to raise himself up by his own efforts:

> O men, . . . your fall accelerates at a terrifying speed – as fast as the widening of the gap between your real appetites and the ever lower forms in which you seek for me.
>
> And, when you, who are but dust, reach the term of your effort, it is but dust that you embrace.

At this point, however, the Redeemer intervenes, and we see that it is by him that everything begins again, or rather is made new. It is Teilhard's *felix culpa*.

> Christ has given me salvation and freedom. . . .
> He restored me to life, with Lazarus – with Magdalen – and set me between himself and men as a nimbus of glory . . .
> He . . . guided men, who had lost track of me, back to the true road I had trodden.
> In the regenerated world I am still, as I was at my birth, the summons to unity with the universe . . .
> My charm can still draw men, but towards the light. I can still carry them with me, but into freedom.[2]

One should not fail to note, again, the role attributed to the Virgin Mary of serving to draw down the Saviour: in this she exercises the fullness of the unitive function which is proper to the Feminine.

> Long before I drew you, I drew God towards me.
> Long before man had measured the extent of my power, and divined the polarity of my attraction, the Lord had

conceived me, whole and entire, in his wisdom, and I had
won his heart.

Without the lure of my purity, think you, would God
ever have come down, as flesh, to dwell in his creation?

Only love has the power to move being.

If God, then, was to be able to emerge from himself, he
had first to lay a pathway of desire before his feet, he had to
spread before him a sweet savour of beauty.

It was then that he caused me to rise up, a luminous mist
hanging over the abyss – between the earth and himself –
that, in me, he might dwell among you.

Now do you understand the secret of the emotion that
possesses you when I come near?

We can see, then, how Père Teilhard associates *eros* and *agape*
in his concept of divine love. At the same time this is a way of
professing the mystery of the Incarnation in its fullest sense.
Moreover, it is precisely what we shall find him saying again,
ten years later, in another form in *Le Milieu Divin*:

Have we ever thought of the meaning of the mystery of
the Annunciation? When the time had come when God had
resolved to realize His Incarnation before our eyes, He had
first of all to raise up in the world a virtue capable of drawing
Him as far as ourselves. He needed a mother who would
engender Him in the human sphere. What did He do? He
created the Virgin Mary, that is to say He called forth on
earth a purity so great that, within this transparency, He
would concentrate Himself to the point of appearing a little
child.[3]

Equally noteworthy, as the poem continues, is the association
we have already met of the Virgin Mary and the Church, an
association so close as to amount to a mystical identification:

Lying between God and the earth, as a zone of mutual

attractions, I draw them both together in a passionate union.

– until the meeting takes place in me, in which the generation and plenitude of Christ are consummated throughout the centuries.

I am the Church, the bride of Christ.

I am Mary the Virgin, mother of all human kind.

Generation and *plenitude:* these two words are chosen deliberately. The first envisages the corporeal body animated by the Word, born of the Virgin Mary; the second, his mystical body, born of the Church. Mary and the Church are each virgin and mother, and since there is but one Christ they are in some way identical in their maternal function. It is an astonishing passage to find written at that particular time. Does it echo what Pierre Teilhard was taught at Ore Place? The idea it expresses is by no means peripheral to dogma; it is, on the contrary, 'one of the major characteristics of the Catholic concept'.[4] It had been stressed by the Fathers of the Church, by Ambrose, for example, Augustine, Ephraim, and Cyril of Alexandria. It played an important part in the thought of the medieval West.[5] 'He whom the Virgin bore, is born again every day by the Church'; there is a 'perichoresis' (alternation) between the two, and if Mary, in giving birth to the One, is thereby mother of the Multitude, so the Church, in giving birth to a Multitude, is thereby in her turn mother of the Oneness.[6] Since that time, this grand concept has been obscured, so that in our own days it can be found only in a very few writers. And yet it is now fifty years since it was reasserted in our own time, and 'in a way as unexpected as brilliant'.[7] Claudel shares with Teilhard the responsibility for this renaissance. 'This woman', he writes, 'who is the Church'.[8] Monchanin finds matter for contemplation in that same concept. Gertrud von le Fort[9] and Edith Stein[10] have both adopted it. Hans Urs von Balthasar developed it more profoundly, and made it current in theological circles, so that it was soon to receive official approval in Vatican 2's Constitution *Lumen Gentium*.[11]

The above contains only a few brief indications. I do not wish at this point to comment in detail on a text which one would have to study almost line by line if one wished to appreciate all the shades of meaning it contains and follow all its many allusions. For the moment, we need do no more than give a summary of the poem's content and the line it develops. From the literary point of view, while it is not lacking in beauty, it seems less successful than 'The Great Monad' – less, too, than 'Nostalgia for the Front' – two pieces whose symbolism is derived from a more immediate concrete experience.[12] The free-verse or 'versicle' form adopted, which appeared in 'The Great Monad' and was soon to be used again in the 'Hymn to Matter',[13] makes one wonder whether it was inspired by Claudel's free handling of the verse form. The suggestion has been made, and it seems likely. In any case, whether it is an imitation or not, it lends itself excellently, as it does in Claudel, to the treatment of a subject in which emotion must be dominated by thought.[14] Teilhard, however, is less completely an artist, and when elucidation seems called for the versicle becomes a paragraph.

Lyrical though the piece is, it is also the work of a scholar, a man who not so long before, during his 'juniorate', had familiarized himself with the classics. A worthy rival of his brother Jesuits and fellow-students – men such as Pierre Rousselot and Joseph Huby, André Bremond and Victor Fontoynont – he had read Aeschylus in the original; when he makes the eternal Feminine say, 'I am the magnetic force of the universal presence and the ceaseless ripple of its smile', it is because he has in mind the line from the *Prometheus Vinctus* about 'the unnumbered laughter of the waves'.[15] The scholar is at the same time a Christian humanist,[16] who can, incidentally, give an answer in an obvious allusion to the Maurrasism derived from *Anthinéa*, which was very much a subject of discussion in Catholic circles in the years immediately before the war: 'The pagans on the Acropolis blame the Gospel for having disfigured the world, and they mourn for beauty. These men are blasphemers.'[17]

Rather than devote further space to literary analysis, it may be better to try to find out from what sources was drawn the thought expressed in the poem, and what were at any rate the most important of its antecedents. We may then consider in what way Père Teilhard developed the theme in his later writings.

2. SOURCES AND ANTECEDENTS

The theme of Père Teilhard's prose poem is one that has been treated by many other writers. It is love, regarded as the great cosmic force.

The first great writer to come to any reader's mind will be Plato. If we combine (with a certain latitude) what the not over-intelligent Eryximachus – 'a pedant and the ancestor of Diafoirus'[18] – says of love, that it is found 'among all living beings', with Aristophanes' myth of the hermaphrodite, and Socrates' final remark that he has been praising the 'all-powerful energy of love' – then we may well believe that in the *Symposium* there can be found some sort of pagan anticipation of our cosmic, evolutive and Christian poem. At the same time, we should note that the first remark holds good primarily in a medical context,[19] and that the emphasis is rather on the two kinds of love; and secondly that it is only by forcing the translation that Socrates' remarks can be made to have a Teilhardian ring.[20] Finally, there is the myth, at once 'burlesque and grand', which Plato attributes to Aristophanes. This, it is true, has some bearing in this connexion, but its significance is not exclusive,[21] and it is only a free interpretation of it that can be read into Teilhard. The association of the two would have a sounder basis, and indeed would be impossible to deny, were one to take into account some passages in the *Phaedrus*, where love is compared to a wholesome fire, melting the hard sheath which prevents the soul from spreading its wings. It becomes even more acceptable if we consider in the *Symposium* the elevating and spiritualizing process described in Diotima's discourse, as reported by Socrates. 'In Diotima of Mantinea, who certainly had no idea of evolution, the rise of love from level to level is a magnificent prefiguration, in non-evolutionist language, of the natural roots of Teilhardian love.'[22]

What is more, Teilhard himself recognized his debt to the *Symposium* on more than one occasion. As early as 1919, in a perhaps over-hasty generalization, we find him expressing his astonishment at the 'incredible' fact that not one of 'our authors' has taken up again Plato's work on love.[23] In several passages he later included the author of the *Phaedrus* and the *Symposium* among those who had inspired him and, when occasion arose, he even borrowed his vocabulary. In 1934, he wrote (in 'L'Évolution de la Chasteté', of which we shall have something to say later): 'Like any other animal, man is essentially a tension towards the completion that comes from union; he is a capacity for love. Plato noted this long ago. It is from this primordial urge that the rich complexity of intellectual and affective life develops, increases and diversifies. However high our spiritual boughs may rise and however wide their spread, their roots lie deep in the physical. It is from these reserves of passion in man that the warmth and light of his soul rise, transfigured. It is in these that there is initially concentrated for us, as in a seed, the essence, distilled to the finest point, of all spiritual development, the most sensitive of the forces that drive it.' In 1940 *The Phenomenon of Man* returns to Plato's theory: 'If there was no real internal propensity to unite, even at a prodigiously rudimentary level – indeed in the molecule itself – it would be physically impossible for love to appear higher up, with us, in "hominised" form. . . . Plato felt this and has immortalized the idea in his *Dialogues*.'[24] Again, in 1945, in 'Centrology', Teilhard tells us that what he has tried to do is to go beyond the attitudes of the psychologist and the moralist, and study love and its ubiquity 'following Plato's line'.[25]

There is, moreover, a Teilhardian form of Platonism which goes far beyond the theory of love. When one thinks of classical antiquity in connexion with Teilhard, it is rather the intellectual legacy of Aristotle, the natural scientist, which comes to mind – unless one goes back to some pre-Socratic 'physicist'. And this is certainly justified. We should not, however, forget the other complementary aspect of a system of thought which cannot be reduced to a single plane of development. It is here that the influence of Père Auguste Valensin, who was later to proclaim himself a 'Platonist philosopher', makes itself felt. Auguste Valensin was the first of those 'outstanding friends' whom Pierre Teilhard found close at hand to 'help me develop my thought'.[26] An ideology is current at the present time which sees in Platonism, in order to condemn it as the supreme aberration, nothing but an exaggerated dualism of body and soul, of matter and spirit – to which is sometimes added, of creator and creature – and there can be no doubt at all but that Teilhard's view of the world and of man is the complete opposite of that dualism. Teilhard tries to discover the 'genesis' and the 'rise of spirit'.[27] He tries to establish a structural relationship between spirit and matter.[28] He accordingly rejects the idea of 'two substances', of 'two heterogeneous . . . things' which are then 'coupled together by accident or force',[29] and 'unintelligibly associated in the living compound', of which the second (spirit) 'would by that very fact be reduced in [Teilhard's] eyes to no more than a shadow', whereas what he wishes to do is the exact opposite – to ensure 'the primacy', or 'pre-eminence', or 'sovereignty', or 'triumph' of spirit.[30] At the same time we can find in Teilhard a complete doctrine of the soul, in strictly logical association with his rejection of dualism, which some

rather biased commentators do not seem to have noticed.[31]
For Teilhard, the 'human sphere' is not only 'the sphere of
reflection, of conscious invention'; it is also 'the sphere of union
between souls'; he urges man to 'find his soul'; in the human
soul he sees 'the first permanent handhold to which the
Multiple can cling as creation raises it up towards unity'. The
world Teilhard loves – and in the light of which he loves the
present world – is essentially 'a world of souls'; for, while the
ephemeral materials from which bodies are made have 'only an
apparent solidity', souls alone are destined to endure. Moreover, 'the true evolution of the world takes place in souls and
in their union'.[32] The mystical body is constructed by integrat-
ing souls into itself.[33] Teilhard's Platonism became gradually
less evident in his vocabulary as he developed his own terminology. It underwent considerable modifications, but it remained
essentially intact.

It is impossible, for example, not to think of Plato when we
read such a sentence as this in *The Phenomenon of Man*: 'Whether
as a force or a curvature, the universal gravity of bodies, so
striking to us, is merely the reverse or shadow of that which
really moves nature',[34] or this, from 'L'Évolution de la
Chasteté': '*The depths we attribute to matter are no more than the
reflection of the heights of spirit.*'[35] When he is dealing with
problems that are expressed in new terms, we can still clearly
recognize the line of thought which is not unjustly known as
'perennial Platonism'. In spite of extremely radical changes,
every age witnesses its revival: and we see this in Teilhard, as
we do, for example, in the twelfth-century Rupert of Deutz
when the latter writes: 'All that Scripture tells us of the love of
God or of God manifesting his love, is incontestably so real and
so unchanging that in fact our physical realities, from which
we draw our metaphors, are themselves no more than shadows
and fugitive images of the eternal truth.'[36] The essay, again, on
'The Spiritual Power of Matter' is undoubtedly a reflection,
Christianized and 'Teilhardized', it is true (for 'the Christian is

more demanding than Plato'),[37] but still recognizable, of the
discourse reported by Socrates and of the conclusion of his
argument, when he eulogizes 'love of that unique, boundless
Essence which penetrates the inmost depths of all things and
there, from within those depths, deeper than the mortal zone
where individuals and multitudes struggle, works upon them
and moulds them'. The 'Hymn to Matter' itself (whose title has
misled some potential readers) evokes our human aspiration to
'come little by little to feel that the individual shapes of all we
have laid hold on are melting away in our hands, until finally
we are at grips with the *single essence* of all subsistencies and all
unions'.[38] The fiery chariot that bears man aloft is the same sort
of symbol, though more violent, as Diotima's mystical ladder.
When Teilhard came to quote, just as they occurred to him,
the names of a number of great men, the natural vigour of
whose work had stimulated the most supernatural interior
lives, the first he wrote down of those 'any one of us could name
in his heart' was Plato.[39] We find him in Peking, in January
1943, rereading the *Timaeus* with great delight; he found it was
wonderful, he said, that after two thousand four hundred
years Plato should still be so fresh an inspiration to us.[40] What
are our theologians waiting for, he asked, echoing once again
the spirit of the Fathers of the Church, to transpose, through
the medium of Christ, Plato's sense of the harmony of the
cosmos?[41]

In short, Teilhard is of great importance to anyone who
wishes to follow up until our own day the long and varied
story of Christian Platonism. At the same time it should be
noted that if Plato saw in love a 'road of beauty leading up to
God', Teilhard saw in the Virgin, the mother of fairest love, 'a
road of desire, a fragrance of beauty', which enables God to
make his way down to man.[42]

Reading 'The Eternal Feminine' reminds one also of Boethius,
when he speaks of love as the universal bond and the principle
of all harmony:

Hanc rerum seriem ligat
Terras et pelagus regens
Et coelo imperitans Amor.[43]

One thinks also of Nicolas of Cusa (d. 1464), whom Teilhard quotes side by side with Plato, pointing out that with him medieval philosophy 'returned technically to the same notion'.[44] Another writer who comes to mind is Marsiglio of Padua, who makes love 'the beginning and the end of all the forces which ensure the order of the world and inspire all creative activity'; there are Marsiglio's disciples, too, such as Leo the Hebrew, whose *Dialoghi d'Amore* base the unity of the universe on love,[45] or the Franciscan Francesco Zorgi, whose *Harmonia Mundi* describes the '*circulus amorosus*' which holds together all living beings.[46]

Teilhard, as we know, refers from time to time to Renaissance scholars; as early as 1916 he had noted their 'irresistible passion for nature, new-found and loved to distraction'.[47] Later, he was to praise the Florentine Platonists for the organic character of their concepts, and one could point to more than one example of correspondence between his own thought and that of Marsiglio Ficino – even though Ficino's Platonist teaching on love has few cosmic echoes, and his '*ars naturalis*' or '*artificiosa natura*' is a principle of movement rather than of union and is not related to love.[48] We should be careful not to omit from the list of Teilhard's great precursors the name of René Descartes, who once wrote: 'There is a single active force in things, love, charity, harmony.'[49] Newton, too, should be included, who thought that forces 'of inordinate strength were required to hold atoms together' and set matter in motion, and could never conceive their existence without a feeling of 'mystery and awe'.[50]

Going further back than Plato himself, we may well think of the earlier philosopher, Empedocles, to whom Plato, too, was undoubtedly indebted. Empedocles, we know, held that the

universe resulted from the union of the four elements, which
were brought together by the great cosmic force to which
he gave the name of love – while the antagonistic force of
hate worked to separate them and reduce the universe to
nothingness. Above all, however, our minds turn to the
two great poets from whom Teilhard visibly borrows, Dante
and Goethe.

Even if Teilhard read the second part of *Faust*, it is doubtful
whether he owes any other precise debt to Goethe, beyond the
actual phrase 'the eternal Feminine', which has become common property. There are, however, two remarkable coinci-
dences. At the very end of his 'symbolic and cosmic' poem[51]
Goethe attributes to the eternal Feminine some part at least of
the role which Teilhard was to attribute to her. His *chorus
mysticus* sings, 'The eternal Feminine draws us aloft'.[52] And for
Goethe, too, this principle is incarnate in a personal being, the
Virgin Mary: the star-crowned virgin, Queen of Heaven, as
represented in Titian's *Assumption*.[53] Goethe, however, has no
idea of ascribing a universal cosmic function to his eternal
Feminine; moreover, being more concerned as a poet to find a
concrete expression of his thought than to conform to some
rule of faith, the true nature of the Virgin could not be
presented by Goethe as it was by Teilhard.

Teilhard had at least some slight knowledge of Dante. He
must have sympathized with the Florentine who was not
afraid of fighting, but whose ideal was unity, and who declared,
when cities and factions were at one another's throats all around
him: 'The world is my country, just as the sea is to the fish.'[54]
He must certainly have heard his friend Auguste Valensin speak
with enthusiasm about Dante when they were novices
together.[55] It is perhaps worth noting, too, that Pierre
Charles, who was the third of that trio, was soon to publish an
article on Dante and mysticism. In this we read that there is a
desire which 'raises up the world, unconscious of its destiny,
towards the universal term, the omega of all reality'.[56] We

mentioned earlier that Teilhard's attention had been drawn again to Dante by a passage in *Études*, in June 1917. He must have been familiar with the well-known lines on love which 'moves sun and stars'.[57] It was from Dante that he borrowed the name Beatrice – though, for the reason we gave, he changed it to Béatrix. This would appear to be all he borrowed, though he may perhaps have remembered the veil which still covers the face of Dante's beloved when he sees her emerging from her *'divina basterna'* like the rising sun, and knows her by 'the hidden virtue which went out from her':[58] thus Teilhard completes the transposition and uses the symbol of Béatrix to stand for the 'veiled virgin'.

Further examples can be found of such parallels between Dante and Teilhard. For Dante, love is the root of all good, as it is of all evil. In *The Divine Comedy* 'love is realized only when it is exteriorized and is widened to the dimensions of the universe'. This love, which is indivisibly both *eros* and *agape*, or which must be conceived as transcending the opposition between the two, is in principle God himself, the most real of beings. Similarly, for Dante Beatrice is not an allegory but a completely personal reality.[59] Without ceasing to be herself,[60] she is transformed, once in heaven, into a symbol or rather 'into an incarnation of the loving Church'; she is 'part of eternal wisdom, and because one cannot with truth speak of part where all compenetrates all, she is that wisdom itself'. The eternal Feminine which she represents 'passes through all the degrees of the real without any loss of continuity' and culminates in 'Mary, the archetype and foundation of the receptive and virginally fruitful Church'. Every one of these characteristics, which are well brought out in Hans Urs von Balthasar's analysis of *The Divine Comedy*, will be found again, *mutatis mutandis*,[61] in the short philosophico-religious poem we are studying. Following Père Auguste Valensin, we should emphasize the last of those characteristics: 'In a certain sense the Virgin Mary may be called the protagonist of *The Divine*

Comedy'[62] – as, even more truly, she is in 'The Eternal Feminine'.

There is, however, an earlier work which both in date and in its astonishing similarities is closer than any other to Teilhard's poem. This is Vladimir Solovyev's (1853–1900) *The Meaning of Love*. And yet, Père Teilhard cannot have read it, because although it was published in 1894 it was not translated into French until 1946. He could have read, either in Hastings during his theological studies, or later in Paris, the little book which Père Michel d'Herbigny brought out in 1911, *Un Newman russe, Vladimir Soloviev*; but in that he would not have found any exact information about the 'eternal Feminine' into which the Russian philosopher condenses his theory. Solovyev had studied science; he was a great admirer of Darwin, and he had been thought of as an obvious candidate for a chair in palaeontology. That, however, is not the really important factor in his kinship with Teilhard. What mattered more was that, in spite of differences of temperament and circumstances, they both went through a similar experience which had a great influence on the development of their thought. We quoted earlier[63] the passage from 'The Mystical Milieu' in which Teilhard refers to what was then a comparatively recent event; Solovyev's account was written later and perhaps with some eye to literary effect. For Teilhard, the experience was a deepening of spiritual awareness in an immediate renunciation; for Solovyev, it was the beginning of a conversion and a return to faith. But there was equally for both of them a sudden revelation of the universal in, or rather through, what each is at pains to call not woman but the Feminine. Solovyev was saved by a young woman just as he fainted and was about to fall under a train. He felt, he tells us, that a wondrous event was taking place in him; with an impact that was 'infinitely soothing, illuminating and peaceful, a wonderful image was reflected, motionless, as though in a mirror'; the girl was 'transfigured' – 'and I knew that in that single image all things were contained; I loved with a new love which was infinite and all-embracing, and in that I felt for the first time the whole fullness and meaning of life'.[64] Later, in *The Meaning of Love*, he explained that 'the heavenly object of our love is only one', it is 'the eternal Femininity'; each individual form is trans-figured into 'the ray inseparable from its resplendent source "the eternal divine femininity"', for 'in the transcendent sphere . . . i.e. in truth, the individual person is only a living, and actual yet indivisible ray, of the one ideal light'.[65]

It is beyond our immediate purpose to examine Solovyev's theory more fully. Both in content and spiritual atmosphere it differs widely from Teilhard's. At the same time a number of characteristics are practically identical in both writers. Solovyev anticipated Teilhard in noting that 'love . . . is . . . an extra-ordinarily complex affair, obscure and intricate, demanding fully conscious discrimination and investigation', and yet the problem has never been raised in a completely precise and conscious way.[66] For Solovyev, love was eminently sexual love, an image of God's love for his Church. By that, however, he did not mean 'physiological union', which, he thought, has no exact relationship to love. He had in mind a cosmic reality, a principle of union the main lines of whose evolution he traced. Seeing, as Teilhard did, that mankind's historical progress takes over from a continuous cosmogonical pro-gress which substitutes for man a super-man, he shared at the same time Teilhard's realization that within our species there can be seen a progressive invention of 'hitherto unknown forms of existence', and that these are due above all to love's advance towards its perfection. As an ideal for the future he accordingly put forward a chaste love, as far removed from sterile emotionalism as it is from carnal appetite; through this man would become open to all his fellow-men and to the whole universe, and so his primitive integrity would be restored, history would reach its term, and death would be conquered.[67]

CHAPTER 3

Sequel to 'The Eternal Feminine'

*

I. TEACHING ON LOVE AND MARRIAGE

From a starting-point in Goethe's phrase and the allegory in Proverbs, Teilhard, like a musician who borrows a theme and develops it in a succession of variations, moved on to an exposition of how he envisaged the role of love in creation.[1] He was drawing, it is true, on his own experience, and taking that special case to bring together in a vital synthesis the view he had for some years found himself obliged to accept, of universal evolution and the central mystery of his faith as a Christian; but at the same time he realized that he was taking up again an idea that was common to many of the 'great philosophers'. He was himself later to rely on the authority not only of 'Plato, the poet' and Nicolas of Cusa (as we have just seen) but also on that of 'representatives of frigid scholasticism', to justify his assertion that 'in its most general form, and from the point of view of physics, love is the internal, affectively apprehended, aspect of the affinity which links and draws together the elements of the world, centre to centre'.[2]

In line with what was his constant aim in every undertaking, Teilhard tries accordingly to breathe new life into this great traditional theme. To do so seems to him all the more important, and indeed more urgent, in that the question of love is the most central of all and has been, he thinks, too much neglected by our theologians.

Love ($\xi\rho\omega s$) lies at the bottom of all that is of concern to man; it is his salvation or his loss, the very stuff, maybe, of which all our great desires are made. Is it not incredible that in all the many centuries in which our writers have been criticizing it and seeking to restrain it, not one . . . has asked himself where that passion comes from and where it is going, what share of evil it contains, and what there is, on the contrary, in its power which should be diligently fostered so that it may be transformed into love of God?[3]

In order to go more deeply into this subject by including it in the whole scheme of his thought, he proceeded to transpose it into the context of evolution. Thus love came to occupy a central position in his thought, just as it lies at the heart of the real:

We may try to reconstruct the history of the world from outside by observing the play of atomic, molecular, or cellular combinations in their various processes. We may attempt, still more efficaciously, this same task from within by following the progress made by conscious spontaneity and noting the successive stages achieved. The most telling and profound way of describing the evolution of the universe would undoubtedly be to trace the evolution of love.[4]

There are a number of great essays belonging to Teilhard's maturity: 'The Spirit of the Earth', 'Sketch of a Personalistic Universe', 'Human Energy', 'Centrology'; in all of these and again in *The Phenomenon of Man*, Père Teilhard devotes a section to this 'strange energy', 'the most universal, most formidable and most mysterious' of all energies. Social institutions hem it in and canalize it; moralists endeavour to regulate it, and in public life a pretence is made of not seeing it. It is an 'untamed force' but at the same time 'a sacred reserve' which is allowed to run distressingly to waste. It is 'the very life-blood of spiritual evolution'. In Teilhard's universe, in fact, which is a universe of centro-complex structure, 'love is essentially nothing other than the energy proper to cosmo-genesis'.[5] Nothing is more essential than a study of love, with a view to guiding it, if possible, and drawing the utmost advantage from it.

Initially, in its most primitive and rudimentary forms, love can hardly be distinguished – or the observer has at least great difficulty in distinguishing it – from molecular forces. Is it not already love 'that is adumbrated and grows as a result of the mutual affinity which causes the particles to adhere to one another and maintains their unity during their convergent advance'?[6] Gradually love emerges. For a long time still, however, it will remain *confused* with the reproductive function'. Starting with man, we shall be able to define love as precisely 'the attraction exerted on each conscious element by the centre which is in formation in the cosmos'. We find then that woman stands before man as 'the lure and symbol of the world'. 'It is fact, that through woman the universe advances towards man.' And Teilhard goes on to say that 'the whole question is that they shall recognize one another'. If they do not, it is an impossible quest, and we shall end with a 'confusion . . . vast and irremediable'. 'The earth is continually dissipating its most marvellous power' in 'pure loss'.[7]

The whole of Teilhard's work can be understood as an effort fundamentally to grasp this manifold reality of love, to trace its history and bring out its value. He is concerned to show us not only its various phases but, even more, its original source to which it is destined to return; for 'it is a love which physically builds up the universe', and in its 'higher and purified form' this 'universal interior attraction' is destined to rejoin that first love. From that beginning the essential energy of the world radiates, and to it it finally and permanently flows back.[8] 'Omega, the sole object of desire'.[9]

In the preceding chapter we saw that a whole line of thinkers had attributed to love the role of a cosmic principle. Similarly, we may now note that another thinker had sought, as Teilhard was to seek, to explain by the action of one single principle all the successive forms to appear in the course of evolution. In this case, however, the principle was completely different. Nietzsche 'defined the atom as a quantity of will to power'; he saw that will to power 'at work in the inorganic, to become still more explicit in the animal kingdom and above all in the world of man (in the form of knowledge, moral science, art, politics and, indeed, religion)'. Beneath each of these various manifestations of life is to be found, he thought, 'one and the same essence, a sort of metaphysical nisus or pressure, which is what constitutes the real; it is not, as is vulgarly believed, and as "the wretched consumptive" Spinoza asserts, an instinct to conserve, but the very opposite, a demand for, and a drive to, transcendence.'[10] Teilhard would agree with Nietzsche in accepting that last phrase. Neither of them, confronted by the rising and irrepressible dynamism of the universe, is content with a 'vulgar', static explanation. However, the extent to which they diverge is soon apparent. Teilhard's realism retains in biology the rigid laws which Nietzsche hypostasizes and magnifies under the name 'will to power'; but the 'drive to transcendence', the ascending and unitive force, as conceived by Teilhard, has characteristics which are the reverse of those found in Nietzsche's principle. It is not surprising that with such a principle as his starting-point Nietzsche violently rejected the Cross, in the Christian interpretation, as the symbol and 'sublimation of impotence', while Teilhard sees in it the 'sublimation of the law that governs all life' and 'the force that elevates the world'.[11]

Further, Teilhard points out that it is 'particularly easy' to find an essential place, as we must, for a phenomenon so fundamental as sexuality in a 'system based', as is his own, 'on union'.[12] On a number of occasions he speaks of human love, the union of man and woman, in terms which are sadly missing from the writings of many more recent theorists, even Christian. He has a lively awareness of Christianity's irreplaceable contribution in this connexion: 'Never', he noted one day as he came away from a conversation with some friends about marriage, 'never had I seen so clearly how true it is that Christian morality is a mountain peak that has been taken, but which very few, by and large, can succeed in holding, and whose possession by mankind calls for a continual battle.[13] He sharply criticized the thesis that 'the fusion of love and marriage is impossible'. He points out that so far as sex is concerned, 'the theory of marriage, which used to be centred on the duty of procreation, is now tending to lay more emphasis on a mutual spiritual fulfilment of husband and wife'.[14] He approves of this development and sees it as a progress; but at the same time he is not blind to the abuses that spring from a possible interpretation of it. Not content with rejecting an unenlightened 'doublehanded self-centredness', he denounces as a 'dangerous illusion, going further than the sensually satisfying temptation of absorption and quiescence', that form of idolatry which keeps itself fresh by trying to find a substitute for the Godhead in the loved being – the idolatry which, in order to glorify lover-and-loved, decks itself out with all the charms that can be drawn from spiritual refinements and analytical subtleties.[15] When lovers 'try to confine the promise the future holds to their discovery of one another' and are thereby in danger of being ensnared 'by the intoxication of bringing a world to plenitude in their own two selves', he reminds them that the law of love, of all love, is to open one's embrace to 'world-wide dimensions'.[16] He shows them, again, that another presence must be 'received at the very centre of the circle in which they sought to isolate their union'.[17]

'Without coming out of itself, the pair will find its equilibrium only in a third being ahead of it' – nor is it only the child Teilhard has in mind. The mysterious 'intruder' who must appear to husband and wife in order to consolidate their union and make it fruitful, is the 'final term' and 'total centre' which will save and fulfil not only their race but their personality. The fact is that the whole effort of life is directed to making it possible to attain the higher form of being which is found in person, and person cannot be realized except in God. Human love, therefore, must be understood as being 'a three-term function: man, woman and God'.[18]

We find a number of occasional later references to the same subject: in 'The Rise of the Other', for example (1942). There he defines love as a twofold force: it is the 'power of producing inter-centric relationship . . . the expression and the agent of universal synthesis', and at the same time it is 'centric power'. 'Like a light whose spectrum is continually being enriched by new, more brilliant and warmer lines, it constantly varies with the perfection of the centres from which it emanates.' The extreme power to love found in man is a consequence of his perfect 'centricity'. Again, in so far as man shows that he is capable of using this power properly, he is 'the most magnificently synthesizable of all the elements ever constructed by nature'.[19] Later, in 1950, *Le Cœur de la Matière* speaks of the real symbol of the heart of Jesus, from which emerges a fire that 'can penetrate all things and gradually spreads universally'. In this symbol Père Teilhard asks us to see the *total amorization* of the universe by Christ. The majority of the passages already quoted urge us to an ascending progression, so that we may see love emerging and becoming interiorized from a starting-point in the most elementary phenomena. There is now a reversal in the point of view: all the earlier stages are simultaneously gathered up in the definitive reality that is intuitively glimpsed. 'After having appeared to be no more initially than the charm or the appeal, and then the operative essence, of all spiritual activity, love tends gradually, as we experience it, to become the main part of that activity – and finally its unique and supreme form. – *Sola caritas*.'[20]

On three occasions, in 1928, 1935, and 1948, Père Teilhard was called on to deliver a wedding address.[21] In all three he took the opportunity of expounding the teaching he was working out in his personal notes and which he was anxious to keep completely in line with Catholic doctrine. In that context he succeeded admirably in presenting his views in an easily assimilated form and with warmth, and without either over-popularizing them or detracting from their vigour.

Even then he could not refrain from going right back to the very beginning in order to bring out the whole history of love. He was at pains explicitly to attach human love – the love of the man and the woman whose permanent union he is witnessing – to something beyond 'the essential basis of every living being, which is its power to love' – and to the prime force which 'constitutes the consistence of our universe', that is to say 'the flame of organization which from the very beginning has run through the world and grown stronger in it'. It is in an appeal to 'the incessantly progressive nature of life' and, more radically still, to 'the very structure of the world' and its 'unbreakable law', that he shows the bride and bridegroom what the structure of their own union must be. He warns them against the great 'temptation of love', which is 'quiescence in possession'; there is nothing, he explains, more sterile than 'an affection closed-in on itself'.[22] It stifles body and soul. Teilhard knows the illusion which seeks to entrap them: for, 'because of the fulfilment it brings, union can appear as a term'. At the same time he warns them: 'You will never be happy . . . unless your two lives come together and bear fruit of one another, launching themselves boldly into the future, in a passionate desire for one greater than yourselves.' He is not afraid to remind the two he is about to bless in the light of their physical union, that ultimately, if it is true that 'the world bears with all its weight on a centre lying ahead of it', it is only 'unions between souls that progress infallibly, and they alone are destined to endure'. You must have faith, then, he tells them, not only 'in the spirit that lies behind you' and 'in the spirit that lies ahead of you', but also – 'and this word sums up all the others – in the spirit that exists *between* you. You are

given to one another as a limitless field for mutual understanding, enrichment and sensitizing. It is above all in a constant penetration and exchange of thoughts, affections, dreams,
and of prayer, that you will come together. There alone, as you
know, in spirit through flesh, there is no satiety, no disappointment, no limit. There alone can your love find air to breathe
freely, and the great gate to the road ahead.'

The conclusion of the address Teilhard gave on 21 December
1948 sums up with supreme clarity the essence of his teaching:

> Between you two there can be no worthwhile union
> unless it be in some higher centre which brings you together.
> I pray that soon this centre may be the child – that, whatever
> happens, this centre may be the excitement and joy of
> discovering and completing one another ever more fully, in
> heart and mind. And above all I pray that in one way or
> another (depending on what is your own individual way),
> this centre may be the God before whom and in whom you
> are going, in one moment, to combine your two lives:
> God, the only definitive centre of existence – not the distant
> God of convention, but God as he must, and as it is his will
> to, manifest himself incommunicably to you, if only you
> obey to the very end the inner force which is at this moment
> working to bring you together.

This brief 'theology' of marriage will appear doubly
remarkable, at a time when even within the Church we sometimes meet the claim to exclude all consideration of God from
the ideal that is offered to human love.

2. 'THE EVOLUTION OF CHASTITY'

Père Teilhard returns to this fundamental theme in an essay
written in 1934 under the title 'The Evolution of Chastity'.
He treats it on the basis of the same principles, but within
narrower limits and, as the title indicates, from a more parti-

cular point of view. On this occasion he had in mind a 'strictly confidential memorandum'. Some months after finishing it he sent it from Tientsin, where he was making his annual retreat, to a number of intimate friends.[23] He was afraid, he told them, that it might be 'misunderstood'. At the same time, he had written it 'without any mental reservation'.[24] 'It's an absolutely honest and disinterested attempt to get to the bottom of a question that seems to me terribly vital and terribly obscure. I have gathered together the most fundamental evidence I've ever been able to find in face of *questions and challenges* that were anything but abstract, so as to build up "the defence" and above all so as to define the value or essence "of chastity".'[25] What he wanted to do, he said also, was 'to defend with all his strength the Church's traditional position in relation to this subject', while at the same time realizing that his explanations and justifications might appear weak or too personal to some.

In the first place he finds that he must accept two facts. On the one hand, 'ever since religions have existed, they have always tended to express themselves, in their highest manifestations, in the form of chastity'. Victory over sexual attraction has been seen by them as 'the supreme expression of the triumph of spirit'.[26] There is, in fact, a deep-seated instinct, a higher echo of 'life's infallible instincts', which suggests to man that at the root of chastity there lies 'something much more valuable than a mere self-mastery': a mysterious, hidden force which can justifiably ensure him a 'certain pre-eminence'. The Church, as the messenger and guardian of the Gospel, has taken over this human instinct; she has purified it, preserved it and given it deeper significance. At this moment it is the Church which is the 'firmest defence of chastity and its richest storehouse'. On the other hand, however, man is essentially 'capacity to love'; he is 'tension towards completion in union', and it is 'from this primordial impulse that the luxuriant complexity of intellectual and affective life develops, rises to higher levels and is diversified'.[27] The problem, then, will be how to combine these two basic assertions without weakening either. Like everything that touches on those areas of being which lie far below the surface, the mystery of chastity will always remain difficult to elucidate. At the same time, we must endeavour to do so, for the Church's teaching on the subject is still largely empirical in nature. A living tradition brings it to us, but this does not dispense us from reflecting upon it, so that we may assimilate it to our own selves. Moreover, 'the empirical character of the Church's teaching is in no way . . . a mark of biological inferiority. On the contrary – the more widely a reality appears to be based on a development and an achievement whose nature is experiential, the greater the probability of its being valuable and definitive. *Provided*, however, *that we try to intellectualize it.*'

In this we see Teilhard's habitual way of approaching a problem. His personal explanations, even those that may be regarded as the most daring, always try (though not always with complete success, one may think) to get back to the practical attitude of 'simple faith' – which he is careful, however, not to exaggerate. We find a similar example of this in another aspect of his teaching on love. 'I spoke of a love', he wrote two years later, 'stronger than sexual attraction, of a love which would embrace the whole earth, of a love which would find the heart of the universe. It might seem that I was speculating on a utopia. But all I was doing in reality was to develop the potentialities contained in the factual reality of Christianity. In the actual simplicity of his worship, the believer perceives and performs all that I seemed to be dreaming of.'[28]

Here, then, Père Teilhard is concerned with an attempt to go beyond the 'ill-assorted reasons' and 'outworn systems' that are often regarded as sufficient, and to develop a line of thought that can answer the doubts of many 'lofty and sincere minds which see nothing morally admirable in the restrictions of asceticism'. It is this that gives his memorandum its twofold aim and orientation: he addresses himself first to theologians, in order to criticize some of their theories or rules of conduct, and then turns back to people who stand outside the Church, in order to justify to them, by what he hopes will be more convincing arguments, the esteem in which virginity is held.

In practice, the theologians make Christian chastity 'a religious transposition of the lover's constancy'. The heart which gives itself to God must not be shared. From this arises the constantly restrictive and negative character of their practical solutions. These are not, indeed, very convincing. It is certainly true that 'our affective potential is a delicate organism whose reserves we too often waste by loving ill'. But does it follow inevitably that the human heart becomes less for one person when it embraces the other 'in another relationship or in a way that recognizes degrees of love'? Even if there can be only one sun in our interior heaven, why can there not also be subordinate stars? Moreover we must not forget that God is not a person 'of the same order' as ourselves; he is 'more profound than we are'; that is why all human love 'is not included in the Apostle's reproach of "producing division"'; it is even permissible to think that God might be better loved through a particular human love:[29] but does it follow that, as some would have us do, we have simply to dissociate 'spiritual virtue' and 'physical chastity'? Should one even listen to those for whom physical union opens the road into a higher life, on the ground that it introduces man into a more profound universe? By no means. It is true, indeed, that like poverty and all the 'evangelical' virtues, chastity is essentially a spirit; 'the material side of virginity, which was important for primitive peoples, has completely ceased to concern us.[30] . . . But has not virginity, at a deeper level than physical integrity, a certain hidden spiritual value, for the sake of which we are again, and more than ever, bound to promote and respect it?'

Two main reasons militate in that direction. The first is

more empirical and less personal; the second, which justifies the phrase 'and more than ever', is closely linked with the whole of Teilhard's thought on convergent evolution, the main lines of which were already firmly established at that time.

First, and whatever one might think 'abstractly', the use of the flesh (*a fortiori* outside marriage) for spiritual ends cannot be a source of freedom. The idea, so prevalent nowadays, that it can, is simply a misrepresentation. It is thought that 'man's powers are magnificently released by physical love. What was already dormant in our souls, it is held, awakes and leaps ahead. Is that completely true? There is another possibility: that, in the dazzling gift of the body, a sort of "short-circuit" is produced – a flash which absorbs and neutralizes a part of the soul. Something is born, but it is for the most part consumed there and then. What constitutes the particular intoxication with the complete act of giving is surely that in it we burn up a portion of our "absolute".' In reality, it is in 'the invisible and, as it were, immaterial zones that true initiation into unity awaits us'. We would be victims of an illusion if we were ready to 'break the bonds of moral duty, of respect and admiration that for centuries of human experience have been woven around the ideal of virginity'. What is more, this would be, in the real sense of the word, a regression. It is here that Père Teilhard introduces his most personal argument: he wishes to establish that the 'sort of absolute superiority' which Christianity attributes to virginity (a position, he reminds us, which it backs with its authority) derives not only from some relative excellence but in fact from 'a perfection inherent in its nature'. So strongly does Teilhard feel this that, after appealing to 'the unitary laws of biological development' (after, that is, applying his general scheme of evolution as a spiritualizing agent to this particular case) he is forced to the conclusion that: 'Virginity is based on chastity as thought is based on life – through a reflex movement, or through one special point.'

Throughout a long first phase of their history, man and

woman, so far as their sex is concerned, were 'completely engrossed with the physical act of giving and concern with reproduction'. Gradually, however, they developed 'around this fundamental act a growing nimbus of spiritual exchanges'. This evolution is still going on. Père Teilhard tries to foresee what will follow from it and to extend it up to its term. Towards the end of his memorandum he suggests a final transformation of love that we may expect in a distant future. It will be so decisive a transformation that for the whole of mankind 'the appeal of the personal divine centre will be felt so strongly as to dominate the mutual attraction' of the sexes.

'At the present moment physical union is still necessary and valuable for the race. Henceforth, however, its spiritual quality is defined by the higher type of union which it first serves as a preparation for and then stimulates. Love is undergoing "a change of state" within the noosphere'. As evolution continues it is carrying us, it would seem, towards a threshold, towards 'one special point'; once that has been reached there will no longer be any 'immediate contact' between man and woman 'who have been chosen to carry the spiritualizing of the earth to its highest degree'; instead, there will be 'convergence above', that is to say convergence in God.[31] This will be a real 'reflex movement'.[32] At present the vow of virginity is taken by some of us as an answer to a special vocation, but it may well be in some way an anticipation or a prophetic announcement of the situation that still awaits us in the future.

It is very evident from what Teilhard says in this essay that if he devoted a great deal of thought to the problems of love, he did not do so simply 'as an abstract exercise', simply for the satisfaction of developing more profoundly his concept of the world and rounding off his teaching on evolution. This does not, however, set it apart from his other writings. We find in it the same basic orientation and the same tendency to construct bold extrapolations. Two years later, in 'Sketch of a Personalistic Universe', he puts forward the same view of the future, though with rather more caution:

> Life, as we have established, does not propagate itself for the sake of propagation, but only in order to accumulate the elements necessary for its personalization. When the maturing of its personality is approaching for the earth, men will have to realize that it is for them not simply a question of controlling births, but of increasing to the uttermost the quantity of love liberated from the duty of reproduction. Enforced by this new need, the essentially personalizing function of love will detach itself more or less completely from 'the flesh' which has been for a time the organ of propagation. Without ceasing to be physical, in order to remain physical, love will make itself more spiritual.[33]

It will be noted that here Teilhard says 'more or less completely'. In 'The Eternal Feminine' he made what would appear to be a much less hesitant allusion to this final transformation.[34] Later, we shall be looking at this passage more closely. As early, however, as 1916 'Cosmic Life' had suggested this transformation: a passage which again describes the evolution of love ends as follows:

> Let us admit, again, that, in its stock, the cosmos can perish, leaving no residue. Who can prove to us that the immortal persons, detached from it in the course of centuries, are not subject to some absolute natural development, that the original small, tart, berries will not be succeeded by plumper and more delightful fruit? Man, through his spiritual soul, steps up into a new ontological and biological level. Who can assure us that no slope rises up from that level, giving access to modes of life we have never dreamt of? Natural evolution, we were saying, seems now to be fully occupied with what concerns the soul. From being organic and predominantly determined it has become pre-

dominantly psychological and conscious; but it is not dead, nor has its reach even been shortened. There are some particularly ancient psychic elements, such as the mutual love of man and woman, in which we can already appreciate the width and richness, the complexity and purity, which the work of time has succeeded in giving to the primitive kernel of a feeling that was instinct with brutish sensation ... Who knows *what astonishing species and natural gradations* of soul are even now being produced by the persevering effort of science, of moral and social systems – without which the beauty and perfection of the mystical Body would never be realized?[35]

What appeared as a question in 'Cosmic Life', as an allusion more or less wrapped up in symbol in 'The Eternal Feminine', and later as a somewhat cautious prophecy in 'Sketch of a Personalistic Universe', is treated more systematically and with great assurance in 'The Evolution of Chastity'. Man, we are told, will master passion and so make it serve spirit. 'Sooner or later, by-passing our incredulity, the world will take this step ... The day will come when, after harnessing the ether, the winds, the tides, gravitation, we shall harness, for God, the energies of love. And on that day, for the second time in the history of the world, man will have discovered fire.'[36]

Teilhard took his stand, in writing this prophetical essay, on the maxim that 'whatever is more true comes to light, and whatever is better is ultimately realized'; but, for all his long-term optimism, he himself foresaw that many would regard such a prospect as Utopian. It seems Utopian, indeed, even to those who do their best to understand it properly and to bring out the loftiness of the inspiration that lies behind it.[37] '*Theoretically*, this transformation of love is possible.' Is the adverb (the italics are ours) sufficient to weaken the effect of the categorical assertions we have just quoted? And are those assertions so convincing that the reader is forced to accept them? Meanwhile, there are two observations that must be made; we shall find that they impel us in two different directions.

Immediately after saying (as we have seen) that 'love is undergoing "a change of state" within the noosphere', Père Teilhard continues: 'and it is in this new quarter that the collective transition of mankind into God is being prepared.' An appropriate comment on this statement is to be found in a letter to Père Auguste Valensin, dated 11 November 1934: '... this metamorphosis [of love] coincides with an *end* reached by fully matured mankind – or simply *limits* the multiplication of the species to the *optimum* demanded by eugenics.' On the one hand, therefore, we are justified in concluding, with Mme Barthélemy-Madaule, that Teilhard postpones the complete 'enfranchisement of the phyletic' to the 'approaches to a threshold of extra-spatial and extra-temporal ecstasis for ultimate mankind'[38] – we may even say, to the appearance of that threshold itself. In that case what we have is an end-concept, purely eschatological. This is the hypothesis suggested by the first half of the sentence just quoted. On the other hand, too (and although this second explanation points in a different direction, it does not contradict the first), what Teilhard now envisages in the temporal future is 'a gradual increase in the spiritual association of the sexes, with a gradual reduction of the "reproductive" side and the physical acts which serve it'.[39] In other words, Teilhard anticipates and regards as desirable, when a certain stage has been reached, a policy of birth-restriction; and this restriction, he hopes, will be made possible by a relative spiritualizing of marital relationships. The ideal he suggests to mankind of tomorrow is not contraception, which would allow a multiplication of the 'physical acts', but the contrary, a reduction of those acts, which will promote spiritual progress.

At the same time, however, there is a little more than this in 'The Evolution of Chastity'. The fact is that Teilhard is led to generalize what is his own situation and to make use of his own experience, and so more or less project them both into the future of the species. He then tends once again to take the process as far as it will go: relative spiritualization becomes absolute spiritualization, but this time it happens in the actual development of history. It may be that he is clothing a correct intuition in a Utopian form. Something, perhaps, is changing socially, and to some degree, in consequence, intellectually, in the relation between the sexes. They are not losing their own special character nor moving towards a uniform equality (Teilhard is opposed to a 'disastrous egalitarianism' and a certain form of feminism was styled by him 'masculinism'); but it may be that man and woman will succeed one day in freely exercising their complementary character more in common and accordingly more normally; they may perhaps develop relationships in which there is place for a variety of shades of association and friendship. What history has hitherto allowed only in comparatively rare cases, might well result in the future in a collective spiritual refinement, for which the feminine element would be chiefly responsible.[40]

It would be the same, of course, with such a development as it is with everything which results from an increase in collective consciousness.[41] Initially, at least, it would not mean greater moral perfection in individuals. As a result of the transformations and discoveries that accompany a certain maturing of mankind, there would be a natural increase in such spiritual love. At the same time, of course, the progress made in this direction would continue to be ambivalent. This is because of a law which Père Teilhard strongly emphasized on more than one occasion, and which we must bear in mind in this connexion if we are not to consider him over-naïve. 'The more subtle and complex mankind becomes, the more numerous the chances of disorder and the greater their gravity; for one cannot build up a mountain without digging a great pit, and every energy has equal power for good and for evil.'[42] For some, accordingly, such a progress would be an occasion for new disorders and new sufferings; in others, however, it would stimulate a higher expression of personality in a spirituality of such purity. In the language he is fond of using, with scientific and pragmatist overtones, Teilhard says that we might thus obtain 'a resultant which carries "spiritual output" to its maximum'. In his fundamental optimism, he is ready to see a first symptom of this in what he can observe of the evolution of morals around him. 'Making full allowance for the phenomenon of moral retrogression and licence, it would certainly appear that the real cause of the present "freedom" of morals lies in the search for a form of union that is richer and more spiritualizing than one whose horizon does not extend beyond the cradle.'[43]

Until that new era arrives (and this symptom pointing to it is still extremely vague) Teilhard is concerned to justify the virginal chastity which is practised today by those who have been called to it, in harmony with the tradition of the Church, with full rigour but without any contempt for the flesh or any pride of caste. With this aim in view, he applies the general principles of spirituality which he has so often explained, first in the essays he wrote during the war, then in his letters to Père Valensin which were intended for Maurice Blondel (1919), and then again in 'My Universe' (1924) and Le Milieu Divin (1927). This, he hopes, will enable him to give a more satisfactory answer to current objections, which he has often met and which a number of the classic explanations, he feels, fail to meet. He has already summarized these principles in a number of words, such as 'traversing' or 'passing through' (traversée), 'transcending' or 'going beyond' (dépassement), and 'detachment by passing through'.[44] Taken by themselves, these words might lead the reader astray. They should be read in their context and in conjunction with the phrase 'creative transformation'. Teilhard attributed great importance to this latter idea, whose full meaning will not be apparent until we have studied it in the next chapter. It is this 'mysterious notion', he wrote on 8 December 1919, which enables us 'to pursue the higher realities *through* the mean husk of all forms, all physical possession';[45] and on 21 December we find a most unexpected comment on an article by his fellow-Jesuit Père Maurice de la Taille on contemplative prayer: 'Its general principle, which seems to me extremely sound, is precisely that of "creative transformation" – the principle which, without allowing any break in the cosmic framework, explains how life comes after matter, thought after instinct, revelation after rational effort, the new earth after the old, etc.'[46] On 20 June 1921 he had just been reading an article by Père de Grandmaison on Fr. William Doyle, an Irish Jesuit killed in the war, and he recognized in Fr. Doyle's attitude the embodiment of his own ideal.

> What I liked was the combination of a life which, seen from the outside, was lovable, gay and full of go, with an inner life of intense mysticism. The 'style' is pretty extraordinary, but the meaning is clear and universal: One must, somehow, live 'eccentrically',[47] without ego-centric gratification. In that lies the whole practical problem of the inner life . . . We must *keep our footing* on the earthly *just enough constantly to go beyond it.*

He was saying the same again, in 1924, in 'My Universe': 'The man who has understood this immense simplicity of things, who has heard beneath the universal din the one unique Note – that man possesses the world. Intimately involved in things though he is through his eager efforts to complete them and understand them, he does not, even so, share their instabilities. He impinges upon them, but he attains God through them. And in the plenitude that flows over him from this *pre-adhesion* to God in All, he cannot say which is the more precious of these two graces: that he has found Christ to animate matter, or matter to make Christ universally tangible.'[48] Again in 1927: 'The light of heaven becomes perceptible and attainable [to the Christian] . . . in the crystalline transparency of beings. But he wants only this light, and if the light is extinguished . . . then even the most precious substance is only ashes in his sight.'[49]

These are principles that hold good for every action and every situation. They express an ideal for the conduct of all one's life. They govern a complete view of the world, and they govern, too, the attitude which, in virtue of its practice of complete chastity, Teilhard regards as the most admirable of all. In 1917, he had written in 'The Mystical Milieu': 'The true union that you ought to seek with creatures that attract you is to be found not by going directly to them but by converging with them on God, sought in and through them. . . . Therefore, my soul, be chaste.'[50] It is exactly the same thought that guides him in the essay we are discussing, and the question he asks in it is exactly the question he was asking on 2 March 1918.[51] He distinguishes 'two solutions, and two roads': one leads to total separation, the more surely to escape every wrongdoing and every danger of wrongdoing. The other accepts the possibility, even between man and woman, of spiritual friendships which are wholly directed towards the quest for God. Of these two roads which, he asks, 'is the right road? On this point there is opposition and even contradiction in the evidence offered by different individuals. By birth, I may say,[52] I was committed to the second, and I have followed it as far as possible. I have, of course, had some difficult sections to negotiate in it, but as I pressed on I never felt that I had grown any less as a person or that I had lost my way.'

What chiefly concerns those who favour the first solution is the dangers inherent in the second. Teilhard was well aware of this, and had referred to them in 'Creative Union': 'We all know that the purest affection can degenerate into a crude form of union; we have all grieved to see a relationship that originated on the highest spiritual plane gradually extend, unchecked, to the flesh.'[53] He now refers to this again, but with this difference, that he does not consider that it entails inevitable degradation.[54] He knows from experience that there are times when we must make a real effort to become 'deaf and blind'; in every case, accordingly, he urges extreme caution. At the same time, however, he wants us to try to distinguish 'what is only prejudice' and what derives from the 'laws of life'. He refuses, accordingly, to confuse, as a certain conventional education does, 'playing for safety with prudence, freedom from danger with truth'. On the other hand, as the passages just quoted make clear, a lofty and strictly disciplined mental attitude is called for in anyone who takes Père Teilhard's second road. Such attitudes, which ensure the 'sublimation' of love in 'plenitude', are hardly common, and do not depend solely on good intentions. That is why his own case, as he describes it himself, seems to us to be somewhat exceptional[55] – as, indeed, we may say of the circumstances in which, under the sanction of obedience, his life as a scientist developed. Moreover, Père Teilhard himself was aware of this. He is careful not to condemn 'total separation' in practice, even though it does not, in theory, correspond so well to his concept of things. Even in theory his criticism is not directed primarily at this 'total separation' but at the notion which makes separation (itself a negative concept) a sufficient definition of virtue.[56] On the other hand, no determining cause can justify our condemning the road he chose and rejecting the reasons he gave for his choice.[57] On 9 May 1916, deliberately using a very strong phrase, he had expressed the wish quoted in our first chapter: 'I pray that Our Lady may keep me from going off the rails in a matter which bears equally on two of her most eminent prerogatives (of being Virgin and Mother).' Both in 'The Evolution of Chastity' and in 'The Eternal Feminine' it is abundantly clear that his prayer was granted.

Teilhard recognized and pointed out the danger which accompanies a deep friendship, even if we assume that gross lapses have been avoided, when it is in danger of monopolizing one's heart; and he recalls, in various ways, the incessant austerities to which a man must subject himself if he is determined not to allow such a friendship to become degraded. During his retreats, he examined himself from this point of view. Knowing that he was exposed, as we all are, to insidious currents or even 'storms' that can drive us before them or sink us, he told himself, for example: 'The road I take must make me (and make all who choose it) more *mortified* (in the true and profound sense of the word: *ex-centred*).' Intimate relationships are accepted by him only with a view to an effort to be made in common, without withdrawing into personal satisfaction: the two friends should help one another to 'recognize and savour the one thing that is necessary' – and if the friendship is with a woman, it should have an influence on the man which assists the continuance of the influence on him of the Virgin Mary. In any circumstances a deep friendship is a difficult thing: its ideal is so lofty and so pure that it calls for the taking of a decisive step, a sort of inner escape and – this is the word that constantly recurs – a reflex movement, if it is to be lived completely and with full freedom of heart.[58] Moreover, we must not imagine that we have effected this reflex movement and taken this step once and for all, so that there is no danger of our withdrawing without noticing it: 'Nothing is easier than to pursue one's selfish interests under cover of growing and of loving in God. The only real protection against that dangerous illusion is a constant concern to keep very much alive (with God's help) the impassioned vision of the *Greater than All*.'[59]

'The more spiritual an affection is, the less it absorbs, and the more it provides a stimulus to action.'[60] That is an excellent criterion. It was the inspiration behind Père Teilhard's advice as it was to the requirements which he drew up for himself. We can see this in a passage from a letter to his cousin Marguerite Teillard-Chambon, dated 25 July 1917: 'Our friendship is precious. I look on it rather as a musical note that gives "tone"

to our whole life. May our Lord help us to make it such as to be wholly transformed into a force that leads us to him, with nothing wasted in fruitless mutual gratification (which would be a waste of energy and love).'[61] There could be no better practical commentary on Teilhard's essay on the evolution of chastity.

In 1950 a sort of appendix was added to that essay in an addendum to *Le Cœur de la Matière*, headed 'Le Féminin ou L'Unitif'. In these few sentences, which contain an admixture of biographical detail,[62] Père Teilhard condensed all that is essential in the ideas he had already long since arrived at on the place of love, considered in turn in the life of the cosmos since its beginning, in the future of mankind, and finally within the mysterious organism of the universal Christ – a series that takes us back to the outlook of 'Cosmic Life'. Once again he identifies, in the discovery of the Feminine, the principle which brings release from the 'mesmerism of the impersonal and the generalized'. He gives a brief explanation of his views on the various forms that can be assumed by the 'fundamental complementarity' of the sexes; and, as an application of his general theory of the relationship between matter and spirit (which he has just outlined once again in this addendum) he then turns to justifying (again as before) virginal chastity, both in its 'hidden essence' and in 'the magnificent task that awaits it'.

Nevertheless, we can hardly say that he is completely successful in carrying out his design, either in the addendum to *Le Cœur de la Matière* or in the 1934 essay. The assured tone of the latter cannot conceal a certain hesitation: this may very well derive from the twofold nature of his aim, which corresponds, as we have seen, to the two very different groups he was addressing. A further criticism is more substantial. Père Teilhard summed up the core of his theory in the phrase 'creative transformation'. By this he meant the transition from physical to spiritual love, which, as he understands it, is a love in and for God. The phrase is happily chosen; but the transition in question, conceived as a 'change of state' and as a true 'reflex movement', nevertheless takes place only within human love. The 'forces of passion' and the 'mystical forces' are shown as still 'associated' in this transformed love – although, it is true, by no means in the same way as they are in physical love – whereas, from the design which emerges from 'The Eternal Feminine', one would expect the mystical forces to spring from the soil of passion. Is not this an indication that the fruitful idea of 'creative transformation' has not been fully exploited?[63] No doubt the double unity, human and cosmic, which every man seeks in 'the Feminine' and in 'the Divine' comes 'basically' from the same 'convergence-energy', from the same fundamental love – and in this sense Père Teilhard could have re-stated his formula and given it its truest meaning: 'There is only one love.' He was justified, I believe, in maintaining this in every case, while at the same time trying to specify the extremely different ways in which convergence is effected. In his 'attempt to draw the full logical consequences of a doctrine of the spiritual value of matter',[64] he certainly had occasion to develop some profound insights, but at the same time it is difficult to believe that he was completely successful in so doing.[65]

All the various essays Teilhard wrote on love, whatever the occasion for which they were written or the point of view they adopted, show a remarkable continuity as a whole.[66] A number of them, even if they do not succeed in satisfying the reader completely, give evidence of a thought that has gained more control of itself than it had during the war period. Not one of them, however, contains more than a portion of the rich substance which we find, for all its brevity, in the more lyrical 'The Eternal Feminine'. Not one of them shows such a luxuriance of thought and imagery or is accompanied by such evocative overtones: nor does any of them reflect so felicitously a certain intuition of what Christianity has contributed to the world and the world appears to be losing – but which will be preserved and so bring about its salvation. For that very reason, none of the essays is so successful in showing us something of the pure and loving soul in which that intuition emerged: and none, finally, advances so boldly into the twin fields of metaphysics and theology.[67]

CHAPTER 4

Dynamic Analogy

*

I. TEILHARD'S USE OF ANALOGY

If we wish to learn something more about Teilhard's thought on the subject of love and the Feminine, we shall have to bring out the formal notion which enabled him to include in one single theme – or in one single category – so many apparently different principles and so many apparently heterogeneous realities: covering, in this way, both matter and spirit, and even the two orders of reality, natural and super-natural, which are distinguished by theologians. The formal notion is not mentioned in the poem, but it runs throughout the whole of it, and it is that which Scholastic philosophy, to which Père Teilhard had been introduced in Jersey, knows as analogy.

His first essay, 'Cosmic Life', is, with 'The Mystical Milieu' (1917), perhaps one of his most markedly dialectical writings (even though the dialectic is still condensed in comparison with what we find in 'Centrology' and 'Outline of a Dialectic of Spirit'). Similarly there is no doubt but that 'The Eternal Feminine' is one in which his use of analogy is most marked. In it we find two distinctly recognizable anticipations of this dialectical form of argument and of this analogy. Later, he was to put a name to them, handle them in a more sophisticated way and (when occasion offered) provide at least a summary theory of their function; and when the two are combined they represent the driving impulse of his thought. Some commentators on Teilhard have not realized this, and have accordingly been seriously misled, just as some readers of St Thomas, too hasty and not sufficiently familiar with Scholastic methods of exposition, have attributed to the author of the *Summa* a doctrine put forward in some objection which he introduces by a *videtur quod non*.[1] Other rather more generous critics of Teilhard have thought that contradictions in the dialectic reflect weaknesses in his thought. In the present case, it is essential to understand the idea of analogy as inherited by Teilhard, and the personal character he impressed on it, if one is not to see in 'The Eternal Feminine' no more than, at best, an imaginative work with no practical significance.

In order to understand Teilhard, then, we must first turn to Thomist Scholasticism. He retained much more than is commonly admitted of the philosophical training he received in Jersey, just as he did of his theological education in Hastings shortly afterwards.[2] Another undoubtedly important intellectual influence was that of his colleague, friend and fellow-student, Auguste Valensin, author of a *Théorie de l'Analogie*, of which Teilhard had a high opinion as guiding and informing both his thought and his interior life.[3] In any case it is a fact that analogy was to continue to influence the whole of Teilhard's teaching. The part it played was of capital importance, and that is a point which should never be forgotten.[4]

Some writers, however, would have us believe that Teilhard was guilty of an unfortunate misunderstanding of the law of analogy, and, what is more, that he is a classic example of a thinker in whom 'univocism', the inability to distinguish, is carried to an extreme.[5] Teilhard, says another writer, 'insists on the univocal character of spirit and nature'.[6] No proof is given in support of this statement: and it would be difficult to find a single passage in the whole of Teilhard's writings in which this insistence is evident, or which even contains that sort of statement. On the other hand, it is not difficult to see how a slight shift of emphasis can lead to such judgments. Teilhard spoke of, and indeed emphasized, 'the homogeneity of the real'; he postulated 'the unity of the stuff of the universe'; and the two

words homogeneity and unity have been translated as univocity.[7] We must admit that, taken out of the context which
explains them, the words in question can lead to confusion, but
the same may be said of the way in which all original thought
is expressed. In using them, Teilhard had no intention of
rejecting an analogical way of thinking; he was reacting against
a mischievous dichotomy which allowed no truly organic
connexion between scientific study of the world and philosophical study of man. This divorce, he believed, could be
attributed both to the materialist scientists and the idealist
philosophers of the nineteenth century, with their present-day
successors. Some of these 'engulf us in the lower mass of
animals', while others 'isolate us, making our group a sort of
driftwood floating without roots on the great waters of the
world'.[8] What he was hoping for, accordingly, was 'to see the
collapse of the wall which improperly divides the sciences of
man from the sciences of Nature'.[9] This is the primary significance of the notion of homogeneity, which is then used to
link together the different aspects that can be distinguished
when we study man himself. This notion, Teilhard wrote, 'is
without doubt of central importance in intellectual, moral and
mystical life. Even though the various stages of our interior life
cannot be expressed strictly in terms of one another,[10] on the
other hand they must agree in scale, in nature and tonality.
Otherwise it would be impossible to develop a true spiritual
unity in ourselves.'[11]

At the same time a certain complication arises from the fact
that on a couple of occasions Père Teilhard uses 'homogeneity'
in the pejorative sense it is quite often given; he applies it in
this way to the theory he is contesting, according to which the
universe is 'gliding down a single slope towards homogeneity
and rest'.[12] 'Once I have discovered Omega', he writes elsewhere, 'all things become for me in some ways the same thing
... But this fundamental unity has nothing in common with a
melting into homogeneity'.[13] It would, in fact, have been

impossible for him not to have used the word in this sense,
which current scientific usage makes unavoidable. On the
other hand, there are times when he regards homogeneity as
an ideal. In a note dated 26 January 1918, he is thinking of
rewriting 'the three sections of "Cosmic Life" in a more concentrated form, "Towards the Homogeneous" '. There are
'three ways', he believes, 'of arriving at the Absolute Homogeneous', but the best of the three would entail concern to
promote 'the work of heterogenization all along the line.'
Similarly, in 'The Mystical Milieu', homogeneity is one of the
three qualities of the universe, in as much as it enables us to see
the divine presence: 'a universal Milieu – a Milieu that knows
no change – a homogeneous Milieu'.[14]

In spite of these variations in terminology there can be no
mistake: Teilhard is at pains to show that everywhere – within
'the homogeneous'[15] and 'the one' – within the cosmos itself
which he studies 'phenomenologically' and without at first
including the relation of the cosmos to God – in all these there
are differences which make it impossible to speak absolutely of
univocity. He points out these differences explicitly enough
for any attentive reader; and, what is more, as we shall see, he
attaches capital importance to them.

The actual word 'analogy' is used more than once by Père
Teilhard, and not in its ordinary sense, nor in a more or less
lyrical context, but to designate exactly what the Schoolmen
mean by it. Teilhard completely adopts the Scholastic use. If,
for example, he wishes to explain the relationship between the
'lower degrees of being' and what he for a time called 'the
universal element' or 'the higher centre' or again 'the form of
forms' (another Scholastic expression), he tells us that the
relationship must be considered 'in conformity with what is
called in Scholastic language the *Analogy of Being*'. He carefully
points out that it is this recourse to the doctrine of analogy
which enables us to avoid the 'aberrations' of 'pantheism' –
'philosophically catastrophic' and at the same time a dis-

appointment to the soul seeking 'the Divine'.[16] He believes, further, that 'the *analogum princeps* of fully constituted being must be the pleroma'.[17] He knows that about matters that concern the life to come 'we can only speak by analogy – as with divine qualities'.[18] He was no more afraid than any other writer to use, when necessary, extrinsic comparisons and analogies in order to elucidate his thought, but he distinguished them perfectly clearly from the only true analogies, which are intrinsic. The former, he said, are no more than 'metaphors', while the latter have a foundation in nature; they 'correspond to a deep bond of nature'.[19] He points out that whenever we wish to move from one degree of being to another, even within this world, we must always apply the necessary 'corrections by analogy'.[20] In short, he is convinced of the 'fundamentally analogical nature of human knowledge'.[21]

There can be no doubt that for Teilhard the world is homogeneous. He even tells us that he is astonished that 'minds better equipped than *his* are not alive to the need for thinking and living a homogeneous world. And yet (this is one of the profound truths that familiarity with science teaches) there is nothing real except the homogeneous (by that I mean that "being homogeneous is an essential precondition of reality")'.[22] Were this not so we could not in fact speak of analogy; everything we said would be ambiguous. There is not only superficial variety, however, within this 'homogeneous' fabric. Thus an 'essential correction . . . must always be applied to our views each time we try to follow any line of reality through a new circle of the universe. The world is completely transformed from one circle to another'.[23] It undergoes not only an enrichment, as though by added attributes, but also an internal recasting. On each occasion, accordingly, it appears in a new form in which the whole of the earlier properties partly subsists and partly assumes a new form – although this does not mean that one can in some way distinguish two separate parts. Thus, in the structure of the universe 'the human world . . .

appears as a zone of continuous spiritual transformation, where all inferior realities and forces without exception are sublimated into sensations, feelings, ideas and the powers of knowledge and love'.[24]

According to the point of view he is adopting or the subject he is concerned with at the moment, we will accordingly find Teilhard emphasizing either the positive or the negative aspect of analogy, emphasizing, that is, either the resemblance or the difference; or, adopting his dynamic approach, we may say, again, that he emphasizes either what remains constant or what is given a new form. In either case he is at pains to maintain the correct balance between the two.[25] His most basic, and most frequently used, categories are analogical. In the case, for example, of the idea of 'segregation' we could show that he applies it in the most diverse disciplines, from geology to Christology.[26] The same is true with the notion of faith, his position towards which he explains in *How I Believe*.[27] We find this, too, in the notion of the cosmos itself,[28] and again in the way he speaks of 'consciousness'; he chose that word, he tells us, using it in its widest sense to indicate every form of psychism,[29] but he does not use it in a univocal sense. For Teilhard, 'life (that is to say, in fact, the universe itself, apprehended in its most active part) is a rise of consciousness'.[30] In other words 'consciousness appears as a cosmic property, variable in magnitude, which undergoes a global transformation'. He then goes on to distinguish what in the lower degrees is no more than a 'germ of consciousness', a 'trace of consciousness', 'elementary soul', 'rudimentary "within" (or immanence)', 'lower states, progressively more ill-defined and diffuse'; or again, what he calls 'rudimentary spirit', 'rudiment of immanence, that is to say spark of spirit';[31] then comes consciousness properly so called, the property peculiar to very large complexes,[32] and finally, in man alone we find 'the reflective' or 'reflective consciousness', bringing with it immanence, autonomy, and freedom. This third sort of consciousness is radically other than the earlier forms; it is a 'fundamentally new type'; it has a value that is not only 'privileged' but 'unique', because in reflection there is no degree: it either exists or it does not.[33] Teilhard is expressing the same idea when he speaks of 'eu-centrism' or when he says that the phenomenon of hominization is defined by the transition from a diffuse state of consciousness to one strictly concentrated in one single point.[34] So true is this that there are only two great mutually opposed categories – the irreflective and the reflective. With man, the world effected its 'break-through into the reflective', which is at the same time a breakthrough into the irreversible (=escape from entropy).[35] From that point onwards one may speak of 'the hominized essence' of the universe.[36]

Teilhard is seeking to improve on the accuracy of Aristotle's definition of man as 'a rational animal' by saying 'a reflective animal' and so emphasizing both the evolutive character of consciousness and the radical newness of its culmination.[37] He refuses to follow Bergson in distinguishing human intelligence from the perfected form of animal instinct as the two extreme terms of two evolutionary lines which are counterparts of one another, thus constituting two sorts of species of the same genus.[38] Thus, in *The Phenomenon of Man*, 'the originality of man is brought out far more strikingly than in Bergsonism'.[39] By stressing the global phenomenon of reflection – apprehended in its objectively discoverable effects – Teilhard retains more effectively than Bergson both the continuity between the animal and man and the *total* recasting which produces the unique value of the 'human stock'. In other words, Teilhard establishes more effectively the analogical relationship (in its twofold aspect) between animal and man: 'For reflection (the essence of hominization) does more than generate ratiocinative reason, by introducing a sort of dichotomy which impoverishes the being concerned: it recasts and transforms animal psychism in its entirety. What, in fact, is man's creative intuition if not an example of reflective instinct?'[40]

In the light of this, the question of the word 'consciousness' and its use to cover so wide a range loses some of its importance. Teilhard's use of the word has been criticized, over-severely, we believe, but not without some justification.[41] It is a pity, in fact, that Père Teilhard had so poor a vocabulary relating to the 'within' of beings (if, at least, it was his normal intention to develop something more than an objective phenomenology). For example he speaks as he feels inclined, of 'spiritual energy' and 'psychic energy'. This accounts for the lack of precision, in particular, in his use of the word 'consciousness' as applied to man, which is aggravated by the fact that, for Teilhard, consciousness is not merely reflection but, more profoundly, love; in fact, although Teilhard normally expresses his meaning in terms of intellectual apprehension, he does not forget that 'centrogenesis' is effected under the influence of the great cosmic force of attraction, of a 'convergent psychic energy' which is individualized at the centre of each being, and which, starting with man, can properly be given the name of love. 'In the zones of the pre-living and the non-reflective', 'strictly speaking, love does not as yet exist.'[42] Again, in spite of Teilhard's explanations, it is difficult to deny that there is a certain 'tendency to pan-psychism' in his thought.[43] In this his position seems further from the contemporary Scholastic position than from that of Leibniz, to whose writings his attention had been drawn by Auguste Valensin[44] and Maurice Blondel,[45] and whose *Monadology* he imitated in his own *Centrology*.[46]

It should, however, be noted that since being is analogical, we are quite correct in using the same words, in particular the word 'being', for both God and his creatures. With this elementary philosophic principle as his justification, Père Teilhard might well have thought it legitimate to use the same word, 'consciousness', to denote the 'within' of beings whose inner essence he himself shows to be extremely diverse.[47] In Teilhard, according to M. Marc Faessler, the word 'is not used in the anthropomorphic sense of the more or less clear intuition which the mind (or its analogue at the animal stage) has of its states and acts; it is deprived of any precise content and used in a *formal and recurrent sense* which means that to each progressive advance in centro-complexification there corresponds an increase of self-determination (and in consequence of self-immanence) in the system in question.'[48] If we accept the analysis of a recent interpreter of St Thomas Aquinas, Père Teilhard could have quoted the example of the Angelic Doctor to support him in this use:

St Thomas measures all being (including inanimate being) by the twin standard of emanation–return to self, or in other words by reflection. The general principle, whose full significance is felt at the higher degree, can be verified no less certainly (if only by its absence) at the other degrees. This is reminiscent of Leibniz, who attributed a consciousness to every being, but one that may be so diffuse as to become an absence of consciousness; Bergson, too, was to make consciousness the very stuff of being. The kinship with the Thomist view should warn us not to be too hasty in speaking of 'monism' . . . It is true . . . that for St Thomas this universal presence of consciousness comes about *analogically*, by an analogy which is precisely the analogy of being. It is because consciousness characterizes being at its highest degree that it must be present in every being – analogically, however, an analogy which at its lowest level is expressed by an absence; the absence would be meaningless, if it were not disappointed expectation, a reverse mould of presence.[49]

The same applies in St Thomas, we know, to the notions of 'natural desire' and 'natural love':

When St Thomas is discussing the reason why a stone falls

to the earth, he says that it is because it has a 'natural love' (*amor naturalis*) for its natural place. Aristotle used similar language . . . When medieval philosophers said that the stone wants to fall they did not mean quite what we do when we say that a man wants to do something. They meant that there is a true analogy between the two, and I believe that they also meant that, in virtue of this analogy, there is some spiritual element in everything that makes up the universe, including even inorganic things.[50]

Similarly Père Teilhard is anxious to establish a link between the human social development and the 'biological'. This second example fits in with the earlier, since, as Père Pierre Leroy explains, if we think of invention in biology 'there must be a certain constructive and creative imagination, and therefore a certain psychism, in the lowest elements of living being'.[51] For all that, Teilhard has no intention of assimilating these two 'circles' of the real to one another. What he wishes to do, he says, is to effect 'an integration (without confusion)' of the former in the latter.[52] This means that even if he emphasizes what, in man, 'relates him to the domain of life', he never, for all that, reduces the human to the biological. His attack on racialism consists precisely in showing that it improperly carries 'the biological, without change or modification, into the human, neglecting what gives the human its specific character'.[53] If Teilhard's language has sometimes led readers astray, it is because in his view the 'circle' of biology goes beyond the normal concept of natural scientists. 'Biology' is to be taken, accordingly, in 'the very comprehensive sense' which, according to Bergson, 'it should have and perhaps, one day, will have'.[54] Teilhard's concept of biology is analogical, and the analogy works *both ways*. It is a reciprocal relationship.[55] 'If it is indeed true . . . that the laws of inorganic matter and the external processes of living matter can continue upwards as far as us, and reappear "hominized" in us, it is because we can, conversely, try to understand them both by making our way towards them from within, there to meet ourselves again, materialised.' All this, however, must be done 'allowing for the necessary analogies'.[56]

This is what Père Teilhard endeavours to establish by applying to the history of life the two concepts of invention and the tool.

To take the first of these, one cannot fully explain the appearance of new zoological characteristics without introducing the influence of 'inventive forces'. 'In order to know how life operates (if it is really life that operates in us), is it not enough to watch ourselves at work', feeling our way, searching and inventing?[57] 'In virtue of analogies which correspond . . . to a deep bond of nature, the development of a phylum is strangely parallel to the successive stages undergone by an invention made by men.'[58] Thus, 'the whole evolutionary process of the organic world becomes comprehensible when placed in analogy with the developments of our human world'. Conversely, however, 'the tool . . . is the equivalent in the human series of the differentiated organ in the animal series; the equivalent, that is to say the true homologue and not the superficial imitation born of a commonplace convergence'.[59]

At the same time, if we are not to distort Teilhard's thought or oversimplify it to an exaggerated degree in either direction, we must bear in mind the analogical character of our knowledge, which is based on the analogical character of reality itself. With Teilhard, who does not use the word analogy lightly, we must recognize, as we pass from one 'series' or 'circle' to the other, the differences which affect them as a whole. Thus we must beware of crudely translating 'the mechanical laws of selection into the human field', even though in that field also, as in the lower zoological groups, we can observe 'the fact of biological competition' and 'the inexorable forms that it takes'.[60] All this confused and disturbing tangle of relationships and differences between the living and the human is explained without difficulty as soon as we discover the law of transposition and transformation which allows passage from one sphere to the other.[61] If, therefore, as we have already seen, 'the world is metamorphosed from one circle to another', then we must accept the vitally important conclusion that nothing is more erroneous and stultifying than 'the alleged uniformity of evolutionary laws and forms at all stages on the zoological ladder'; 'at the very bottom (to which we are finding our way) there is a biology of viruses and genes, sharply marked off from that of cellular beings. And in any case what is quite certain . . . is that it is becoming imperative to distinguish at the other end, at the very top, a special biology of man, called for and determined by the breakthrough into reflection.'[62]

2. TRANSPOSITION INTO DURATION

What we have seen so far would be sufficient to convince us that, contrary to what we might have believed, 'the notion of analogy or correspondence plays an essential part in Teilhard', and that he does not conceive being as one single plane but 'in depth, as a network of unified planes'.[63] If univocity is thus denied even inside our experiential world (the field of observation covered by Teilhard's phenomenology), how much more must we reject it as existing between that field of observation and the other 'sphere' of the real[64] – between the being of this world and the being of God! Already, however, several of the texts and examples quoted suggest a further consideration. These examples taken from the field of evolution draw our attention to the new and original element in Teilhard's concept of analogy.

Teilhard himself shows us this in a single word. His own concept, he tells us, was not produced out of nothing. 'It is the ancient scholastic truth, but rejuvenated in the light of duration.'[65] Whatever the position might be in other worlds that one might imagine constituted in some different way (idle though such a speculation would be), it is within duration that the world is metamorphosed, and not in accordance with some ideal plan. Such is 'the particular ordering of our world, in which everything is made by the transformation of a pre-existing analogue'.[66] Transferred from the spatial to the temporal, the 'circle'[67] becomes a 'stage'; in consequence, the analogy, which now relates 'the various realms of a universe whose structure is temporal' – and this means, also, relating the successive stages of its evolution – 'becomes genetic and dynamic'. This is in a way an 'evolutive projection of Aristotelianism';[68] but this 'rejuvenation' of the 'ancient truth' is far from robbing the theory of analogy of its emphasis and power; on the contrary 'one can press it much further than in an immobile world-structure'.[69]

'To press much further' can only mean to bring out each of the two antithetical and simultaneous characteristics, as inseparable as they are opposed, of analogy, which asserts both similarity and dissimilarity at the same time. Translated into terms of duration, these two characteristics become continuity and discontinuity, constancy and emergence, recurrence and novelty; and we may go further and add, alliance and opposition, extension and turning back or reversal. What gives intelligibility to the coincidence of these contraries or, we may say, the unity of these pairs, is the idea of 'mutation', 'transformation' or 'metamorphosis'.[70] No idea is more fundamental to Teilhard's thought, and he found it surprising that many even intelligent people had such difficulty in understanding its full import. Thus in *The Phenomenon of Man* Teilhard often speaks of 'general transformation', of 'particularly critical form of transformation', of 'critical transformation', of 'accelerated transformation', of realities 'undergoing transformation', of 'a figure that has become transformed', etc. Similarly he speaks on many occasions of 'metamorphosis', 'twofold and radical metamorphosis', 'essential metamorphosis', 'hominizing meta-

morphosis', 'the heart of metamorphosis', 'the metamorphosis
of reflection', 'the internal agonies of a metamorphosis'.[71] On
one occasion he goes so far as to use the paradoxical expression
'an evolutionary severance'. What he means by these words is
something that happens at the crossing of a 'threshold', on
arrival at a 'level', on breaking through a certain 'critical
point'. This produces a 'change of state' which, at least in the
most advanced cases, can amount to a 'change of nature'.[72] As
Jean Lacroix was later to say, in almost the same words, 'the
"step of reflection" is possible only through an advance which
certainly uses vital forms but at the same time negates them'.[73]

Whether it be, then, the 'emergence of the microscopic from
the molecular, of the organic from the chemical, of the living
from the pre-living', etc., 'one thing is certain . . . a metamorphosis of this sort could not be the result of a simple
continuous process'.[74] Thus we ourselves participate in this
essential happening, which itself does not re-occur at each
'threshold' in precisely the same form: 'the entirely new in-
sinuating itself into the heart of the monotonous repetition.'[75]
For, 'it is the characteristic proper to higher life that it recasts
the lower elements, breaking the continuity with their specific
orientations and tendencies'.[76] 'Without a long period of
maturing no profound change can take place in nature. On the
other hand, granted such a period, it is inevitable that something quite new should be produced.' 'With hominization, in
spite of the insignificance of the anatomical leap, we have the
beginning of a new age. The earth "gets a new skin". Better
still, it finds its soul.'[77]

As the cosmos evolves, we have this horizontal projection
from the vertical, static system of degrees of being; and here
again there is analogy, in the strict sense of the word, because
we are dealing with a genetic relationship between two beings,
two types of being, the second of which is both completely like
the one from which it is produced, and completely different:
in the Scholastic phrase, *totum non totaliter*. While the new

reality is not completely new, the old reality is none the less
given an entirely new form by this process of evolutive birth.[78]
If, for example, we consider the case of the appearance of man,
in whom animal life is continued, we shall nevertheless have to
say that his appearance is the result of 'a mutation from zero to
everything'.[79] In this conclusion, the analogy is stressing
difference even more than resemblance; in a letter, Teilhard,
after underlining that man is *rooted* in the universe, underlines
twice the RENEWAL introduced by his appearance.[80] Indeed,
'by the sole fact of his entering into "Thought", man represents
something entirely singular and absolutely unique in the field
of our experience'.[81] As in the real order of genetics, so equally
in the ideal order of 'essences', to be linked together does not
mean being identified, and because one thing follows on
another, both are not therefore one and the same thing.[82] 'Experientially, spirit emerges in the world only upon matter that
is progressively more fully synthesized' – but the essential point
is that this is not the simple development of spirit from matter; it is the new principle of a new synthesis:[83] 'a synthetic
[i.e. a synthesizing] principle'. 'In the field of cosmic evolution,
the One chronologically presupposes, and structurally inte-
grates, the Multiple.'[84] This does not, however, mean 'that the
One is made up of the Multiple'. That view 'would be the
materialist illusion, which consists in regarding the elements of
the analysis as "more real" than the terms of the synthesis'.[85]
Putting it in general terms, we must say the exact opposite, that
'the formula of the world (if we may use so deceptive and
pretentious a phrase) is not development of one thing *in*
another, but one thing with another *as its occasion*, of one thing
upon another'.[86] In short, we must not confuse a 'law of genesis'
with a reduction to the same.

It follows that the transformation which characterizes
transition from one analogue to another may perfectly truly be
called 'creative transformation'[87] (which, as Teilhard explains
later, can be effected only under the influence of Omega).[88]

This will result, for the two analogues, in a relationship which will be as much one of opposition as of alliance, and in some cases much more so. And this will apply most of all to the relationship between matter and spirit. Sometimes Père Teilhard is concerned to demonstrate the necessary connexion between the two, joining issue with 'naïve idealists', who, as we have seen, fail to recognize the homogeneity of the real or, in other words, the unity of the world (or 'universe');[89] at other times he refutes those who would explain everything as an unfolding of matter and thereby lapse into univocity – in this case, materialism – and emphasizes the other aspect, the no less indispensable 'opposition' between the two: emphasizes, that is, the transcendence of spirit.[90] 'Passing from one platform of existence to another, living properties survive only by transformation or transposition.'[91] In describing this access to 'an entirely new biological plane',[92] as in the similar cases of 'major discontinuity', Teilhard uses again the words 'revolution', 'turning back' and 'reversal'. In man, for example, he says 'the pressure of life tends to be transformed, to turn back, into vital drive'.[93] In slightly tentative language, he even accepts the words 'break'[94] and 'rupture'.[95] These are hardly too strong to express the effective transition from one 'sphere' to the other, the real 'sublimation' of the real.

All these last words serve in a way as the link between Teilhard's analogy and his argument. A typical example of the transition from one to the other, or rather of their coincidence, could be found actually in human history, the example of the war-peace relationship. We know that Père Teilhard refuses to allow man to be shut up 'in a certain number of circles which he will never be able to break'; he rejects the 'organic necessity of wars'.[96] However, like Bergson, he believes that there is a 'deep-rooted instinct for war' in human nature, and he does not put so much faith as Bergson in 'a return to simplicity', in which men could take the initiative and so get rid of this instinct by suppressing the causes of international conflict.[97]

He does not therefore see peace – effective and desirable peace – as simply the opposite of war; he does not define it negatively as the cessation or absence of war, as so many naïve pacifists do:[98] if peace is to be achieved, it can only be as 'a sublimated form of war', 'war carried beyond and higher than itself'. Men will always have to fight. The ideal of quiescence, of pleasure-seeking tranquillity, of facile, unadventurous happiness, is not only unworthy of man, but also full of contradictions. It would produce a fatal boredom from which every sort of evil would again be born. Moreover, 'a world quietly at rest' is impossible; it is incompatible with our progressing universe. What men must do is to make up their minds to fight together 'for a goal which unites our energies instead of dividing them'.[99] The spirit of conquest and discovery must absorb 'the whole vital force contained in the spirit of war'.[100] The 'human fascicle' must weld itself into one for a great enterprise, the 'vast battlefield of the earth',[101] so that 'brotherly emulation' may take the place of 'hostile competition', and that all the feeling for war may in future be diverted to 'dangers or conquests outside humanity'. 'The whole phenomenon, in fact, is reversed.'[102]

If we then look at the relationship between the natural order and the supernatural, we shall see that it follows the same laws, but again it does so analogically. Just as Père Teilhard distinguished, but did not separate, matter and spirit, so he makes a complete distinction between the two orders. We find this on many occasions,[103] and it is mostly in so doing that he introduces the words 'turning back' and 'reversal',[104] 'metamorphosis' and 'transformation', the concrete synonyms for which are 'death' and 'ecstasis'.[105] At the same time, of course, he brings the two together; here again he recognizes the duality, and rejects the dualism[106] – not that he refuses to retain the truth to be found in 'the old intuitions of a cosmic dualism'.[107] He tries, therefore, to make us see the supernatural order as born, in man, from a natural foundation – appearing, that is, *upon* the natural order (just as he showed spirit appearing *upon* matter) – as a higher principle, to synthesize the elements and at the same time raise them up to a life and so transform them. 'Just as spirit appeared in man by making some sort of use of the rudimentary forms of instinct, the supernatural is continuously being formed by the super-creation of our nature.'[108] And 'the sense of the omnipresence of God . . . sur-creates and supernaturalizes the identical physiological energy which, in a mutilated or misdirected form, produces the various styles of pantheism'.[109] There is accordingly a real 'dynamic continuity from the natural to the supernatural';[110] since, however, it is 'continuity of discontinuity', it cannot, any more than the continuity of earlier examples, operate without a complete recasting[111] – or rather it is even more dependent on it. There is an abrupt threshold to be crossed, involving a 'transformation', a 'transposition', a 'mutation', a 'turning back' (for the final transfiguration Teilhard goes so far as to speak of a 'point of annihilation'). In this case again it may rightly be described as a dialectic.[112] It is what we would now call, to use words that had not yet become popular in France when Teilhard was writing, the transition from *eros* to *agape*.[113] It is a passing through fire, 'fire which devours', which is at the same time 'fire which transfigures': but this fire 'must have something to fall upon, otherwise nothing will be consumed or consummated' – nothing will be devoured or transfigured.[114] And just as animal realities – hunger, love, the feeling for conflict, the hunting instinct – are still with us, 'recognizable though hominized',[115] so supernatural charity, for example, is nourished by our natural capacities for love while at the same time it transforms them.[116] 'Human passions are not directly orientated to the heavenly Jerusalem; and yet we advance towards heaven only by, of necessity, spreading our sails to their wind'.[117]

A year before the composition of 'The Eternal Feminine', Père Teilhard was writing:

God has not seen fit to create in us a new and distinct centre of affection, through which we might love him. In accordance with the particular ordering of our world, in which *everything is made by the transformation of a pre-existing analogue*, it seems evident that, initially, divine Charity exists in us simply as the flame, supernaturalized and purified, that is kindled at the prospect of the Earth's promises. It could never possibly persist in a heart that had ceased to be fired by the quickening contact of tangible realities. Great love of God normally presupposes the maintenance of a strong natural passion. If the tree which is deprived of the soil that nourishes it withers and dies, are we justified in hoping that grace will make it grow green again in order to graft itself onto it?[118]

And a year later, he was again to write:

Transformation, in that the supernatural actually re-arranges the elements of this world, to the point of making them truly *more* and *other than they were* – but also transformation in the sense that the natural elements are absolutely necessary to this work of salvation, providing it with its fuel and with a suitable material. The supernatural fullness of Christ depends upon a natural fullness of the world.[119]

It is the concept, again, of universal analogy that inspires Teilhard when he writes: 'There are other peaks between us and the chasm of the supernatural . . . One prepares for the decisive metamorphosis through a series of moultings which are models of this ultimate change of state, though of a much lower order. There is a sort of continuity in the successive discontinuities which the creature passes through on his way to God.'[120] If the Cross means 'breaking with the world', it is, precisely in that, 'the sublime aspect of a law common to all life'.[121] Everything is not univocal, but everything *holds together*.[122]

CHAPTER 5

The Transformations of the Feminine

*

I. THE HISTORY OF LOVE

The fabric of the poem we are studying is woven, as we have already said, from universal history, since the creation of the world to its consummation in God. Thus we are shown the chief metamorphoses of the principle which Teilhard at first, in neutral and general language, calls the *Universal Feminine* or the *Eternal Feminine*. We follow its various analogical expressions, not so much in empiric chronological order as in a dialectic; at times this dialectic, which is a 'history of salvation' in the widest sense, carries us to a higher level, at times it brings a change from positive to negative. Thus we already have here a realization, in a sort of poetical anticipation, of the programme which he was to indicate in 1931 in a sentence, already quoted, from 'The Spirit of the Earth': 'The most telling and profound way of describing the evolution of the universe would undoubtedly be to trace the evolution of love.'[1] In so far as we succeed in doing this, disclosing, as we do, 'what deep-rooted power lies hidden' under the various forms of love, we shall have discovered 'the great secret of the cosmos'.[2]

As we have seen, however, evolution presupposes both continuity and discontinuity: in other words, transformation. This word recurs on a number of occasions in connexion with the evolution of consciousness. The universal love, which mankind needs, the love to which it aspires in order to become total, and which only Christ 'in the full realism of his Incarnation' makes possible, 'is not a mere sporadic accident'; 'it appears as the higher term of a transformation which has already begun in the mass of the noosphere'. We must, then, make our way much further back into the distant past of the world – climb, that is, much lower down the tree of life, or even right into the soil in which it is rooted – if we are to distinguish the first analogies of this love, so barely embryonic, so fantastically rudimentary, as to be imperceptible.

The whole vocabulary of analogy discussed in the preceding chapter comes into play at this point. To designate the depth of the transformations that occur during the process, or of the successive 'changes of state', one of Teilhard's favourite words is 'metamorphosis';[3] when, however, he is speaking of the spiritual progress which is effected under the radiating action of Omega, he is more inclined to use the word 'transfiguration'; to denote the unforeseeable mystery by which 'spiritualized love' can give the penetrative power (through the limitless potentialities of intuition and the mutual relationship it produces), he prefers 'sublimation';[4] finally, there is the arduous character and the element of rupture contained in the final transformations, which take place under the 'substantial' and 'mortifying' influence of Christ.[5] The word he uses for this reflex movement is *retournement* ('turning back', 'turning in' or 'return'). We have already met these words, which are part of Teilhard's regular vocabulary. To some extent, moreover, they are interchangeable.[6]

In its most primitive, and still completely rudimentary state (which in the course of time will perpetuate itself in the material zone of the cosmos), 'the essential Feminine' – another name for the principle of love – is simply 'the unitary aspect of beings'. It is 'this force of condensation and concentration' without which they would return to the non-being of pure multiple, and under the influence of which they unite in progressively larger and more complex syntheses. Later, in the essay which schematically summarized the history of his thought, he spoke of it as the universal 'unitive cement'.[7] Even into atoms it introduces 'a vague, persistent anxiety to emerge from the annihilation of their solitude'. It is this principle of love which animates and fosters the 'vast process of arrangement' to which the essence of 'the whole cosmic event' may be reduced.[8] 'Driven by the forces of love, the fragments of the world seek each other so that the world may come into being.'[9] Thus love is 'the energy proper to cosmogenesis'.[10] Hidden 'beneath as yet barely conscious affinities', it is 'the charm woven into the world to make it amalgamate'. Its power, however, is not exhausted in this charm, or rather this charm is not exhausted in this first effect. It is already, at the same time, the 'ideal held up above' the world, 'to draw it aloft'. It is a principle of union, but it is also a principle of spiritualization; the two go hand in hand. Five months earlier, Père Teilhard was explaining this in 'The Mystical Milieu':

> The true union that you ought to seek with creatures that attract you is to be found not by going directly to them but by converging with them on God, sought in and through them. . . . It is . . . by making themselves more spiritual in the embrace of God, that things draw closer to each other and, following their invincible natural bent, end by becoming, all of them together, one.[11]

Here we meet, in its root form, Teilhard's well known axiom,[12] whose true significance has first to be asserted in a restricted form: there is no convergence without ascent. We may say that it sums up the whole of Teilhard's moral teaching on love.

We can at the same time understand the basic reason for the opposition between Teilhardian time and Freudian time, between Teilhard's universe and Freud's. Teilhard, as we have seen, and as he asserted on countless occasions, unreservedly recognized that 'the energy which feeds our interior life and weaves its fabric, is primordially of the nature of passion'.[13] In this idea he was to see 'the surest basis of psychoanalysis'. The idea, however, is no more Freudian than it is Platonic. Teilhard had illustrated it in 'The Eternal Feminine', and had again found confirmation for it in the *Phaedrus* and *Symposium*, which he reread in Alsace in December 1918, long before he studied Freud.[14] It lends itself to many interpretations, and it can be included in many different, even contradictory, syntheses. It is in no way a summary of Freud's philosophy, nor does it betray Freud's basic approach. For Teilhard, the spiritual forms of love, which result from a 'sublimation' and which are still 'passion', are due to a specifically 'creative' transformation of their lower, passional, basis: in other words, if there is to be a *real* sublimation[15] and a *real* transformation, there must necessarily be a 'sublimating' and 'transforming' agent.

When Père Teilhard first met Freud's writings, he deplored some unintelligent criticisms launched against him. He refused to agree with those who condemned Freud *en bloc*. For his own part, however, he was already raising the essential objection, that of Freud's accepting, as he was obliged to do, only a deceptive 'sublimation', which falsified the meaning of all spiritual life, while neglecting – for his silence on this point was in fact a negation – the positive source of the 'sublimating' and 'transforming' agents.[16] His own attitude to Freud was explained in 1950, in *Le Cœur de la Matière*. He describes how he found himself gradually driven to formulate his concept of anthropogenesis, which governs his idea of man, and how he was led to postulate 'the primacy of spirit, or, which comes to the same thing, the primacy of the future';[17] he then goes on, without discussing the value of Freud's discoveries, to say: 'At this point, I might well find myself confronted with Freud's unconscious . . . My position was henceforth permanently settled. For I had seen, once and for all, that, left to itself, the world falls forward into equilibrium, with all its vastness and all its weight, not in the direction of obscurity but towards the light.'[18] At first reading this might seem rather sweeping. It is an incidental comment, in which nevertheless Teilhard brings out again and transposes into terms of time the distinction, too often overlooked, between 'psyche' and 'pneuma'. It is a criticism of Freudianism whose essential point is not Teilhard's own. Other writers had already formulated the principle it rests on, and the Abbé Jules Monchanin had made the same criticism, pointing out the 'incurable sadness of Freudianism' which arises from 'what is fundamentally a return to the past' – the past 'in which complexes are formed' – whereas what should be asserted is 'the primacy of creation over what is given'.[19] 'Archaeology of the subject', in Paul Ricœur's phrase, 'without teleology'.

Teilhard, however, does more than adopt this criticism as his own, and so put forward against Freud's 'sombre theories' a vague theory of hope; and there is something more than an unerring instinct behind his refusal to accept the tyranny of that 'sinister pair' Anagke and Logos.[20] Some of the force of his criticism comes from its coherence with the whole body of his thought, as it emerged from his endeavour to organize it with increasingly professional vigour.[21] Thus he found himself obliged to put forward a sort of inverted psychoanalysis; the aim of this would be to help the subject to decipher 'in those areas of himself which are still ill-explored and unexplained, the great aspirations' which lie dormant at the heart of mankind: psychoanalysis is, in fact, 'not for release but for commitment'; to 'make man look into himself, not in order to dispel phantoms but to give body to, to bring under control and satisfy, certain important needs or essential demands which are stifled in us (or which stifle us) for lack of being expressed and understood'. This would be the way in which to bring out the greatest human truth which lies hidden not in the determinations of the past but in a process of transcendence which opens up into the future.[22] A better name for this, rather than psychoanalysis properly so called, would be 'psych-energetics'.[23]

Teilhard knows the 'enigmatic power of love' – enigmatic, and 'yet the inspiration of genius, of the arts and all poetry'; but he sees beyond this. He sees affective forces emerging from

this enigmatic power, increasing in strength and sharply distinguished from any sort of 'backward-looking emotionalism'.
Beneath it he discerns 'a formidable creative impulse', which
has so far been held almost completely in reserve; what we have
to do now is not simply to master or 'suppress' it, but to
contain it so that we may then release it and make use of it. Man
will not be fully man until he succeeds in doing this.[24]

Père Teilhard believes that he will succeed if he wants to,
thanks to the very strength of the evolutionary movement
which is carrying him along, provided he knows how to apply
it. A rise of spirit is being produced, whose purpose is to lead
hominization to its term. As we have already seen, the extreme
form in which Teilhard pictures this rise is described in
'L'Évolution de la Chasteté'; and we have already remarked on
the Utopian element it seems to contain. In 1934 it brought
objections from Père Auguste Valensin, to which Teilhard
could only answer: 'I know very well that I have on many
occasions laid myself open to the reproach of not knowing
what I was talking about.' As it turned out, it would appear
that before long he was obliged to abandon some part at least
of his dream for the future. On the other hand, it may well be
(again, as we suggested earlier) that all he had intended to do,
in the case of mankind taken as a whole, was to indicate a
probable direction. He was right about the direction, and it
was one which a Christian can understand. His forward looking has greater educative and tonic virtue for mankind – because its truth is more real – than the most perceptive of
backward looks.[25] When Teilhard tells us that man's centre
of gravity lies ahead of him, he is using the language of the
Gospels.

All the main principles behind this concept of the world
which runs through his theory of love, are already affirmed in
'The Eternal Feminine'.

Nevertheless, within the whole body of his writing, the
philosophy of love was to be developed on an even wider

scale. For the sake of brevity, we have had practically to leave aside in this study the question of love considered in God and in the creative act;[26] the same is true of the whole social aspect of the problem, which nevertheless was one to which he continually attributed central, and even increasing importance. We have confined our study to the themes set out in 'The Eternal Feminine' or to themes directly connected with them, from the twofold point of view which determines them, that of the spirituality of marriage and that of the religious vow of chastity. Within this range of thought, however, there is complete coherence. Père Teilhard noted 'the extraordinary increase in personality' produced by a 'great human affection'. It was within society that he looked for the conditions that allow perfect development of the person. Are we not justified in hoping that the future will bring the ascent to the threshold opening into consciousness of a 'sense of man' (from which is born co-feeling with the other), which is still largely overlaid? In that case the personalizing power of love would not be confined to a few special, limited cases. A 'universal human love' would emerge, without which society will never be able to organize itself except at the expense of person:

> Love has always been carefully eliminated from realist and positivist concepts of the world; but sooner or later we shall have to acknowledge that it is the fundamental impulse of Life, or, if you prefer, the one natural medium in which the rising course of evolution can proceed. With love omitted there is truly nothing ahead of us except the forbidding prospect of standardisation and enslavement – the doom of ants and termites. It is through love and within love that we must look for the deepening of our deepest self, in the life-giving coming together of humankind. Love is the free and imaginative outpouring of the spirit over all unexplored paths. It links those who love in bonds that unite but do not confound, causing them to discover in their mutual contact

an exaltation capable, incomparably more than any arrogance of solitude, of arousing in the heart of their being all that they possess of uniqueness and creative power.[27]

A bewitching ideal, indeed! How could it possibly come true? For, 'does it not run counter to the nature of effective powers to be extended to too great an object?'

Père Teilhard never had 'any illusions about the degree of incredibility' in such a hypothesis: was it not, he asked, of the same family as 'squaring the circle' and 'perpetual motion'? Nevertheless, he wondered for some time whether 'under the irresistible influence of the forces that are bringing them together' men might not come to love one another – 'as a normal expression of their behaviour'. He believed that he could already feel this new mankind 'stirring beneath the old'. It is to this we owe the simile of the travellers in the ship – one of the finest passages he wrote, but also, without any doubt, one that will have done most to cause him to be treated as a Utopian visionary.[28] Nevertheless, his thought is more realistic than a passage like this might lead one to imagine. He is convinced, it is true, that a certain 'sense of man', in which the 'sense of the cosmos' takes on concrete reality and reaches its peak, is 'the most fundamental form of all passion' to be found in man. It is the root basis of a 'universal love'; and that love is not only possible in itself – it is 'the only complete and final way in which we are able to love'.[29] It is essential, however, to understand on what conditions it will be possible for such a love to be realized in this present life. If man – whether individual man or the whole human race – is left to himself and shuts himself up in himself, then the sense of man will never triumph and yield its richest fruits. Instead of the 'mutual sympathy' we dream of, what in fact prevails, and may well prevail for ever, is much more a 'mutual repulsion'.[30] Every effort, therefore, aimed at unifying the world is pregnant with the direst threats: it seems certain, if successful, to stifle life, to convert it into terror and tyranny. The forces of unification even now operating might well lead us into 'the worst forms of slavery'. 'Brought to a halt at the collective', 'mankind, so extolled for the last two centuries . . . is now a terrifying Moloch.'[31] Does this mean that the drive which is behind the world's ascent must in the end be pulled up short?

Even so, Père Teilhard retains his belief in the capacity to love which, he says, 'still slumbers in the human mass'; but it can be awakened only by 'the radiant influence of Omega'.[32] In other words, we are looking for a solution to the problem of social unity which at the same time will bring freedom; we dream that through 'the centric power of love' the very pressure of numbers and the increasingly close and numerous ties of the collective may assist the 'ascent into the personal', and that 'conspiration of the human monads' may be fully realized – but this is completely impossible without the effective action of a higher energy, the magnetic pull of a personal, loving, centre recognized by man 'at the heart and summit of the world'.[33]

Turning then to 'the Christian phenomenon', Teilhard found there the 'real, existential value' lacking to his dream. In it he recognized the action, as yet partial and far from complete, of this 'universal love', a 'specifically new state of consciousness' which man cannot acquire by himself and without which the life of mankind will never be really human. In it he saw, born of the Gospels, 'Christian love'.

'Christian love is incomprehensible to those who have not experienced it. That the infinite and the intangible can be lovable, or that the human heart can beat with genuine charity for a fellow-being, seems impossible to many people I know – in fact almost monstrous. But whether it be founded on an illusion or not, how can we doubt that such a sentiment exists, and even in great intensity? We have only to note crudely the results it produces unceasingly all round us. Is it not a positive fact that thousands of mystics, for twenty centuries, have drawn from its flame a passionate fervour that outstrips by far in brightness and purity the urge and devotion of any human love? Is it not also a fact that, having once experienced it, further thousands of men and women are daily renouncing every other ambition and every other joy save that of abandoning themselves to it and labouring within it more and more completely? Lastly, is it not a fact, as I can warrant, that if the love of God were extinguished in the souls of the faithful, the enormous edifice of rites, of hierarchy and of doctrines that comprise the Church would instantly revert to the dust from which it rose?'[34]

This is not a facile piece of apologetics on Père Teilhard's part. He sees further and more clearly than many critical observers who cannot perceive anything but the always glaring pettinesses of the 'only too human', or than many others who are blinded even before they start by the tendency to masochism which is so distressingly prevalent today. Teilhard can recognize in our history the irreplaceable contribution of the Gospel: and he is a realist again when he locates in a love of God, which comes from God, the only energy capable of producing an effective love of man, truly universal and saving.[35] His realism, however, does not exclude the hopes that are prompted by charity: Christ has revealed to men a new dimension of the universe and gives them the strength to enter into it.

The same essential views were given their final expression in Le Christique, an essay written in New York and dated March 1955 (Teilhard was to die on 10 April): in this he speaks of the real possibility of a love, a true love of God, as attested by Christian history: 'it is undeniable that the most ardent collective centre of love ever to appear in the world is burning hic et nunc in the Church of God'; it is impossible for human consciousness, however intense it may be or can become in each one of us, to establish a religion of love, the religion which is as essential to man's life in society as it is to his final aspiration;

on the other hand, however, there is the 'extraordinary and momentous power of "pan-amorization"' possessed by Christianity, which must ensure its central directive position, provided sufficient attention is given to it; but to appreciate it fully we must get to the very core of it. And then, 'in a world that without any doubt opens up at its peak *in Christo Jesu*, there will no longer be any danger of our dying for lack of air to breathe – and, correspondingly, what comes down from those heights is not only air, but the radiation of a love'.[36]

2. *AB INITIO AD AETERNUM*

To return to 'The Eternal Feminine' itself. If its nature is as we have described it, it is not surprising that, from the very first stage in its progress, it is worthy of being conceived under the biblical symbol of Wisdom: the operative Wisdom which collaborates in God's work. *Ab initio creata sum.*

As its divine origin indicates, this text already suggests, to anyone who is familiar with the traditional interpretation in the Church and with its applications in the liturgy, what the complete fulfilment of the eternal Feminine will be. We should not seek here for anything analogous to Bulgakov's sophiological theories. Wisdom is not a hypostasis which, in its created aspect, is realized in the Virgin. As in the liturgy, it is a symbol. There is, however, a coincidence that is worth noting. Not only, as we have seen before, do Teilhard and Claudel agree in mystically identifying the Church and the Virgin in one and the same evocation, but they agree also in designating both under this same symbol of Wisdom: both writers, moreover, having first given the symbol a much wider significance – Claudel wishing to 'see in Woman an image (or adumbration) of divine Wisdom', and Teilhard recognizing in her at first an ambivalent principle, whose knowledge 'is of good and evil'. We might wonder whether there is not in one of the two, Teilhard or Claudel, some reminiscence of the other. This, however, would appear to be impossible. Claudel obviously could not have known the poem written at Verzy during the Great War, and himself referred only much later to the eighth chapter of Proverbs (the lesson for the Feast of the Immaculate Conception), which he came across at the time of his conversion.[37]

It is I, says Teilhard's Wisdom, who am the bond that holds together the foundations of the universe: 'every monad, be it never so humble, . . . obeys in its movement an embryo of love for me'. Gradually, with the appearance of life, the Feminine is differentiated, is individualized, and is stabilized in tangible forms: sexuality properly so called is born.[38] Yet, all through its progressive advances and new forms, the basic characteristics of the Feminine remain: it is only that they are made to carry an increased consciousness, and, simultaneously with the patient development of the process which, at the human stage, will incarnate the Feminine in Woman, in the double character of wife and mother, the Feminine – that single, shifting ray – continues its work of universal animation.[39] Everything great, in every order, that man will achieve, will be due to its hidden activity:

> Man, nature's synthesis, does many things with the fire that burns in his breast. He builds up power, he seeks for glory, he creates beauty, he weds himself to science. And often he does not realize that, under so many different forms, it is still the same passion that inspires him – purified, transformed, but living – *the magnetism of the Feminine*.[40]

In woman herself, beneath individualized characteristics, it is always the same 'great hidden force' which draws man; it is 'the mysterious latency, that has come to him in this form in order to lead him captive'. It is 'the world's attractive power imprinted on human features'.[41] Woman 'is the symbol of all those things whose mutual fulfilment can be looked forward to in the universe'.[42]

In this the reader will already have noted a further resemblance to Claudel. This same fundamental characteristic is found in Claudel's doctrine of love. 'I am the promise which cannot be kept, and it is that very failure which constitutes my charm': Teilhard's eternal Feminine, whose attraction leads beyond itself, might well be the speaker. In Claudel, however, it is Lala, the disturbing, bewitching heroine of *La Ville*, who uses the words. We have two interpretations of the common basis of this thought that Woman symbolizes the world, which ultimately means the unity mankind seeks; and it is not long before the two follow directions so different that in one phase they become contradictory. Claudel's hero, forced to make a decisive choice between the 'heart-rending mirage of the absolute, and the absolute in its inapprehensible totality', 'between the silence of God, the prospect of his absolute desire, and the shattering, exhausting satisfaction of that desire concentrated on a being here below', found that it was possible for him 'to love a creature as much as God'. He recognized, then, in Woman the 'sudden, triumphant rival of the hidden God'. For Teilhard, on the other hand, it was not so much Woman as the 'Feminine' which appeared directly as the symbol through which the reality of the whole breaks through and insists on recognition. For Claudel, the whole is sought (though it is an illusion) in the individual being: 'You can only give it', says Pélage to Prouhèse, 'things that are limited.' For Teilhard, all individual beings must be found (really, with no illusion) in the whole, and that is what the symbol means for him. The fact is that both writers are transposing their own experience. At a later stage, however, the two concepts come together again: free from the illusion which led him astray, Claudel's hero – Rodrigue in *The Satin Slipper* comes to mind – finds in suffering 'the strength to take the measure of the absolute which animates him'; in him, spirit ultimately 'conquers in the transfiguration of noonday'. What had been for him mirage becomes image, and, as in Teilhard, all that matters henceforth is convergence on God.[43]

The Claudelian adventure, or roundabout approach, is included, moreover, in the passage in 'The Eternal Feminine' which traces the history of the Fall. Man has had a distinct glimpse of the ambivalent mystery of the Feminine. It is this which has disturbed him and made him waver between fear and worship. But the mirage proved stronger for him than the truth. We saw earlier that what we are told under these symbols is the whole history of human love, of temptation, sin, the Redemption, and we need not go into that again. Saved and freed by Christ, the magnetism of the Feminine has become pre-eminently *Virginity*, the principle henceforth indispensable to man's recovery.[44] In this change – and none more radical could be conceived – the universal Feminine has remained itself. Perfect chastity will bring about the final flowering of its stem:

> The man who hearkens to Christ's summons is not called upon to exile love from his heart. On the contrary, it is his duty to remain essentially a man.
>
> Thus he has an ever greater need of me, to sensitize his powers, and arouse his soul to a passion for the divine.
>
> For the Saint, more than for any other man, I am the maternal shadow leaning over the cradle – and the radiant forms assumed by youth's dreams – and the deep-seated aspiration that passes through the heart like some undisputed alien force – the mark, in each individual being of Life's axis.
>
> Christ has left me all my jewels.
>
> In addition, however, he has sent down upon me from heaven a ray that has boundlessly idealized me.

Since this metamorphosis, the result of 'the Christian influence', the universal Feminine answers to a new name: it is now *the Feminine Ideal*. By that influence, even in the order of natural activity, a new impulse has been given to its development. The Christian revelation of love, refining and widening the powers of the soul, stimulates a higher form of humanism. But above all, the feminine ideal calls out, through its charm, 'an effort of arduous purification' to which every man is summoned.

No concession, accordingly, is made to hedonism. And yet, 'arduous purification' is not a mere 'breaking-off'. In a phrase Teilhard was to use later, it is 'spiritualization by emergence'.[45] Here, again, we have just seen, a certain continuity persists. As he wrote, in 1919, in 'The Spiritual Power of Matter', 'purity does not lie in separation from, but in a deeper penetration into the universe'.[46] So it is, as explained by Teilhard, with peace in relation to war.[47] The feminine ideal does not lose itself, like an alien force, in the great cosmic current; it is only as seen by the individual that it appears, at first, to do so. On the contrary, it springs from 'the axis of life' and in its own way it carries still further the drive of the initial principle. It is, we should note, precisely in connexion with 'the spiritual forms of love' which when their time comes graft themselves upon its 'lower form', that not long afterwards we find Père Teilhard speaking of 'creative transformation'.[48] To bring out the contrast in continuity, he borrowed the two words Plato uses in the *Phaedrus*, '$\xi \rho \omega s$', he says, 'has become $\pi \tau \xi \rho \omega s$';[49] the great cosmic force has become a summons to the 'liberation of souls'. But, he goes on to say, Plato could have no more than a hint of the meaning of chaste love, for this is not revealed except in Christ.[50] 'What a strange, mad force the heart is', he says later, in a passage which must reflect an intimate and personal experience; 'nowhere else does life seem so rich, so new-born, and so disturbing. How are we to transfigure this without impoverishing it? That's the whole secret of creation.'[51]

It is at this point, however, that the universal Feminine, which has become more exactly the feminine attraction and has then been metamorphosed into the feminine ideal, is for the first time given a proper name; and this immediately gives it personality. We know from this that we have just made our way into a completely new order. It is here, in fact, that there finally appears in the poem itself the name which stands in the dedication which follows the title. 'Reflected in the face of Béatrix [are] the dreams of art and of science towards which each new century aspires', and in her 'ever-changing perfection' are embraced 'the aspirations of each new generation'.

One of these aspirations, and the loftiest, is precisely Teilhard's own: 'the love of the cosmos which I would like to safeguard', he wrote a little later again, from Strasbourg, 'is a chaste love, centred outside self, "enucleated", in tension towards God, animated by him'.[52]

> Since the beginning of all things, Woman has never ceased to take as her own the flower of all that was produced by the vitality of nature or the art of man.
>
> Who could say in what climax of perfections, both individual and cosmic, I shall blossom forth, in the evening of the world, before the face of God?
>
> I am the unfading beauty of the times to come – the ideal Feminine.
>
> The more, then, I become Feminine, the more immaterial and celestial will my countenance be.
>
> In me, the soul is at work to sublimate the body – Grace to divinize the soul.
>
> Those who wish to continue to possess me must change as I change.

It is the dream of a love that is 'changed', transfigured; of a love that has become completely limpid, such a love as the spiritual man acquires after a persevering effort of purification. It will be recalled that some months earlier Teilhard wrote in 'The Mystical Milieu', 'that no blemish may separate him, by so much as a single atom of himself, from the essential limpidity, he labours unceasingly to purify his affections and to remove even the very faintest opacities which might cloud or impede the light'.[53] The next year, the closing words of 'Hymn to Matter' reflect the same dream: 'Raise me up then, matter, to those heights, through struggle and separation and death; raise me up until, at long last, it becomes possible for me in perfect chastity to embrace the universe.'[54] The dream was to be given fuller expression later, as we have seen, though not without 'a certain ambiguity',[55] when Teilhard came to write his essay on the evolution of chastity. Here he does no more than sketch in a rapid outline of his dream, without our being able to say whether we should see in it the Utopia of a distant future for the earth,[56] or rather the hope and prophetic announcement of the final transfiguration. He is dreaming of a collective sublimation of human love, 'of a universe that is completely made virgin'; the dream is based on the possibility of a certain 'transparency of matter *in relation* to spirit'.[57] He has in mind a total dissociation between 'the essence of the Feminine', which remains, and 'the sexual', which passes away: passes away, that is, unless one means an entirely 'sublimated' sexuality, or 'a spiritual application of the sexual relationship' carried to the extreme limit at which it is transformed, between man and woman, into 'peaceful friendship' – even though it can still be 'passionate' in Teilhard's sense of the word.[58] Teilhard himself tells us the twofold origin of the dream – which brings us back to firmer ground – and so makes it possible to understand its nature more clearly. In the first place, as we saw in chapter 3, it arises from 'a profound instinct' in mankind which cannot but contain some hidden truth.[59] Secondly, and even more, there is 'the empiric evidence of Christianity' which derives from the Gospel: 'the solid platform built up by two thousand years of Christian experience'. However, the faith that every Catholic has in the eminent value of virginity is one thing; quite other are the attempts, sometimes more fortunate, sometimes less, to justify it intellectually that have been made in the course of centuries by theologians, spiritual writers or preachers. Dissatisfied with what he found in contemporary writers, Père Teilhard decided to work out his own explanation for himself, introducing considerations that were to some degree novel. He did this, we know, realizing that he could never be completely successful, but at the same time convinced that the practice of the Church always remains 'the basic foundation, the firmest, that all the philosophies can do no more than illustrate, with more or less accuracy'.[60]

But he went further than this. In 'L'Évolution de la Chasteté' the subject he was treating (as the title indicates) did not allow him to consider more than the spiritualization of love, its liberation from the flesh. In 'The Eternal Feminine', on the other hand, while the cosmic picture knows no limits, the human picture itself is also much wider. Since 'the attraction of the Feminine' can be seen in it as the source of all higher activity, 'the feminine ideal' must now apply its work of sublimation to each one of these activities, just as it does to love. Under the influence of its charm, a progressive condensation is effected; a unity is formed from above; one single object eclipses all the others, the one object which was sought through all the others, the only one to be ultimately worthy of engrossing man's attention:

Behold!
The centre of my attraction is imperceptibly shifting towards the pole upon which all the avenues of Spirit converge.
The iridescence of my beauties, flung like a mantle over creation, is slowly gathering in its outlying folds.
Already the shadow is falling upon the flesh, even the flesh purified by the sacraments.
One day, maybe, it will swallow up even art, even science – things loved as a woman is loved.
The beam circles: and we must follow it round.
Soon only God will remain for you in a universe where all is virgin.

It is God who awaits you in me!

'A universe where all is virgin' (or, more literally, 'a universe which is completely made virgin') – we can now see the truly total range of this phrase, which was not apparent when we quoted it earlier. Using language that gradually unfolds its meaning (even if it is open to objection) it is an evocation of the 'beatific vision', the final term to which the feminine ideal, the fruit of revelation, is leading us.

Meanwhile, the feminine ideal is only a transitional concept. The abstract form in which it is still expressed will ultimately have to be replaced by a personal reality. Like Auguste Valensin, Pierre Teilhard was a consistent personalist. In his youth he may well have experienced the 'fascination of the impersonal and generalized' and confused them with the universal; but as soon as he began to develop his thought, he made a complete change of direction. That is why, among other reasons, the attempts to more or less equate Teilhard's dialectic with an Hegelian type of dialectic seem to us to be doomed to failure.[61] As early as 1917, he was describing 'the circle of person' as the innermost and most real circle in the 'mystical milieu', at the centre of which he placed the being who 'has a name and a face . . . Jesus'.[62] His personalism, for which he was later to be at pains to construct a sounder foundation, was always to retain a realist, concrete flavour. Here, again, we should note the essential difference from Dante. In *The Divine Comedy*, when the poet meets Beatrice on the Mount of Purgatory, she says to him: 'Look at me well: truly am I, truly am I Beatrice.'[63] They both then pass through into heaven; but then comes the moment when, as Virgil faded away before Beatrice, so Beatrice fades away before St Bernard, who has been appointed to present Dante to the Virgin Mary. Thus Beatrice and the Virgin Mary are two distinct persons. In 'The Eternal Feminine' the personalism is no less emphasized, but there is only one person in it, not two. Béatrix (whose lack of identification is stressed by Teilhard's spelling) would be only a symbol, if she was not, rather, a pseudonym. She is shrouded in a veil. The mystery of the Feminine, in its purest essence, will not be revealed until the end. At the same time there is agreement between Teilhard and Dante. For each of them, the transformations and sublimations of love effected under the influence of Christianity,[64] which lead them away from Plato,[65] presuppose the whole of Christian reality, whose character is eminently personal. It is this which explains in particular the passage from Teilhard quoted earlier, and which we shall be considering again, about the Incarnation of the Word of God, drawn down to earth by the wonder he had created for that very purpose: 'I am Mary the Virgin.'

Following out the plan of this chapter, we should, however, note once more how a certain continuity persists from beginning to end, through all the most unexpected transformations; how, according to the point of view from which we look at things, a certain totalization is effected or, on the contrary, a certain distillation or spiritual purification. The principle of analogy governs everything, bringing about the unity of the whole vast curve. This is brought about by the constant use or repetition of certain words. At the very beginning the essential Feminine, starting its career in the most material and ill-defined forms, said: 'In me is seen that side of beings by which they are joined as one, in me the fragrance that makes them hasten together and leads them, freely and passionately, along their road to unity.' And now we find her who is finally about to pronounce her name, the woman blessed among women, explaining her unitive function in the same words:

> If God, then, was to be able to emerge from himself, he had first to lay a pathway of desire before his feet, he had to spread before him a sweet savour of beauty. . . .
>
> Lying between God and the earth, as a zone of mutual attraction, I draw them both together in a passionate union.

Particularly striking is the recurrence in each passage of the adjective or adverb 'passionate' or 'passionately'. We find it as early as 1916 in the introduction to 'Cosmic Life',[66] and it reappears in many later writings, as does the corresponding noun 'passion' and such adjectives as 'impassioned'.

In man, 'evolution . . . must, becoming conscious, fasten passionately upon itself';[67] in him, this evolution is being continued in 'a consciously and passionately willed deliberate act'.[68] According to Teilhard, man has the 'passion for the absolute'; he has an 'impassioned awareness';[69] his view of the world is 'both intellectual and impassioned';[70] it is an 'ardent vision', 'an impassioned vision of the earth';[71] man nurses in himself 'the sacred and impassioned hope of attaining fuller-being';[72] Teilhard would like to kindle in all men 'the passion for unity', more ardent than 'the passion for destruction' which is satisfied by war;[73] he associates 'passionate and legitimate love of earth's highest aggrandisement' with 'the sole quest for the Kingdom of Heaven';[74] he 'feels and loves the whole passionately';[75] he experiences 'passion for the divine',[76] the 'passion for union with God' and to fulfil his will; he 'will not shrink from a passionate questioning . . . concerning his God';[77] he is like 'Jacob passionately wrestling with God';[78] he 'seeks passionately for God in the heart of every substance and every action';[79] so absorbing is this quest that one might, paradoxically, define his basic attitude to every thing and every situation as a 'passionate indifference'. His effort is directed 'towards one unvarying goal, ever greater, and passionately loved';[80] he 'follows passionately' the current of life which is carrying him to that goal; it is precisely in virtue of his faith that he has a passion for the things of the earth, and he overcomes obstacles with the help of 'an added passion, a new sense of purpose';[81] this makes him 'love passionately' the 'most obscure' tasks, and in every one of them he finds 'a root identity of passionate interest and devotion'.[82] He is enamoured of purity, because purity unifies 'the inner powers of the soul in the act of a single passion'.[83] 'Through its evolutionary peak', that is to say through Christ, the vision of the world bursts upon him as 'passionately seductive';[84] this 'passion for Christ' seizes him,[85] and he fulfils his quest in an 'impassioned enfolding ... in the arms of the Cross'.[86] He admires the inspired 'passion' of a Paul, an Augustine or a Teresa.[87] He would wish ultimately to know but 'a single passion', or in other words 'a single "mysticism" '.[88] Teilhard tells us himself in *Le Christique* (1955) that ever since the time of 'The Mass on the World' and *Le Milieu Divin*, he has always contemplated the same fundamental vision 'with the same sense of wonder and the same passion' – the 'burning vision' of a 'universe a-flame', of a universe that is 'not impersonal and closed, but opening, beyond the future, into a divine centre'.[89]

In this vocabulary of passion (which is analogical) we have an excellent expression of one of the characteristics both of Teilhard's thought and of his concept of the universe. At the same time, it should not be misunderstood. The passion of which he speaks in these last quotations, whatever its natural substratum may be, is far from being a fruit 'of flesh and blood'. Its principle is not human. It is a force, says Teilhard, which I cannot give myself; 'it is a *primum datum*', and it eludes me as soon as I rely on myself to retain it.[90] We may certainly wonder whether in some particular instance the introduction of such passion into his thinking might not have brought with it some lack of moderation, impairing the objectivity of his view. We should, however, beware of a general rejection of his attitude; the fact is that there may well be 'domains of reality or, more precisely, of withdrawal from reality, in which the most complete detachment represents the effective cognitive approach'; but this is not the case when our purpose is to see into the real 'in its concrete infinity';[91] and may we not be justified in seeing in what characterizes Teilhard's thought and his universe what is also one of the characteristics of Christian thought and the Christian universe? 'Christians', M. Émile Bréhier has written, 'do not preserve, when confronted with the universe, the serenity of the Greek sage; they have an impassioned vision of it and, instead of making passion a lower form of the life of the spirit, they include it among the governing forces of the universe.' And is not this Christian attitude already prepared and prefigured by what Yahweh offered his people and demanded from them, the bond of a 'passionate relationship'?[92]

In the supernatural domain, passion is not extinguished (as the examples quoted make clear), but sublimated. But the conjunction it effects in this final stage is no longer a conjunction between earthly beings, but one 'of heaven and earth' – a spiritualized earth. This is the reality extolled, throughout Christian tradition, by commentaries on the Song of Songs.[93] If the universal ascent, under the influence of the feminine ideal, towards the beatific vision seemed (in our account above) to assume the appearance of a Platonic ascent, the reason is that this ideal, even when given the name of Béatrix, was still no more than the veil shrouding her who was to draw God down to earth. But what of her who borrowed the tongue of Wisdom to describe to us her long and dramatic history? From afar off, she prepared that 'conjunction of heaven and earth' stage by stage; finally she was herself realized in the woman who directly initiated it. We might think, then, that she would be destined to 'disappear as a useless handmaid', to vanish 'like a shadow before reality':

> Those who love me should dismiss this fear.
>
> Just as participated being is not lost when it attains its principle – but, on the contrary, finds fulfilment in melting in God . . .
>
> So the Cosmos, when divinized, will not expel my magnetic influence by which the ever more complex and more simplified fascicle of its atoms is progressively more closely – and permanently – knit

I shall subsist, entire, with all my past, even in the raptures of contact with God . . .

When you think I am no longer with you – when you forget me, the air you breathe, the light by which you see – then I shall still be at hand, lost in the sun I have drawn to myself.

In this blessed contemplation, in the union of heaven and earth, prepared since the beginning of the world, inaugurated in the bosom of the Virgin and now consummated, no more than a momentary relaxation of the tension which flings the elect into God and absorbs them in him would be sufficient for them once again to see 'playing over the surface of the divine fire' the image of her in whom all this is summed up – 'the ever-living series of allurements – of forces that one after another have made themselves felt ever since the borderline of nothingness, and so brought together and assembled the elements of Spirit – through love.' This image, this bond, this unity in the series, is the *Eternal Feminine*.[94]

Neat epitaph

CHAPTER 6

'The Veiled Virgin'

*

I. TEILHARD'S SYMBOLISM

After telling us in *The Phenomenon of Man* that 'driven by the forces of love, the fragments of the world seek each other so that the world may come to being', Teilhard immediately adds that 'this is no metaphor; and it is much more than poetry'. In his eyes, it is certain truth, whether you care to call it physics or metaphysics. That the realization of this truth through the various phases of the world's history or the various types of beings which make up the world is analogical, in no way detracts from its character of truth: 'but it is a truth whose observable manifestations show us only the outside: we cannot divine it straight away, as, for example, when we observe the phenomenon of gravity':

> Whether as a force or a curvature, the universal gravity of bodies, so striking to us, is merely a reverse or shadow of that which really moves nature. To perceive cosmic energy 'at the fount' we must, if there is a *within* of things, go down into the internal or radial zone of spiritual attractions.
> Love in all its subtleties is nothing more, and nothing less, than the more or less direct trace marked on the heart of the element by the psychical convergence of the universe upon itself.[1]

Even if there is something 'much more than poetry' in such views, it is none the less true that in expressing them Teilhard was trying to organize scientifically an intuition which is shared by poets. Here again, as so often, he comes close to Claudel, when the latter says that 'what is tension in matter is intention in spirit'.[2] He is akin, too, to Baudelaire, 'the Platonic poet', searching out the laws of 'universal analogy';[3] or to Benjamin Constant, for whom 'there was a great correspondence between moral and physical beings'.[4] We find a similar affinity in Pierre Emmanuel, when he says that 'a generalized symbolism transcends objective separation and restores effectiveness to signs in the affirmation of mysterious solidarities'.[5] An even better comparison, perhaps, would be with Pascal, whom many readers would be less inclined to suspect of insubstantial 'poetry'. It is true that Pascal defined with magnificent precision the infinite distance which separates 'the three orders' and the 'impossibility in nature of rising from one order to another'; but at the same time he was very much alive to the 'analogies and correspondences between the different levels of the real'.[6]

Only a couple of days before starting on 'The Eternal Feminine' – on the very day on which he was thinking of calling it 'Before a Veiled Virgin' – Père Teilhard was in fact copying into his notebook one of Pascal's *Pensées*, which he had just been reading in Émile Boutroux's *William James*:[7] 'Everything is one – the one is the other – like the three persons.'[8] Pascal, it is true, had also said, 'Everything is one, everything is different',[9] but at the same time he had thought that 'all things are held together by a natural though imperceptible chain which links the most far removed and different things';[10] and this view had led Pascal to criticize – as Teilhard was to do in more positive terms[11] – over-specialized scientists, 'imperfect scientists', as he called them, 'shut up in the narrow limits of their discipline which they thereby make it impossible for themselves to understand correctly'.[12] Again, as Teilhard was to be, Pascal was much more concerned to bring out the 'remarkable connexion by which nature, always enamoured of unity, brings together things apparently so far removed from one another'.[13] This is precisely what Teilhard was to say, in very similar language: 'Have we not known for a long time that the true advances of science consist precisely in discovering the hidden links uniting orders apparently very far apart?'[14]

Such a concept of the universe, which in no way rules out the use of strict analytical method but rejects 'the analytical illusion',[15] has much more than its scientific fruitfulness to recommend it. It shows a definite kinship to 'the mystical feeling', if it is true that, considered in its natural roots, this feeling is essentially (as Teilhard says) 'a sense and a presentiment of the final and total unity of the world, beyond its present, sensibly apprehended, multiplicity'.[16] The unity, however, of which he is speaking is not Baudelaire's 'deep and darksome unity'; it is not confusion but 'harmony'.[17] Just as it does not abolish the distinction between sources of knowledge, so it retains both the distinction between beings and the hierarchy of orders which are linked together by an omnipresence,[18] and thereby symbolize one another. This is what Newman noted when he said: 'The very idea of an analogy between the separate works of God leads to the conclusion that the system which is of less importance is economically or sacramentally connected with the more momentous system.'[19] This idea of analogy suggests that one system should be seen through the other; and so the development of a certain type of symbolism is encouraged and justified.[20]

This is exactly what we can see happening to Pierre Teilhard during the war years which brought the first flowering of his genius. His intuitions were later to seek a more strictly organized form, applying to this end all that he never ceased to acquire in the course of an incredibly active career; but first they became embodied and developed in the invention of a number of great symbols. In their very variety, almost all of these have this property in common,[21] of being more than a reinforcement drawn from the world of sense or imagination. On the other hand, they are in the first place existentially experienced realities, seen as such; they are facts of experience, and every time they are described or evoked they give us an autobiographical document. On the other hand, they emphasize a real relationship with what they symbolize – a relationship which at the same time, as we shall see, varies greatly according to the circumstances of each case. In 'Christ in the World of Matter' we have the three symbols of the picture, the monstrance and the pyx, that is to say of the heart of Christ and the eucharist, envisaged in their actual reality and with their origin in the part they played in Père Teilhard's interior life or priestly ministry. In 'La Nostalgie du Front' and 'La Grande Monade', we have the symbols of the front line and the moon, two things that are also very real, and evoke wartime nights in the trenches. And finally, in 'The Eternal Feminine', we have Béatrix.

The three symbols in 'Christ in the World of Matter', it is true, already contain the very reality which the story is going to bring out in sensibly apprehensible form. In the first of the three stories, the action of the heart of Christ, imposing its form on the universe without either absorbing it or being absorbed by it, is symbolized by a 'vibrant atmosphere' which 'radiated outwards to infinity'. In the first place, even so, this heart was seen only as something painted in a picture. In 'The Monstrance' and 'The Pyx',[22] it is the consecrated host itself, seen with all the realism of faith, which arouses in the narrator the symbolic images which will give the believer a glimpse of its power of universal penetration, but also of inexorable discrimination, and at the same time will show him the mysterious gap, impossible to bridge, before Christ reveals himself to him fully when earthly life has reached its term. We know that the literary form Père Teilhard adopted in these stories was suggested to him by Robert Hugh Benson's *The Light Invisible* which he had read in June 1912 and, he said, had greatly admired.[23] It is only the second story, however, 'The Monstrance', which, in the opening scene, is directly inspired by one of Benson's, 'In the Convent Chapel'.[24] The first starts from a picture with which Père Teilhard had long been familiar, and the third is based on his experience as a priest-stretcher-bearer, carrying the blessed sacrament on his person; 'thinking of our Lord, so close to me, since the pyx is lying on my heart, and so far from me, since I am so little penetrated by him, I resolved, etc.'[25] In any case, one has only to read the collection of imaginatively mystical stories contained in *The Light Invisible* to realize how far apart the two authors are – as far, one might say, as *Crime and Punishment* is from a straightforward detective story.[26]

The symbols we meet next are more complex. In 'La Nostalgie du Front', the front line, before being given any symbolic function, is extremely real, seen and lived as such. It is the front line that many others who fought in the same war have described or tried to describe. It does much more, too, than serve as a colourful background for what the writer has to say: it is the front line itself, in its full reality, which arouses in him the feelings he wishes to describe. We must, however, try to understand the direction in which it arouses them. We must see how its symbolic significance grows deeper step by step.

At the outset, one simple observation will prevent us from being misled. In this essay, Teilhard's subject is not, as some have thought, the war, but the *front*. Anyone who survived that great cataclysm, and has had experience of life in the trenches, will immediately appreciate the difference. And many of them will be able to bear witness – though they may not have been so clearly aware of it and may not have analysed it so exactly – that they themselves experienced something of the same sort as that which they find in Teilhard's essay. They will recognize themselves in it, although that does not mean that they can be suspected in the least of having a war-mongering spirit. In the dozen pages or so of 'Nostalgie' the word 'war', it will be noted, occurs only four times (it could hardly be completely absent from an account by a man on active service) but 'the front' comes in twenty-one times, not counting similar expressions such as 'the line' or 'the shore'. In this piece, which is all symbol, it is not the war which provides the symbol, even though the war was its occasion – an occasion forced on the writer – and the place it occupies for a time,[27] as a fact, in the history of man and his progress is indicated towards the end of the article. The source of the symbolism is the front, the front line. We must not confuse nostalgia for the front – which Teilhard was never to lose and which many other survivors of the war of 1914 were also to experience – with nostalgia for the war.[28] In 1950, writing in *Le Cœur de la Matière* about this article, he refers in similar terms to the 'atmosphere of "the front"'. Once again, it is in fact in itself, in its real existence as lived by Pierre Teilhard and his comrades, that the front line is said to be 'fascinating'; it is the front line which arouses in him that 'feeling of fulfilment and of the super-human' which he fears he will no longer experience when the war is over. But this is not quite, in fact it is not even at all, because it is the firing line: if one saw in it only the firing line 'the sights you see and the life you lead would be more than you could bear'.[29] The real reason is that it is *the Front*.[30]

In this advanced position, one has left behind 'the daily slavery' of the countless banalities which make up the normal life of today; there one 'bathes in the pure real, outside all conventions'; there one breathes 'an immense freedom'; and there, for the reflective mind, is a ready symbol heralding 'a more intimate liberation – liberation from evil egocentrism and narrowness of personality'. So true is this, that 'going up the line is an ascent into peace'.[31] Even so, this first emancipation is still only the outer fringe of a more exalted freedom. The atmosphere of the front, 'pure and subtle', is also 'full of substance and nourishment', for, breaking through all social distinctions and barriers, it is charged 'with the vast presence of man', 'it is permeated by a vast presence which is sheer man'.[32]

There, the individual soul expands to the dimensions of the 'soul of the whole', in a detachment from its own self which is 'inexorably effected' by the 'magnitude of the common task and the imminent danger of death'.[33] It is, in short, 'a heaven-laden air that one breathes there'.

There is, however, something more to explain the extra-ordinary vibrancy of these pages written on returning from the front: something which, without in any way robbing this 'sublime area' of its tragically real character, transforms it – on this occasion only for Teilhard himself – into an immense forward-looking sign. And it is here that we cannot but admire the strength of symbolic imagination shown by one whom we may regard either as a prophet, or, if we like, as a visionary or a creator of myths. The vision that Teilhard was always, from that time, to retain, seen through 'the firing line, the exposed area corroded by the conflict of nations', was 'the "front of the wave" carrying the world of man towards its new destiny'.[34] It is indeed a 'shore', but such a shore as would border an ocean in which the tide never ceases to rise. It is no longer the line of division between two camps, between the two halves of mankind confronting one another, slaughtering and paralysing one another: it is the great line of attack, the ' "front-line" of humanity',[35] the line of man's advance, as it impressed itself on him one evening in concrete form when his unit was being relieved:

Now the Chemin des Dames was being completely swallowed up in darkness. I rose to go down to my billet. And as I turned back to take a last look at that sacred line, the warm and living line of the front, in a flash of half-formed intuition I thought I could see it taking on the form of some higher, very noble, entity: I felt that it was coalescing as I watched it, but that it would have called for a more perfect mind than mine to grasp it and understand it. I thought, then, of those fantastically vast cataclysms which, aeons ago, had only animals to witness them. – And it seemed to me, at that moment, that confronted with this great thing that was coming into being, I was like a dumb beast whose soul is awakening and can perceive groups of correlated realities and yet cannot see what it is that holds together the single reality they represent.[36]

Here again the relation of the symbol (present reality) to the thing symbolized (reality in the future) is a real relationship. There is not only an intelligible connexion between the two, a relationship between sign and thing signified: what the writer wishes us also to understand is that the symbolizing reality (the war front, which at the end is compared to a 'cataclysm' of nature) contributes to the coming into being of the symbolized reality, to the formation of 'this great thing that was coming into being', to the new advance of the human front which has been glimpsed, is hoped for, and foretold.[37]

There was an interval of four months between 'La Grande Monade' and 'La Nostalgie du Front'. As Teilhard himself was to note later,[38] there is a continuity between the two. This does not mean that there is repetition – the theme is carried further, and this, as we shall be seeing, involves a reversal of approach.[39] So the vision he has glimpsed now unfolds itself, and it is the moon, rising over the trenches, in this same front line, which will give definition to its features. Here we no longer have the symbolic gradation of the first of these two essays. 'La Grande Monade', that 'slightly crazy fantasy',[40] which is perhaps Teilhard's literary masterpiece, is made up of two contrasting parts. The moon is first taken as a symbol 'of the thinking earth', in other words of unified mankind rising up in one great unanimous effort; and then suddenly it becomes the symbol of cosmic death. Without examining here the details of the symbolism or even the basic principle behind his thought,[41] we may simply note that if in the first part the moon serves purely as a symbol, in the second part it is indeed the realness of the 'dead star', 'the implacable mirror' reflecting the future of the earth, which stands as a supreme warning to men and urges them to take thought.

2. MARIAN THEOLOGY

We come, then, to 'The Eternal Feminine', written only two months after 'La Grande Monade'. Here again we have a symbolic writing, but, as we have already seen, one conceived in a new form. In this third composition the relation of symbol to reality is both similar to and at the same time different from that in either of the two earlier pieces. It can be properly understood only if we recognize in it the application of one of the fundamental themes in Teilhard's thought: that of the union of the personal and the universal. A fortnight after finishing 'The Eternal Feminine' Père Teilhard was to give this theme its first, more abstract, expression in 'Mon Univers' (14 April 1918); shortly afterwards he tried to put it more exactly in two versions: first in 'Forma Christi' (December 1918), and then in 'The Universal Element' (January 1919). These were preliminary to his more fully worked out syntheses, of which we need mention here only one, with the significant title, 'Sketch of a Personalistic Universe' (1936). The principal application of the theme was to be contained in the doctrine, dear to Père Teilhard, of 'the universal Christ'. In this poem, however, the personal reality directly concerned is not Christ, but the Virgin Mary.

At the outset the reader might think that this is one more example of the old method, common to all primitive poetry as it is to all allegory, which consists in personifying a principle. Whether spontaneous or made with conscious art, this method obviously cannot give the principle in question a personal individuality. The universal Feminine, like the biblical Wisdom, speaks in the first person, making itself known, at the beginning, only as the 'essential Feminine'. As the poem proceeds, the personification becomes more marked, starting from the moment when the principle is given a proper name: Béatrix. Nevertheless one may still question whether this Béatrix may not still be an abstract figure. She does not, it would seem, correspond to any real being in the universe.

Nevertheless, we already know that this is a mistaken conclusion; we have learnt as much from Teilhard's preparatory notes. Béatrix is the veiled virgin.[42] The real being has not yet been disclosed, but is indeed there, beneath the veil. It was there from the outset, hidden at the heart of the principle. It existed before all other creatures – as did Wisdom itself – and the 'essential Feminine', or the 'universal Feminine', was no more than what we might call the veil of its veil. But if we are to be sure that this interpretation has a solid basis, if, that is, we are to bring out its full meaning, we must once again remember what, in Teilhard's view, is the true relationship between the personal and the universal. It is not the universal which takes on for us the appearance of the personal in order that it may make itself apprehensible by giving itself mythical expression; the universal does not become more or less personal and so acquire an added attribute. It is the personal which becomes universal, to the degree in which (subject to certain conditions) it realizes more profoundly its own specific character. Universality is the prerogative of the strongest personality.[43] God, apart from whom nothing subsists, is pre-eminently the personal being, and it is for that very reason that nothing subsists apart from him: even more, too, for that very reason, he is the 'personalizing' being. In becoming universal, Christ is not dissolved in the universe; he is the 'plasmatic principle' of the universe, he exercises upon it his 'enveloping and unifying action' and imposes his form on it:[44] and that is why we can speak with equal justification of both a 'Christified universe' and a 'universalized Christ'.[45] Similarly, in 'The Eternal Feminine', Père Teilhard does not identify a universal principle with the individual being who is the Virgin Mary, in a way which detracts from that individual being. On the contrary: it is not an abstract principle which is personified in the Virgin – it is the Virgin, existing in her own individuality, who is universalized in the principle. When, much later, Teilhard summed up one of his meditations in the words: 'Annunciation: mystery of the Feminine',[46] he was not enclosing the Virgin in the mystery of the Feminine; it was the mystery he saw enclosed in the Virgin, and receiving its fullest significance from her. Even more emphatically, then, the Virgin Mary is not for Teilhard a sort of literary personification or allegory, used to make some general idea intelligible in poetical terms. If, then, we speak of symbol, we shall not be saying that in this context the Virgin Mary is the fully realized symbol of the universal Feminine, but rather that this universal Feminine must be understood, in its pure essence, as the Virgin Mary.

This is of prime importance. In 1928, Père Teilhard was already able to say that the history of his interior life was that of a 'quest for progressively more universal and perfect realities'.[47] A year earlier, in those pages of 'The Mystical Milieu' which echo with such vibrancy the experience on which 'The Eternal Feminine' is based, he had brought out, in his outline of the cognitive process, the fundamental development of that quest:

> We imagine that in our sense-perceptions external reality humbly presents itself to us in order to serve us, to help in the building up of our integrity. But this is merely the surface of the mystery of knowledge; the deeper truth is that when the world reveals itself to us, it draws us into itself; it causes us to flow outwards into something belonging to it, everywhere present in it, and more perfect than it.

This 'something', rather clumsily suggested in this passage – this reality which the purely matter-of-fact man can hardly perceive but which remains even when the world 'withdraws from us' – this, Teilhard goes on to say in the next paragraph, is 'the unique essence of the universe'.[48] It is what he was a little later to call 'the concrete universal'.[49]

Teilhard and Blondel both use the expression 'concrete universal', and both give it the same fundamental meaning. Both, again, carefully distinguish the universal from the general. For Blondel, the concrete universal is fully realized in the actual being of the supremely personal God. 'True unity', the unity which pantheism looks for but fails to find and to which Christianity leads us, 'consists', said Blondel, 'in the presence in us and in all things of one and the same real mediation, of a concrete universal which, without being involved in the imperfections of creatures and their finite mode of being, is nevertheless, itself and complete, in all things.'[50] More precisely, the Christian recognizes this concrete universal in Christ, man, and God, who is 'the universal cohesive bond, the *vinculum vinculorum*, the supreme, single constituent which contributes to the firmness of the whole. He is the cohesive bond of whom St Paul said, *in quo omnia constant, Primogenitus omnis creaturae*, of whom St John says that 'all things were made by him and that without him all that is, would be nothing.'[51]

We find what is fundamentally the same idea in what Hans Urs von Balthasar says, speaking, from the historical point of view, of 'the two great limitations which characterize the finite being':

No individual being can as such be the universal, and no universal can be the individual. – But . . . in Christ it is God himself who comes. Christ is neither one individual among others (since he is God in person), nor is he the norm in the sense of a universal (since he is a completely concrete individual) . . . He is a 'concrete Universal', a 'universal Concrete' . . . Philosophically speaking, we may say that the Phoenix – that is to say an individual which in itself exhausts its whole species – is an impossibility. Theology, on the other hand, starts from the Phoenix, Christ, who, in as much as he is this individual being, is the universal (since he is the absolute norm): Christ, who precisely in as much as he is this contingent being in history, is the indispensable Law set above all history and all nature.[52]

This notion of concrete universal obviously presupposes for Teilhard, just as it does for Blondel and Balthasar, a certain identification of the personal and the universal. At the same time we must add that the identification is to be conceived in a particular sense: God is 'universal personality';[53] he is not universal principle personalized by man; the 'personal-universal' is the 'supreme personality'.[54] Taken in the contrary sense, the identification would replace the ontology of personal beings by a mythology of abstractions. It would produce a new 'gnosis' (or let us rather say, following St Irenaeus, and preserving the true force of a Pauline word, a 'pseudo-gnosis' or perverted gnosis). If, however, the identification is understood in its true sense, it constitutes an attempt to probe the mystery more deeply; it is a legitimate step towards 'understanding the faith'. There is, in fact, no doubt about the true sense. In contrast with every form of 'gnosis', Teilhard's teaching is a realism, and a 'personalist' realism. He has, it is true, 'a dominating sense of the universal', to the point where, as he tells us himself, 'he cannot appreciate anything except on the scale of the universal';[55] everything he wrote, moreover, is a confirmation of this. Yet his universe is none the less a 'personal universe'. This personal universe is in no way the improper personalization (or the mythical personification) of an impersonal. It is 'the centration of the universe by a supreme person',[56] by a supreme 'someone': 'Common sense is right. It is impossible to give oneself to anonymous number. But if the universe ahead of us assumes a face and a heart, and so to speak personifies itself (not, of course, by becoming a person, but by charging itself at the very heart of its development with

the dominating and unifying influence of a focus of personal energies and attractions), then in the atmosphere
created by this focus the elemental attraction will immediately
blossom.'[57]

Towards the end of this same year, 1918, in which he had
written 'The Eternal Feminine', Père Teilhard blames Meister
Eckhart, in one of his reading notes, for having sometimes, at
least in the language he used, confused the concrete universal
with an abstract universal.[58] Teilhard's own God, 'universal'
because 'hyper-personal', is the complete opposite (here, again,
it is Teilhard himself who makes this clear) of 'this common
foundation of the tangible-element of all elements, support of
all substances' that one might obtain by abstraction or that one
might apprehend 'through the relaxed and diffuse before there
is any determination or any form'.[59] Similarly, Teilhard's
Christ is completely different from that of Hegel, for whom
'the Christ of history is, in comparison with the religion found
in mind and truth (which may be identified with reason and
philosophy), inessential and contingent'.[60] Teilhard's Christ,
like Blondel's, 'is truly the centre and cohesive bond of the
whole body of monads destined to build up glorified man'[61] –
he is 'the universal Christ',[62] but this is because he is in the first
place God incarnate, God-man, Jesus, the being born of the
Virgin. Thus he is both personal and universal.[63] The Virgin
(and this is where we meet the boldness of Teilhard's Mariology) is closely associated with the personal and universalizing
work of her son. To understand this association is to 'universalize Our Lady' and at the same time to understand how much
she is 'truly unique: *Virgo Singularis: Χαίρε, μόνη*'.[64]

We find something that in all essentials corresponds exactly
to Teilhard's teaching, even though it is less complex and not
so structurally complete, in a work published sixteen years
after 'The Eternal Feminine' by a writer who could not have
read Teilhard's poem. Gertrud von le Fort's *Die ewige Frau*
is essentially the Virgin Mary: it is Mary who 'gives form to

the metaphysical mystery of woman and makes it conceiv-able'; it is in Mary that 'the mystery of the Feminine as such' is concentrated, with 'its metaphysical and cosmic qualities, its place in the religious scheme, its origin and end in God'.[65] Gertrud von le Fort realizes, just as Père Teilhard did, that this mystery has been through a number of preparatory phases: 'before Mary came the Sybil'; she knows, too, that at first the face of eternal woman is veiled, and 'that it is for God alone to raise the veil he has imposed'.[66] In this, however, there is again nothing that impairs or distorts in the slightest degree the unique and pre-eminent reality of Mary. At the same time, we may say that this idea of the 'eternal woman', in spite of its cosmic qualities, falls short, by a long way, of Teilhard's idea of the eternal Feminine.

There are other, older doctrines which, without always being more cosmic, offer a similar concept of the 'universalized' Virgin. In his *Traité des saints Ordres*, the theologian-poet Jean-Jacques Olier hailed in Mary 'the universal creature'. He urged his reader to contemplate in her, unified in its pure quality, the sum of perfections dispersed in all the members of the Church.[67] In so doing, Olier was reaffirming the old medieval doctrine which identified in Mary the unique 'species' within which the whole 'genus' is included or from a starting-point in which all grace is transmitted to the 'genus'. In one word, which Paul Claudel was to adopt again and amplify, Mary was seen as the 'form' of the whole Church: in her ineffable person, said Claudel, she 'is the form of the Church, the form of humanity, and the form of all creation'.[68] This doctrine itself, however, was but a particular application of the great theme which has dominated scriptural interpretation, and all Christian thought, throughout the centuries. We find it in a sermon of St Bona-venture, expressed in terms that could not be more explicit. Commenting on the symbol of the Ark of the Covenant, St Bonaventure sees in it, in the allegorical sense, an image of the Church; in the tropological sense, an image of the soul of the blessed; in the anagogic or mystical sense, an image of the heavenly Jerusalem; but all these senses converge on a peak which brings them together and transcends them, to denote mystically the unique wonder of the Blessed Virgin Mary: pre-eminently the Ark of God's Covenant with man in Jesus Christ.[69]

Père Teilhard made no attempt methodically to combine his thoughts on the Blessed Virgin into a body of doctrine, any more than he did with any other of the mysteries of the Christian faith. His Marian theology can be deduced only from occasional passages. Nevertheless its characteristic features are sufficiently numerous, well marked and consistent with one another, to give it a definite form. To use a term which Teilhard applied to all his teaching, his Marian theology is 'hyper-catholic'. Some readers might feel that it goes too far. Those who have seen (mistakenly, we believe) a 'gnosis'[70] in his Christology will be inclined to say the same about his Mariology. Here we may say no more than that it is expressed, occasionally, in terms that are undoubtedly justifiable theologically but are not necessarily a matter of faith.

In seeing all the 'chaste essence of the Feminine'[71] realized in Mary, Père Teilhard thereby attributes to the Virgin, considered in what is most concrete, individual and intimately her own in her personality, a sort of universality which is analogous to the universality he recognizes in Christ.[72] In consequence, we find in Teilhard, in his piety as in his teaching, a constant parallel between the Son and his Mother. Of both he resolves 'to make them more real in his life'.[73] Just as Christ is 'Our Lord', so Mary is 'Our Lady'. He was always particularly fond of that name for her – 'Our Lady', 'Notre Dame' – by which he had been taught as a child to address her, and which reminded him of the old basilica in Clermont, Notre-Dame-du-Port, and his own school, Notre-Dame-de-Mongré. (It was the name, too, that St Ignatius Loyola used.) He believed that it was natural for a Christian 'to love Our Lady passionately'.[74]

A note written in 1917 establishes a sort of equivalence between 'Our Lord, perfect man' and 'Our Lady, the ideally pure woman'. It was Teilhard's practice, at the end of his annual spiritual exercises, to add to St Ignatius's '*Sume et suscipe*', which is addressed to the Lord, a consecration to the Virgin: '*O Domina mea*' – just as he did in his school-days, as a sodalist. Within the mystical body, he believed, Mary fulfils a 'mysterious function which is complementary' to Christ's: for each one of us she serves as the necessary 'introducer'.[75] Similarly, he establishes a parallel between Our Lord's Ascension and Mary's Assumption, applying to each the same text from St Paul's Epistle to the Ephesians. Even if we cannot say of the Virgin, as we do of Christ, that she 'descended', we can nevertheless say that she 'ascended, that she might fill all things'.[76] And that is why, like Christ, with whom she is henceforth fully associated, she is 'universal': with Christ, 'she has filled all things'.

It was on 15 August 1940 that Père Teilhard applied in this way to the Virgin Mary the text from the Epistle to the Ephesians (4: 8–10). Ten years later he had no difficulty in understanding the definition by Pius XII of the dogma of the Assumption. In his correspondence he even gave a psychological justification of the definition. It is worth mentioning this incidentally, but since it was no more than a passing comment there is no need to dwell upon it. It does, however, serve as an example to illustrate his general theory of the way in which the Christian revelation fits in with our natural aspirations. 'I am too conscious', he wrote when the papal definition was announced, 'of the bio-psychological necessity of the "Marian" (to counterbalance the "masculinity" of Yahweh) not to feel the profound need for this gesture.'[77] A little later, he said the same thing in more general terms, when combating Jung's thesis that the increasing dominance of Mariology in Catholic mysticism 'was the work of women, who are determined to see themselves well "represented" in the structure of the Kingdom of Heaven'. Such an interpretation seemed to Teilhard not only superficial but false. He quoted against it the history of Christian spirituality, which shows that those with the greatest devotion to the Virgin were men, and he expressed once again his conviction 'of the irresistible Christian need' which legitimate development of the cult of Mary serves to satisfy in the Church: the need to correct 'a dreadfully masculinized' conception of the Godhead.[78] For his own part, Teilhard liked to think of God, to entrust himself to God, as to a great maternal force.[79] This is a characteristic that he had in common with Père Auguste Valensin – and one that is very much in keeping with the Catholic ethos: in the sacred Psalms which the Church puts every day into the mouths of all her priests, does not God appear 'alternately majestic and "maternal" '?[80]

This extempore psycho-analysis (the letter just quoted was addressed to an enthusiastic psycho-analyst) does not justify the conclusion that Père Teilhard wished to make Mary the counterpart of some goddess or to include her in the divine Trinity! He himself corrected, though with some clumsiness, the paradox of his statement, by specifying that it can only be a question of an 'outer atmosphere or envelope' and not of God himself.[81] Like all of us, Mary is a creature; when we consider her in her life on earth, we see her above all as the perfect model of what the creature should be before the face of God. We know how, when Père Teilhard is speaking of the mysteries of the Immaculate Conception and the Annunciation,[82] he urges us to contemplate her in her open, receptive attitude. He also asks us to admire in her the virtues of faith, purity, humility, fidelity, and silence: the 'static virtues', which are eminently the Marian virtues, and in which he also sees the eminently 'operative virtues'. In an intentional paradox he compares them to a 'huge fire', 'a mighty torrent'.[83] Speaking of the contemplative, the man visited by God, through whom 'as though through a sacred door opening on to the universe, God passes . . . and spreads his radiance', Teilhard wrote:

Seeing the mystic immobile, crucified or rapt in prayer, some may perhaps think that his activity is in abeyance or has left this earth: they are mistaken. Nothing in the world is more intensely alive and active than purity and prayer, which hang like an unmoving light between the universe and God. Through their serene transparency flow the waves of creative power charged with natural virtue and with grace. What else but this is the Virgin Mary?[84]

From the very outset Mary was, indeed, this transparent medium. Purity is 'the inward tension of the mind towards God'; it is 'the rectitude and the impulse introduced into our lives by the love of God sought in and above everything'. It is, Teilhard tells us again, 'in spite of outward appearances, essentially an active virtue, because it concentrates God in us and on those who are subject to our influence'.

The inward tension of the mind towards God may seem negligible to those who try to calculate the quantity of energy accumulated in the mass of humanity.

And yet, if we could see the 'light invisible' as we can see clouds or lightning or the rays of the sun, a pure soul would seem as active in this world, by virtue of its sheer purity, as the snowy summits whose impassable peaks breathe in continually for us the roving powers of the high atmosphere.[85]

More than any other creature, the Virgin Mary practised this 'active virtue', and practised it incessantly. In Our Lady, 'all modes of lower, restless, activity disappear within this single, luminous, function of drawing God to oneself, of receiving him and letting him penetrate one's being.'[86] Those men and women who are like Mary have had 'the better part'.[87]

With this solid basis for his Mariology, Père Teilhard was in no danger of falling into those distortions of a cult of Mary whose roots, sometimes more obviously and sometimes less, are independent of the mystery of Christ. With his keen perception, he was conscious of the danger for what he called 'the greatest Christic' that might arise not from the development of 'the Marian' but from allowing it to get out of hand.[88] There is no doubt, too, that he would have had reservations about some exaggerated forms of devotion to Our Lady; nor can we find in Teilhard certain individual expressions of faith or devotion such as we meet in his contemporary, Louis Massignon, whom at the same time he admired.[89] This sort of caution, however, did not arise from any doctrinal 'minimism' or frigidity. It comes as no surprise to learn that he always loved the rosary – a prayer so pure and simple, 'an expansion . . . of the Ave Maria', which can become mere routine but can also become contemplation, as Teilhard once explained in a wartime sermon.[90] It is a prayer in which the whole mystery of salvation comes to life again, and which is instinct with the feeling of human misery, cured by the refreshing message of the Gospel.

If Mary is, as Teilhard says, 'the Pearl of the Cosmos' and 'the link with the incarnate personal Absolute',[91] she is in consequence very much an element of the cosmos. At the same time, she is set 'above the world and church as a never-fading nimbus',[92] and since the day of the Incarnation she is inseparable from her son. Therefore Père Teilhard accords to her 'an essential role in Christic evolution' or 'Christogenesis', by which he means in evolution activated, dominated, penetrated, vivified by Christ,[93] that so his mystical Body may progressively be constituted. Mary already shares in her son's 'dominating influence'. With him she forms 'the fully-developed centre' of the 'new earth'; around this centre 'the nebula (of the elect) is in process of segregation and concentration'.[94] So strikingly pictorial an expression of the dogma reminds us of one of the masterpieces of Byzantine iconography: the majestic central group in which Virgin and Child are one indissoluble whole so powerfully conveying an intense mystical feeling – such a group as can be seen, for example, in the apse of the Cathedral of Torcello. We can appreciate, too, how Père Teilhard, prompted by his own intuition, revived the ancient patristic and medieval theme: that he saw the Virgin, as again he saw her son, mystically identified, in a certain aspect, with the Church. Or rather, to put the two in the correct order, we can appreciate that he saw the Church mystically identified with the Virgin.

But this is not all. If it is true that 'the directness of the vision of God is not a denial of the mediatorship of Christ as man',[95] it may well be that in order fully to understand Père Teilhard's thought and decipher the final section of his poem, we must say something similar of the Virgin Mary. When Dante had entered Paradise, St Bernard urged him to look upon the face of Mary, 'for that is the face most like unto Christ' and 'its brilliance alone can fit you to see Christ'.[96] Similarly, for Teilhard, the group of Mother and Son still remains indivisible, but in a unity that is stronger and more mysteriously suggested. 'The Feminine' is a 'component' of the universe – provided that it has been followed to the zenith of its ascent. At every degree, and therefore again at the highest degree, the Feminine is the 'unitive aspect' of the real. 'Its progressive development (not its suppressive)' has given 'the Virgin, who gives Christ' – and who gives him to us for ever.[97] Immediately after revealing its purest essence, its unique and definitive essence, in the words 'I am Mary the Virgin', the eternal Feminine – the pellucid ambience – thus fully vindicates her name by speaking of her eternal role.[98]

PART TWO

TEILHARD AND THE PROBLEMS OF TODAY

*

CHAPTER I

The New Approach

*

In spite of the great differences that still persist between countries or continents, a number of facts are beginning to emerge which are common to mankind as a whole. A mixture of joys and sorrows, of painful disappointment and hope, is shared by a number of observant and thoughtful persons in almost every quarter. Throughout the whole world such men 'see themselves sharing a common history';[1] they know that they are confronted by a 'common danger' and experience.[2] For the first time in the existence of the human species, and in spite of the terrible divisions produced by world wars and the conflict of great ideological systems, a longing for real unity is making itself felt. Suffering and destitution of every sort, more keenly felt than ever, are not weakening confidence in the ability of scientific and technological progress to produce a better life. Notwithstanding all the disheartening experiences, all the selfishness, misunderstanding, and inertia, a great effort is being made on all sides to promote an economic, social and cultural development that we can only call – human. Obstacles may rise up again as fast as they are removed, but even so it is becoming more and more impossible not to be conscious of the emergence of a grand concept, which only yesterday might have been regarded as madness: the concept of 'working to construct the world'.

We know, too, how much the Catholic Church is encouraging all her faithful to pursue this line – urging them to get rid of the narrow-minded polemical approach that has so often, during these last centuries, clouded their view and paralysed their activity, and exhorting them to take an active part in this progressive movement: as, indeed, is demanded by that love of man, that 'cult of man'[3] which our faith inspires in us. A new significant example of this is the recent encyclical *Populorum Progressio*: nor can we fail to see the surge of energy that Vatican 2 produced in the Church, the boundless goodwill of many Christians, the general spirit of enterprise and initiative – all these indications of a new approach that are to be found in every quarter.

Both inside and outside the Catholic community, the writings of Père Teilhard de Chardin have made a very great impact; and without doubt this is largely because readers have found in them both an agonized awareness of the same dangers and the same fundamental aspiration. Undeterred by disappointments, 'stronger than every obstacle and counter-argument',[4] we find in Teilhard the same hope and the same eagerness to get to work. It is because Teilhard's teaching gives definite expression to these hopes and fears, because it indicates them and guides them, that he is so widely read.

One of the chief signs of Père Teilhard's originality – one of the marks, we might say, of his genius – is that he was a generation ahead of his contemporaries. What we feel today, what is tending to become part of every man's consciousness – sometimes even becoming a commonplace (with the consequent inevitable simplifications and distortions) – this young Jesuit was already thinking out and expressing, as he meditated in his solitude, over half a century ago. Towards the end of his life he wrote: 'Like a doctor at a sick-bed, we often wonder why all around us we should see this hitherto unknown amalgam of anxieties and hopes bringing restless uneasiness to individuals and to nations.'[5] Teilhard was to endeavour to build up a foundation of Christian hope, a 'faith in man' which will triumph over our anxieties. This he began to do as early as the First World War, when men were divided more bitterly than ever before. Writing in little exercise books, during intervals of rest between spells in the front line, he was already giving an initial form to the great dream of unity whose structure and conditions he was later to seek ever more earnestly to define. 'Even here, in this battered hovel at Avocourt, where shells may at any moment surprise the unfortunate passer-by, I can feel my soul swelling in the great hope of things to be done tomorrow, after the war.'[6]

'In its essence', he wrote again, 'the mystical feeling is a presentiment of the total and final unity of the world, beyond its present, sensibly apprehended, multiplicity'[7] – apprehended, moreover, painfully. Such a feeling, however, is not sufficient in itself. In Pierre Teilhard it is combined with an outlook on the world's progress which is such as to inspire consequent action. Unity has to be built up. A certain unity can be realized in history. There is a future to be constructed, an earth to be constructed, a world to be constructed.[8] The Construction of the World: that is precisely the title he gave to the first section of one of his essays:

> The world is under construction. This is a fundamental truth which must be understood at the start, and so thoroughly understood as to become habitual and more or less natural to our thought. At first sight, beings and their fate may possibly appear to be distributed by chance, or at least arbitrarily, over the face of the earth . . . [as though] the universe from the beginning to the end of its history [were] like a sort of vast flower-bed in time and space in which the flowers are interchangeable at the gardener's whim. This view seems at fault. The more we reflect, making use of what we have learnt from science, philosophy and religion, each along its own lines, the more we see that the world must be compared not to a bundle of elements in artificial juxtaposition, but to an organized system, informed by a broad unity of growth proper to itself. . . . Something is afoot in the universe, a result is working out which can best be compared to a gestation and birth: the birth of a spiritual

reality formed by souls and the matter they draw after them. Laboriously, by way of human activity and thanks to it, the new earth is gathering, isolating and purifying itself. No, we are not like flowers in a bunch, but like the leaves and flowers of a great tree, on which each appears at its time and place, according to the demands of the All.[9]

Nevertheless, we must be careful not to make a mistake about this. In its Constitution *Gaudium et Spes* the Council, it is true, urges us to follow this course and so construct the world, but it would not have us lose our way. It points out to us, in the first principles of our faith, the only permanent foundation, the only permanent conditions, the only ultimate Term to be envisaged in such construction; and it shows us the only spirit in which it is rightly to be undertaken. This, again, is precisely what Père Teilhard sought to do. In this connexion it is important to establish the true meaning of his thought against interpretations and applications that do violence to it. 'Teilhardian optimism' has become a catch-phrase, but, in the sense in which it is sometimes understood, it is doubly erroneous. Père Teilhard never envisaged an idyllic future for the world; he did not cherish the Utopia of a world to be built 'like a nice comfortable home'; nor did he ever think that evolution would lead the world to salvation by a natural development. He completely rejected the myth of a Golden Age.[10] We shall never understand his teaching if we omit from it, first its transcendent eschatological outlook, and, secondly, the central consideration of freedom, which includes the ever-present danger of defeat.

Were the cosmos to be no more than this present world, improved to any degree we may care to imagine, no thought could be more resolutely anti-cosmic than Teilhard's. 'As the years go by, Lord, I come to see more and more clearly, in myself and those around me, that the great secret preoccupation of modern man is much less to battle for possession of the world than to find a means of escaping from it. The anguish of feeling that one is not merely spatially but ontologically imprisoned in the cosmic bubble . . .'[11] 'To know that we are not prisoners, to know that there is a way out, that there is air, and light, and love, somewhere, beyond the reach of all death!'[12] The reader will no doubt have noted in the passage quoted earlier that Teilhard does not envisage the birth he hopes for ultimately – the birth of a 'new earth' – simply as the result of an immanent transformation of the species, nor does he locate it in a temporal future. He sees it as a 'new beginning in a quite new realm', as the coming of 'the spiritual reality formed by the souls of the elect, united in their divine homeland'.[13] That passage, moreover, was quoted from an essay entitled 'The Significance and Positive Value of Suffering', an excellent illustration of the fact that Teilhard was prepared to accept the extremely rigorous conditions that alone can make the great dream of unity something more than a Utopia. The pure heart, the believers, the faithful, 'the contemplatives and the men of prayer' with whom 'the sick and suffering' are urged to associate themselves – it is they who, pre-eminently, have the duty and power to sublimate and spiritualize the progress of the whole human convoy. 'In suffering the ascending force of the world is concealed in a very intense form.'[14]

With this goal in view, the Council urges us to reflect on the relationship between the Church and the world; and here again we find that the necessity of their unity occupies a key position in Teilhard's thinking. Both come from the same God, Creator and Redeemer, and the Christian cannot conceive them separately. Throughout his life, he continually came back to this principle, as a reference to his correspondence will show. We find it in such intimate letters as those he wrote to his friend Père Auguste Valensin, as to a true spiritual director:

'The Lord has led me along such unexpected roads that I am relying on him to use me for his greatest glory. If only I could in some small way serve this great cause – the only cause that ultimately matters to me – of deliberately amalgamating Christian life with the "natural" sap of the Universe' (Holy Saturday, 1922). Again, a few years later: 'I think that it could serve the Kingdom of God if there were produced, from some ebullition deep within us, a compound of passion for the world and passion for God' (27 June 1926). Later again: 'Instinctively, and particularly during the last ten years, I have been offering myself to God as a sort of trial ground, so that he may effect on a small scale the fusion of the two great loves, love of God and love of the world – without which fusion, I am convinced, no Kingdom of God is possible' (31 December 1926). As early as the introduction to the first of his essays which we possess, written at the front in 1916, under the title 'Cosmic Life', he was already saying: This 'is written . . . because I love the universe, its energies, its secrets, and its hopes, and because at the same time I am dedicated to God, the only Origin, the only Issue and the only Term.' This, in one form or another, is what he was to continue to say until the end. 'The majesty of the universe' was always to make him recognize 'the primacy of God'.[15]

How, in the light of our faith, we are objectively to conceive the relationship between the world and the Church, or between the construction of the world and the coming of the Kingdom of God; or, again, between mankind's temporal development and its eternal destiny; what help is to be found towards answering those questions in Père Teilhard's writings; how those writings offer us a view of the future – and, still more, a 'will for the future'[16] which is based on 'the substance of the Christian faith' and so lifts the cause of the betterment of man above the purely natural level – at the same time saving us both from all forms of sterile pessimism and from all left-wing and right-wing 'progressivist hot air':[17] these are matters that I, and other writers, have tried to explain elsewhere.[18] I have also on several occasions pointed out where there are weaknesses in Teilhard's thought – a 'trial ground' cannot help producing some failures – and what criticisms may legitimately be made of it.[19] In what I am writing here, I have another purpose in mind. It will be something more simple, an attempt to show that provided we understand Teilhard's work as what it really is, then, no matter how we judge it, we will find that on certain points of vital importance it provides a valuable prophylactic: it safeguards us against certain disorders which, here and now, may well paralyse the impulse which uplifts the Church of Christ. To put it more positively, it is an attempt to examine what basic support each one of us can find in Teilhard's work if we are to act in a way that is fruitful and aimed in the right direction. It is not that we can expect him to give us ready-made answers to all the practical and theoretical problems raised by the new approach we now have to adopt. Some of the problems that are most vital to us are already rather different from those that Teilhard had to deal with. We are confronted by obstacles that arise from possibilities which did not exist in his day. Nevertheless, what he has to say will serve us not merely as an example but as a guide and a stimulus.

It is beyond my present scope to offer a complete analysis or summary of Père Teilhard's religious thought or a vindication of the man himself as a person. On the other hand, in view of the renovation in the Church and the new spirit which can now be distinguished as it strives to express itself, it would be out of the question to confine ourselves to purely negative criticism or to treat them with reserve. Here again Père Teilhard is at hand to warn us against so grave an error. 'Sharing the troubles and ambitions of one's own time is completely different from sharing current failings and prejudices. Sharing in the first sense will always produce a positive reaction and give us something new.'[20]

We must, then, commit ourselves whole-heartedly to the road traced out for us by the Council, throwing down, when need be, with the boldness of faith, the obstacles that bar our entry.

CHAPTER 2

Crisis

*

It would be idle to try to shut our eyes to the multiplication in the last few years of the symptoms of a spiritual crisis such as has seldom before shaken the Church. The modernist crisis at the beginning of this century can hardly be considered as more than a hint of what was to come. It was only in certain places that it took an extreme form and since it was almost entirely confined to intellectual circles it did not have a marked effect on the whole body of Christian consciousness. Today's crisis is the no doubt inevitable backlash both of the rapid advances and the upheavals of all sorts whose pace has been accelerating since the war of 1914. 'The feeling we have of being on the crest of a wave' is no illusion: 'we are in truth standing at the point of transition from one era to another' (Karl Rahner). It is indeed 'a change of age', as Teilhard was already saying in 1925, foreseeing the crisis that was bound to result. It will be, he said, 'a crisis of cosmic nature and magnitude', and is heralded by a 'deep and universal confusion' in men's minds.[1] In such words he expressed the fulfilment of what, as we saw in the preceding chapter, he had been anticipating. He was saying the same thing again in 1936, in 'Thoughts on the Present Crisis', which emphasized that 'mankind has just entered into what is probably the most extensive period of transformation it has known since its birth'.[2] It is 'the very foundations of the human *anima religiosa*, on which the Church has been building for two thousand years, which are changing in dimension and nature. Need we wonder that the whole edifice is being shaken by this deep-seated movement?' Again, in 1941, he spoke of our 'passing through a crisis';[3] and in 1947, after a brief historical survey of the changes that have taken place in man's consciousness during the last centuries, he came to the conclusion that 'a spiritual crisis was inevitable: it has not been slow in coming'.[4] At the time when such statements were made, they might well have astonished many minds, at least in so far as they affected the Church. Others, while agreeing with them, would have been far from understanding their full import or would have regarded them as exaggerated. Some, who considered themselves realists, would have once again dismissed Teilhard as a visionary; but as things now stand it calls for no great perceptiveness to see that it was he who was the realist.

All of us, then, are now involved in a general crisis, which may rightly be explained as a crisis of growth and which may very well make itself felt as such. It is the crisis of a world 'opened up no less than exploded'. It is the coming of a 'planetary world', on the threshold of which we are witnessing the collapse of much that man has built up which we might have thought indestructible; but at the same time it is a world within which, we may hope, 'the mingled dust of great cultures will rise again and recoalesce'[5] to give us a new structure, greater and finer. Meanwhile, however, the crisis is producing a general confusion of turbulent movements. Neither in their underlying causes nor in their essential characteristics do those which are today being produced inside Catholicism have anything to do with the recent Council. The Council was in fact summoned, as a result of a prophetic instinct in which John XXIII rightly recognized the influence of the Holy Spirit, in order to overcome the crisis by guiding its energies and correcting the deviations it might entail, in the only effective way: that is, by a summons to an inner renewal and rejuvenation of the whole Church.

Further, one has only to read the conciliar documents – for all the frequent weaknesses and occasional lack of precision in the drafting, which themselves reflect the situation they were designed to remedy – to appreciate the wisdom, the balance, and the profound sense of tradition which is inseparable from the boldness of the Pope's summons. The Council leaves hidebound conservatism behind and opens a door which allows us to get back to the central core of tradition, where alone promise of life can be found. It came as a shock. For many it was a brusque awakening – others saw it as a thaw – which will have a salutary effect. If 'the huge wind of the Council raised a great cloud of dust', and if 'the Spirit of God is shaking his house as of old he shook the upper room',[6] then we may well rejoice. Already, as I began by pointing out, we can see here and there the emergence, both in social activities and in doctrinal research, of wholesome new movements, for which the Council is responsible. There is no need to be dismayed, or even astonished, if some disorder is to be found in such a hive of activity – if there is some turbulence in the wake of this great ship – or if we meet some 'ill-controlled outbursts':[7] it was only to be expected that the open-mindedness advocated by our bishops, while stimulating a great deal of valuable work, would at the same time produce a certain amount of mental confusion. One of the most perceptive of the advocates of the new attitude gave warning of this danger in St Peter's, but saw in it no reason for resisting the inspiration of the Holy Spirit.[8] However, for the reasons already mentioned, there is another factor in the present crisis: and unless both pastors and faithful make a combined effort to face it, it might well completely distort the Council's work and, in fact, cause it to be a complete failure. We are already, only too often, hearing such ambiguous expressions as 'the post-conciliar Church' or 'the new Church', and this introduces the danger of the establishing of a Church other than that of Christ – if, indeed, we can use such a word as 'establish' to designate a phenomenon that is primarily one of abandonment and disintegration.

This warning does not come only from those who regret the old days, from hard and fast traditionalists or those who oppose change as a matter of principle, from 'integralists' or from those who worry unduly or are intellectually timid, afraid of anything new. They include some of us who are doing most to bring about the new attitude that is needed. Even before the Council, some of these men had given evidence of bold foresight. Later, in Rome or elsewhere, a number of them worked for the Council and are still determined to do all they can to achieve its ends. Here it will be sufficient to recall, among many others, the powerfully urged warning given by Dr Josef Ratzinger on the Bamberg Catholic Day in July 1966, together with an important earlier address by Cardinal Dœpfner on 8 February; we might mention, too, the articles on change and continuity in the Church published by Père Yves Congar in 1967;[9] or the moving shorter papers which Dr Hans Urs von Balthasar has been bringing out between the publication of his major works; inspired by a deep and pure Christianity, these make an appeal to our conscience to which we cannot be deaf. There are, again, all the editorials in periodicals, the investigations, the observations which the most sympathetic Christians feel obliged to issue.[10] We know, too, that Mgr Dumont and Père Maurice Villain have pointed out the threat to the future of the ecumenical movement constituted by the present crisis; and we have the unmistakably clear declarations of the former Secretary of the World Council of Churches and his successor, in which they ask for the brotherly help of theologians in overcoming the new difficulties. To these, I need hardly say, we may add Paul VI himself, who, with as much tact in personal relationships as vigour in the presentation of doctrine, is continually introducing a note of warning into his exhortations to develop a new spirit.[11] In spite of his clearness of vision and the authority of his words, a number of Christians have for too long been hesitant about echoing them in public. We cannot, however, continue for ever to be silent, when we see in so many cases such a failure to exercise Christian intelligence, and the lightness with which some of the clergy, without sufficiently taking into account the authority their position gives them, put out so many misleading ideas which have not even the merit of being the fruit of personal reflection. Are we for ever to be 'the bewildered or distraught witnesses' of this 'denial of the reality of the faith', this 'fantastic playing-down of Christianity'[12] which naïvely regards itself as the last word in progress? Plenty of discussion and questioning may well be a healthy sign; but the universal spirit of inquiry which has made its way into the Church in a form which 'cuts everything down', and so comes as a shock to those of simple faith, would prove fatal to many if it did not stimulate a demand for clarification.[13] As an English observer recently wrote, one might have thought that the solid structure of the Catholic Church would have enabled it to be the only one of all the Churches to escape the crisis of our generation; but this is no longer so, and so we now come up against the formidable question: 'Will the Catholic Church herself remain God's witness among men or will she, rather, become an anthropocentric society?' Making due allowance for the rhetorical form of expression, that question undoubtedly hits the vital point.

Once again, on the morrow of a Council, small groups of impatient people are going too far. They did this, though in a completely different direction, in the sixteenth century, after Trent, when the excessive zeal of some of the Counter-Reformers supplanted that of the Catholic Reform; it happened again in the nineteenth century after the first Vatican Council; and now a number of such extremists are trying to use the present transitional period to promote their own views rather than wholeheartedly adhere to the Council's decisions. The very efforts made by many Catholics whose good intentions are neither well-informed nor properly coordinated are, for the time being, producing anarchy. Enthusiasm is taking the form of an extremism which seeks to introduce changes that are superficially acceptable but have no doctrinal basis. All these reactions, however, are inevitable accidents. As Oscar Cullman has said, they are secondary effects, the marginal by-products of every renaissance, earlier examples of which, he emphasizes, were also provided by the Protestant Reformation.[14] They are human manifestations, too merely human to cause anxiety or even to call for too much attention. But what we can see today goes deeper. In his well-known letter to the Duke of Norfolk, Newman complained of the 'wild words' of men who had become occasions of scandal, and in an address he gave about the same time he pointed out the great danger he saw looming up over the spiritual horizon: 'The spread of that plague of infidelity, that the Apostles and our Lord Himself have predicted as the worst calamity of the last times of the Church.'[15] Newman, however, could have had no idea that these two sorts of evil were one day to combine and produce a single more formidable danger that would threaten to introduce infidelity into the very heart of the Church of Christ. The evil which now imperils men's minds is no longer only that of an apostasy by immanence, but also (and on this point M. Jacques Maritain's diagnosis is correct and confirmed by observers who are very far from always sharing his opinion) the evil of an ' "immanent" apostasy'.[16]

This does not mean that we must abandon hope. The believer never has occasion to display pessimism, even if he has occasion for distress. Times of crisis will always be for him pre-eminently times for hope. He knows, too, that much less is heard of conversions than of desertions: that the fruits of prayer and charity do not lend themselves so readily to fine speeches as does theorizing about personal relationships; that the 'Kingdom of God comes by stealth' and that purifications of the faith are effected in many minds by ways that are more effective and hold more promise for the future than a certain type of writing would lead one to believe. The believer knows that he himself is supported by the vast army of silent and faithful Christians in whom the power of the Spirit of God will always be stronger than any other. In his eyes present-day experience confirms, moreover, one of Maritain's favourite axioms, that 'the history of the world progresses *simultaneously* along the line of evil and of good'. Today we can see 'the effects of this twofold simultaneous progress bursting out explosively'. Over forty years ago, Père Teilhard de Chardin, in a different context, made a similar observation: 'A wind of revolt is passing through our minds, it is true. But, born of the same growths of consciousness, another breeze is blowing through the human masses; one that draws us all by a sort of living affinity towards the splendid realization of some foreseen unity.'[17] We may remember, too, Hölderlin's remark that with the danger comes the life-line. Above all, we know that the Spirit of Christ watches at all times over his Church and never ceases, in spite of every obstacle, to provide the impetus she needs. To quote Newman again, whom Teilhard greatly admired and with whose mind (surprising though it may be to some) he felt a very close kinship: it is wonderful to see 'with what hesitations and uncertainties, with what interruptions and divergencies to right and left, with what reverses, and yet with what sureness', today as yesterday and as in her distant past, the Church continues to move forward.[18]

Nevertheless, we must constantly remember that nowhere is it laid down that this Church is to be completely sheltered from every scourge. Here and now, with the suddenness of an epidemic, an evil has spread throughout her members: and it has originated not from some powerful, wrong-minded, intellectual source, as happened in the case of certain heresies, but from a sort of collective loss of balance. In those who have been infected by the evil, all the vital points seem to be threatened at the same time. Suddenly discovering all the problems and imagining that no one has yet seen them, they allow themselves to be persuaded that in every order the most disastrous solutions must be accepted. This produces an attitude of contempt, which is often based on ignorance and then becomes wilful ignorance and refusal. The result of this is that the Catholic conscience is cut off from all its sources of nourishment; it becomes atrophied and so finds itself empty of all resources, helpless, and an easy prey to every form of seduction from outside. It can no longer see itself except as what an unbelieving world conceives it to be. Lacking any power of discernment, and completely inconsistent, it then becomes vulnerable to every unbalanced perversion that can corrode its faith. If, in addition, the Catholic is emotionally infected, if he turns away in disgust from the Church, from her tradition, from the Christian virtues, the interior life[19] and prayer, and takes pleasure in what is a caricature of them – if the Gospel no longer has a message for him, it is hardly to be wondered at that his mind accepts unresistingly any new 'Gospel' which, while still calling itself Christian, claims to take the place of the Gospel of Christ.[20]

Where such a state of mind prevailed it is obvious that the teachings of the Council could not fail to be distorted; just as serious examination of so many very real problems raised by the present crisis would become impossible. It would mean the end of all progress in Christian thought and life, and paralyse all profound research. *Aggiornamento*, openness to the world, adaptation, rejuvenation, ecumenism, the spirit of dialogue – all these, excellent when understood in their real sense and when they develop as the blossom and fruit of a living faith, can in practice become a pretext for their opposite and disguise a surrender more or less all along the line. Anyone who has his eyes at all open can find examples of this for himself. If we gave way to the pressure of propaganda and allowed ourselves to slide down that slope, we should soon have to speak not of renewal and dynamic progress but of decomposition and liquidation. The hope aroused by the Council would be swallowed up.[21]

To sum all this up in a few very simple propositions – for this is no time for subtleties or marginal problems – we may say that in the present confused situation both the temptations that assail us and the considerations that we must take into account are principally concerned with three fundamental things: faith in a personal God; faith in Jesus Christ (with the destiny it opens up for us as its corollary);[22] and finally faith in the role of the Church of Christ. For many of us these three things are in practice one and the same, and in present-day conditions, when Christian faith loses its vitality, the process of their successive abandonment follows a pattern that has been well analysed by Madeleine Delbrêl. Contrary to what might be logically expected, 'a world which is dechristianized seems to empty itself from within, first getting rid of God, then of the Son of God, then of the divine element the latter communicates to his Church, and it is often the outer surface which collapses last'.[23]

As Oscar Cullman said in Rome itself, on one of the last days of the Council, 'it would be regrettable if the reaction against mistaken forms of renovation were left to the opponents of any form of renovation: for the reactions of the latter are always equally mistaken' and provide an excuse for an aggravation of the evil.[24] These one-sided appreciations, which see only the danger and know no remedy for it except to take a harder line, contribute to the devitalizing of the Church and close it to the Spirit of God. We have only to call to mind the eminent and regrettable example of the ageing Bossuet. A far surer safeguard against these dangers, which at the same time does not act as a brake on our enthusiasm, is to be found, I believe, in the writings of Père Teilhard de Chardin and in his personal behaviour. On countless occasions he expressed his views on the three fundamental points just noted; in connexion with them he set out to ask, and asked himself, many questions which are closely allied to ours, and the very way in which his thought was organized focuses attention on them. In 1944, in a short 'Introduction to the Christian Life', he wrote some words that we may take as a guide: 'A threefold faith is the

essential and sufficient foundation of the Christian attitude:
1. Faith in the (personalizing) personality of God, the focus of
the world. 2. Faith in the divinity of the historical Christ (not
only as prophet and perfect man, but as an object also of love
and worship). 3. Faith in the reality of the Church phylum, in
which and centred on which Christ continues to develop, in
the world, his total personality.'

There are many things, it is true, that we may criticize in
Père Teilhard. If we wished to make an equitable judgment
of the religious part of his work and at the same time to
indicate the limits, in two directions, of its significance, we
should also have to bear in mind the two following facts.
Firstly, in many cases he did not wish to do more than speak
in the light of his personal vocation, which he knew to be (as
he admitted) his own particular vocation, without claiming
that, in concrete details, the line of conduct he was trying to
follow could be universally applicable; without claiming, too,
that his point of view would enable him to see and expound
the whole truth. On more than one occasion he warns the
reader of this: 'Your call [addressing the Lord] has innumerable
different shades of emphasis: each vocation is essentially
different from the rest. The various regions, nations, social
groupings, have each their particular apostles. And I, Lord, for
my (very lowly) part, would wish to be the apostle – and, if I
dare be so bold – the evangelist – of your Christ in the
Universe'.[25]

Secondly, the period in which Père Teilhard lived, and
particularly that during which his thought had taken shape, is
no longer ours. He often wrote as a reaction against certain
ways of life or certain theological concepts which were very
prevalent, particularly in France, towards the end of the
nineteenth and the beginning of the twentieth centuries.[26] This
means that there is in Teilhard's work – as there is in that of
every great writer – a critical and polemical element which
must be seen in its historical context. This cannot be too much

emphasized if we are not to be guilty of anachronisms and of making a number of serious mistakes. The circumstances of his career were such that he was unable, later, to keep in close touch (except in very restricted circles) with the evolution taking place in the Church. Finally, what he had to suffer until his very last years at the hands of an 'integralism' which nobody nowadays would be ready to defend, was not calculated to open his eyes, but rather to harden his attitude – in spite of a sincere desire to submit to criticism. This resulted, on the one hand, in some over-narrow idiosyncrasies and, on the other hand, in his presenting his views sometimes in an over-schematic and summary form, and offering judgments that were too one-sided. Nevertheless, even those who for these two reasons or for others would be the most allergic to Père Teilhard's thought, need have no fear in sharing his approach to the three-point faith-sequence described above.

It is not possible here to do more than give some brief indications of how it is worked out. Only a complete reading and close study of his writings could bring out its full convincing force. Moreover, I must emphasize again that it would be wrong to maintain that Père Teilhard, whose quest was never satisfied, was always successful in finding a fully satisfactory way of expressing his thought, even on the three points mentioned. *A fortiori*, we cannot say that it covers the whole ground or gives the answer to every question. Père Teilhard de Chardin is only one voice, speaking very imperfectly from one angle, in the great Catholic symphony, in which voices correct one another, modify and complete one another. Together they make up the great harmony of sound which continually calls back the very essence of our being to our one Master and Leader, Christ Jesus.

CHAPTER 3

A Personal God

*

Père Teilhard de Chardin once denounced 'the sophism which consists in eroding the solid foundations of the Christian faith on the pretext of encouraging its full and free development'.[1] It is a remark that we may well take as our text. The Second World War had strengthened the conviction he formed during the 1914 war: from Peking, in December 1939, he wrote: 'At the root of the major troubles in which nations are today involved, I believe that I can distinguish the signs of a change of age in mankind.'[2] What was taking place, he thought, was something that might rightly be called a 'moulting' (we find the same sort of expression in the recent Conciliar Constitution *Gaudium et Spes*)[3] which must necessarily affect even the 'religious outlook'. It must therefore entail a new approach in the very exposition of the Christian faith. Moreover, 'however divine and immortal the Church may be, she cannot completely escape the necessity for periodic rejuvenation to which all organizations are subject, no matter what their nature . . . Christianity already has two thousand years of existence behind it . . . the time has come when it must undergo the necessary rejuvenation through the infusion of new elements.'[4]

Père Teilhard, however, believed in divine revelation. In addition (as those last quotations already indicate), this 'moulting', this 'rejuvenation' – or, as he also called it, this 'renovation' – must, he believed, be the effect not of a break in continuity, but of an authentic development.[5] Newman's essay on the development of Christian doctrine had given him matter for much lengthy reflection on both the Church's vital and doctrinal progress and, by transposition, on the evolution of the cosmos.[6] Even if he was always 'reaching out to "What is coming",' at the same time he knew and asserted that 'What is coming' 'can only be born of fidelity to what is';[7] in other words, everything must proceed, not from a relaxation or adulteration of the traditional faith, but from the very opposite – from a deepening of it.[8] 'Let my faith, unhappily, relax and immediately the light is extinguished, everything becomes dark, everything disintegrates.'

This faith was in the first place, as the foundation on which everything else rested, faith in God. At the same time as Père Teilhard diagnosed a 'change of age' for the human species, he also located (surprising though this may seem at first) the cause of the world cataclysm in the fact that men had despaired of God's personality.[9] And it was with this in mind that he made clear to his superiors his desire to engage wholeheartedly in what he called 'the battle for a personal God'.[10] This was in 1940. Next year, during his retreat in Peking, he noted that in the matter of God, the *Christian specific act* consists in an 'affirmation of personality and transcendence':[11] 'tenacious personalism' is the phrase he used at about the same time; an 'uncompromising affirmation' which he makes his own and adopts fully.[12] The contrast he often draws between the two mystical systems which, in his view, divide the world between them – the mysticism 'of the East' and the mysticism 'of the West' – is essentially based on the fact that the former, which he rejects, is a mysticism of the impersonal, while the latter is 'the mysticism of personality'.[13] Rightly, then, has it been said that in Teilhard's thought 'everything rests upon the principle of the person'.[14]

Père Teilhard is continually urging us to see God himself at work in the cosmogenesis which is prolonged in noogenesis. This proposition is central to both his philosophy and his spirituality, so much so that 'seen by us' in the creation which it animates in order to unite it to itself, Teilhard's Omega

appears initially as 'already partially actual' and at the same
time 'partially transcendent';[15] but a second phase of the
demonstration leads us to recognize the absolutely transcendent
character of God himself, the 'only true Omega'.[16] It is
essential, Teilhard makes it clear, at all costs to maintain God's
'primordial transcendence', his 'transcendent reality'.[17] On one
occasion, with ruin and disaster on all sides, he could not, even
so, suppress his 'triumphant joy, based on [his] conviction of
the transcendence of God'.[18] He knows that this God is a
living God, a loving and kindly providential God, who can
reveal himself and has in fact revealed himself. 'Once we
admit the personality of God, then the possibility and even the
theoretical probability of a revelation – that is, a reflection of
God in our consciousness – not only present no difficulty but
are eminently in conformity with the nature of things . . .
Since man is personal, a personal God must influence him at
the personal level and in a personal form – intellectually, that
is, and effectively. In other words, God must "speak" to him.
As one intelligence to another, a presence cannot be silent.'[19]

Such an idea of God is for Père Teilhard the supreme truth.
Neither his faith, nor his competent knowledge of Christian
tradition nor his philosophical thought, nor his inner experience, can for a moment be reconciled with the puerile
antithesis – which some offer as the last word in criticism and
proof of adult mentality – which contrasts an interior God
with a God regarded as 'external' and 'spatial'. It is an artificial
contrast, which we are constantly seeing reasserted, between
a transcendence which is the fruit of a credulous imagination,
and an immanence which proceeds, as Léon Brunschwicg said
not so long ago, from 'a reflection in depth'. For Teilhard knew
(and his knowledge is shared by the humblest believer, even if
he cannot explain it in learned words) that the language of
faith cannot dispense with symbols; faith uses expressions
which have a sensory and imaginative origin, but it is none the
less independent of 'a whole body of imagery which too often

is believed to be essential to it'.[20] He knew, and saw only too clearly, that if the real is a sphere, God is at the same time its centre and its circumference and 'fills the whole sphere'.[21] He is the 'Centre who spreads through all things', the centre whose 'immensity is produced by an extreme of concentration'.[22] In contrast with this world,[23] he embraces all things 'and imprisons none'.[24] He is at the heart of our being only because he extends infinitely beyond it; he is at once near and distant, intimate and inapprehensible. On countless occasions, following many other writers, Père Teilhard repeats in his own words the great St Augustine's phrase, '*Deus interior intimo meo et superior summo meo*'.[25] He is the 'real centre' and 'unifying energy' of the cosmos – *rerum, Deus, tenax vigor* – God can be this only if he is the being 'distinct from the cosmos', 'independent of the Cosmos', 'present' since all time – *immotus in Te permanens* – so much so that the conjunction of the cosmos and God, the supreme end of creation, will always be an 'hierarchic conjunction'.[26]

Père Teilhard was deeply convinced that faith in the divine personality is one of the 'deeper axes of Christianity'.[27] In Christianity he saw 'the saviour of the personal' in a society which is continually tempted to dissolve or stifle it. On the other hand, he was very much alive to the 'anti-personalist complex which paralyses us'.[28] He noticed it most particularly in the world of scientific thought, just as we can notice it again in vast sectors of philosophical thought, and one of his chief preoccupations was to demonstrate its vanity. The unbelievers he mixed with, who were often his friends, were fascinated by 'the modern discovery of those vast diffused unities of energy and matter'[29] and regarded 'dogmatic personalism' as 'decidedly out of date': Teilhard set out to explain to them that on the contrary it represents 'what is most progressive and best adapted to our own time'.[30] What he wished for was the reappearance at last 'in our modern universe' of 'the face of God':[31]

God . . . is almost inevitably conceived by a modern positivist as an ocean without shores, in which all things are totalized by loss of themselves. Our generation . . . seems to understand pantheism only in the form of a dissolution of individuals in a diffuse vastness. This is an illusion, caused by the fact that the unity of the world is wrongly sought, by influence of the physical sciences, in the direction of the increasingly simple energies into which it dissolves: God is ether, they would have said some years ago. A completely different result is obtained if one tries . . . to extend the universe in the direction of personality, that is to say of synthesis. Then God does not appear in the fanning out but in the concentration of the stuff of the universe; not as a centre of dissolution, but a focus of personalization. *He is spirit.*[32]

Père Teilhard realized that before his contemporaries could be given back a sense of divine personality a number of obstacles had to be removed. Hence, in the first place, the insistent care with which he defined and rejected 'all that is bad in anthropocentrism'[33] – the anthropocentrism which even before reducing the stature of God, begins by reducing that of man. For all that, he is very far from losing himself in a vague 'cosmic feeling' in which 'the nebula of the ancient paganisms' would be given a new spell of life. If he hailed 'the dawn of the whole over the horizon of our individual preoccupations', it was not in order to interpret it, as others had done, as a sign that Christianity was approaching its end: 'Is not the anthropomorphic form of worship, based on faith in a personal God, about to be replaced by the cult of totalitarian realities like the world and humanity?' 'The present situation', he replied, 'and the probabilities for tomorrow both appear to me very different. No object . . . could claim to totalize the energy of mankind on itself unless it possessed a soul and was "someone". Remaining in the condition of impersonal collectivities, earth and humanity are therefore definitely powerless to support and maintain the spiritual vigour of the world. So long as they remain inchoate the tide raised by their gravitational pull is certainly destined to fall back formlessly on the beach. Both must assume a definite form. But precisely why should they not both succeed in taking soul and personality by drawing near to the God whom they seemed about to abolish?'[34]

It is this that is behind the care he took solidly to establish the classic distinction between individual and person: a distinction which Maurice Blondel and Jacques Maritain were similarly to be at pains to revindicate as a counterblast to the extravagances that can be produced from a Christianity which is not wholeheartedly lived and thought out. He knew that death must make us subject to the 'expansion which totally de-individualizes, but personalizes, singularizes and consummates *in unum*'.[35] The restrictive individuality which has to disappear was, in Teilhard's view, this 'envelope' not only of 'wilful selfishness' but, more radically, of 'organic isolation' which 'separates the monads';[36] it is 'the impenetrability, the mutual exclusion of being by being';[37] it is, as another writer says, 'the invisible barrier which keeps beings as far apart from one another in life as the stars in the sky'.[38] Teilhard does not regard this as an evil thing, but as something provisional. 'The true ego grows in inverse proportion to "egoism". Like the Omega which attracts it, the element only becomes personal when it universalises itself.'[39] At the same time, however, in a positive sense, understood as a distinct existence, individuality is still present and gains strength in the process of personalization, and is even included among the attributes of Omega.[40]

From the same source is derived, more particularly, Père Teilhard's criticism of a somewhat crude way of representing God in the likeness of a 'great landowner administering his estate'; he speaks on another occasion of 'a great landowner of the neolithic age.' He registers his reaction against a 'certain creative paternalism', 'a certain neolithic paternalism', which is too often presented as the true essence of the Gospel;[41] whereas it is in fact a conception of God, finally and permanently left behind by man's progress, which had been forestalled by the Gospel revelation. 'This conventional picture, which is too well justified by appearances, corresponds in no way to the dogmatic basis or point of view of the Gospels.'[42] There is nothing to be shocked at in such expressions, nor should their significance be exaggerated. Their slightly polemical tone is unmistakable. Thrown into the arena of public discussion at a critical time and exploited in a spirit foreign to them, they may seem at least imprudent. In reality, they are used to support observations that are made not to belittle but to enhance the personality and fatherhood of God.[43] In using them, Père Teilhard is helping to restore the authentic notion of that fatherhood, in which he sees even the essence of Christ's message. God, he says, is 'Father', which means in essence that he is Person, that is love, personal love, summoning man to 'personal union with him'.[44] He would not have Christians allow the God of the Gospels to grow cold in their embrace. He well knows that if the word 'Father' is analogical, it is in God that it is confirmed in its fullness. He knows that this word 'does not express a vast projection of the infantile and subjective ideas which tends to enslave the human being in a pre-rational way', as we are sometimes asked to believe, but draws its strength 'from God who, creating all things, frees the creature by his own divine freedom'.[45] What is more, he echoes the thought of his intimate friend Auguste Valensin, who wrote in his diary: 'The concept of fatherhood as applied to God has been distorted; it has been debased; God-as-love has been made into a daddy-God.' At the same time, however, Père Valensin also wrote: 'Fatherhood is love carried to its perfection. Those who overlook the revelation of this love are dreadfully unfortunate without realizing it; but those who are most to be pitied are those who have received the wonderful tidings and give it only cursory attention . . .'[46]

The same fundamental concern is always to be found behind Père Teilhard's explanations of the impossibility, even in our earthly society, of bringing about a truly human order – or of maintaining in clear-sighted men the zest for progress, for 'fuller being' – or again, for each one of us, of loving other men in a real and practical way – or finally (which comes to the same thing) of attaining happiness[47] – without the vitalizing, magnetic reality of a personal love, 'a centre of loving energy'.[48] Both these last points are worked out so fully and frequently by Père Teilhard, and they are so closely woven into the texture of his thought, that the quotation is superfluous.[49] A single passage will be sufficient, in which the doctrine of the impersonal is rejected as a betrayal of spirit: 'In all the systems of human organization battling before our eyes, it is assumed that the final state towards which the noosphere is tending is a body without an individualized soul, a faceless organism, a diffuse humanity, an *Impersonality*!

'Now once this point of departure is accepted, it vitiates the whole subsequent progress of the operation to the extent of making it impractical. In a synthesizing process, the character finally impressed on the unified elements is necessarily that which permeates the active unifying principle. The crystal assumes geometrical form, the cell animates the matter that joins it. If the universe is tending finally to become *something*, how can it keep a place in itself for *Someone*? If the peak of human evolution is regarded as impersonal by nature, the units accepting it will inevitably, in spite of all efforts to the contrary, see their personality diminishing under its influence. And this is exactly what is happening. . . . [It] is treason against the spirit.'[50]

Finally – and here Père Teilhard shows a profound agreement with one of the essential themes of Christian philosophy – he tries to make his reader understand, or at any rate grasp some idea of, the relationship between the concept of an infinite of condensation (which is the only real infinite) and the mystery of the divine personality (of the hyper-personality, which is 'personalizing personality').[51] The believer receives an additional assurance of that mystery from the revelation of the Trinity.[52] It is a mystery which, far from inhibiting thought (as is sometimes believed), allows the mind to share in an endless quest for and worship of *Deus semper major*. It was this same mystery which prompted St Gregory of Nazianzus, for example, to say – in language which perhaps has for us today rather too Neoplatonic a flavour – 'It is impossible to express the greatness of God in words and give him a name, but it is still more impossible to understand him'.[53] The same quest inspired the thought of St Augustine, to take another example, when he never wearied of explaining that if we are to find we must search, but we must also find in order that we may always search: '*Si comprehendisti, non est Deus; ut inventus quaeratur, immensus est; si finisti, non est Deus.*'[54] We find the same in St Anselm, when he defines God not only as the being 'than whom no greater can be thought of' – '*quo magis cogitari nequit*' – but also, in virtue of that definition, as being 'greater than can be thought' – '*majus quam cogitari potest*'.[55] St Thomas Aquinas, again, tells us in the *Summa Contra Gentiles*: 'We have true knowledge of God only when we believe that he exceeds in his being everything that it is possible for man to think of him', and adds: 'Our conviction that God is above all that can be thought is strengthened by divine revelation which offers us something that goes beyond reason.'[56]

Similarly, Teilhard says that God is 'more remote than all and deeper than all'.[57] Not only must we constantly be at pains to 'keep very much alive the impassioned vision of the *Greater than All*',[58] but we must also yield to the force which impels us to 'the search for the "ever-greater God"':[59] for, if God is 'complete in relation to himself', at the same time, 'for us', he is 'continually being born'.[60] He 'does not offer Himself to our finite beings as a thing all complete and ready to be embraced. For us He is eternal discovery and eternal growth. The more we think we understand Him, the more He reveals Himself as otherwise. The more we think we hold Him, the further He withdraws, drawing us into the depths of Himself. The nearer we approach Him through all the efforts of nature and grace, the more He increases, in one and the same movement, His attraction over our powers and the receptivity of our powers to that divine attraction.' The same will hold good of the divine *milieu*, into which the action of faith allows the believer to penetrate. 'Incomparably near and perceptible – for it presses in upon us through all the forces of the universe – it nevertheless eludes our grasp so constantly that we can never seize it here below except by raising ourselves, uplifted on its waves, to the extreme limit of our effort: present in, and drawing at the inaccessible depth of, each creature, it withdraws always further, bearing us along with it towards the common centre of all consummation.'[61]

Such passages bring home to us the full force of the necessity recognized by the philosopher when he warns us that 'theism has constantly to battle against the temptation to confuse God with an intelligible content which does not even transcend the spiritual activity which asserts it'.[62] Moreover, we find in them, in a form that springs from personal experience, an accurate comment on the traditional teaching reaffirmed in the thirteenth century by the fourth Lateran Council: '*Inter creatorem et creaturam non potest similitudo notari, quin inter eos major sit dissimilitudo notanda.*'[63]

Père Teilhard's realism, the solidity of his spirituality and the healthy vigour of his thought, were not shaken by apparently more subtle or more sublime speculations. Moreover, he understood perfectly that while analysis is an excellent tool, 'an admirable and powerful instrument for dissecting the real', it is not a key to knowledge of being: 'What we are left with at the end of the operation of analysis, far from giving us the permanent essence of the world, is progressively nearer to nothingness.' He realized, too, that intellectual criticism, legitimate though it is in every order, is at the same time not the only nor the highest use of the intelligence.[64] These two instruments of progress must themselves be criticized and allotted their correct place. If their sovereignty becomes unduly exclusive, they become agents of the worst form of retrogression. They destroy man in destroying his object. The impersonalism to which they lead is simply a stage on the road to nihilism. 'The personal elements in the universe', says Teilhard, 'would return to disorder (that is to say to nothingness) if they did not meet some super-personality already actualized, to dominate them. Therefore to balance our activity, there must be in the world around us not only the expectation, but the already recognizable face of a universal personality. Nothing less is needed . . . to preserve the powers collected in the heart of the individual, of societies and of the world itself from going badly astray.'[65] He was, then, faithfully reflecting his own thought, when in private conversations he repeated: 'God is person, God is person! A God who was not personal could not be God.'[66]

God's universal presence – his immanence, active immanence in the world – whose part in cosmic evolution was one of Père Teilhard's favourite themes, was for him what it was for the whole of Christian tradition, the necessary corollary of God's transcendence. As early as 1916 'Cosmic Life' had expressed this in an outburst of lyricism:

'The fundamental substance within which souls are formed, the higher environment in which they evolve – what one might call their own particular Ether – is the Godhead, at once transcendent and immanent, *in qua vivimus et movemur et sumus* – in whom we live and move and have our being. God cannot in any way be intermixed with or lost in the participated being which he sustains and animates and holds together, but he is at the birth, and the growth and the final term of all things. Everything lives, and everything is raised up – everything in consequence is one – in Him and through Him.

'Worthily to describe the rapture of this union and this unification, the pantheists' most impassioned language is justified, whether unspoken in the heart or given expression by the tongue: and to that rapture is added the ecstatic realization that the universal Thing from which everything emerges and to which everything returns, is not the Impersonal, the Unknowable and the Unconscious, in which the individual disintegrates and is lost by being absorbed: it is a living, loving Being, in which the individual consciousness, when it is lost, attains an accentuation and an illumination that extends to the furthest limit of what is contained in its own personality. God, who is as immense and all-embracing as matter, and at the same time as warm and intimate as a soul, is the Centre who spreads through all things; his immensity is produced by an extreme of concentration, and his rich simplicity synthesizes a culminating paroxysm of accumulated virtues. No words can express the bliss of feeling oneself possessed, absorbed, without end or limit, by an Infinite that is not rarefied and colourless, but living and luminous, an Infinite that knows and attracts and loves.'[67]

Thirty-six years later, in 1952, a San Francisco newspaper reproduced a French press agency report according to which 'Père Teilhard's God was becoming a God immanent in the evolution of the world'. He protested vigorously against this allegation. 'What annoys me in this business', he wrote at the time to Père André Ravier, 'is the crude way in which I am made to jettison a divine transcendence which *on the contrary* I have spent my whole life in defending – while trying, it is true (as everyone does, but in my case using the properties of a universe in process of cosmogenesis), to reconcile it with an immanence to which, as is universally agreed, an increasingly more important and implicit part must be accorded in our philosophy and religion.'[68] The immanence of which Teilhard is speaking is in fact the immanence of a God (and of a Christ) who dominates, animates, upholds and vivifies the world, in direct contrast with the God 'immanent in evolution' attributed to him. It is thus that he often prefers the word 'Presence', which has a personalistic ring.[69] His doctrine of 'devine omnipresence'[70] which is essentially that of all mystical thought in the Christian tradition, in particular that of St Ignatius Loyola's *Meditatio ad amorem*, is the very opposite of the immanentism he was accused of. 'God is above ourselves.'[71]

On another occasion Père Teilhard wrote: 'The spiritual value of a man . . . depends on the degree of reality that God has assumed for him: not on the degree of speculative or even affective perfection, but, I repeat, on the degree of reality.'[72] This was one of the fundamental themes of his meditations every year during the first days of his retreat. 'What we lack is the sense of the reality of God, of the fullness of faith.' We must 'give to God – as the saints do – His true value of reality'.[73] God, therefore, was not for Père Teilhard a mere philosophical concept. His transcendence and his personality – his transcendent personality – was not for him the result of a mere conclusion, of a pure objective affirmation. In moments of recollection he placed himself where he could contemplate and be wrapped up in 'the unique greatness of God'.[74] His inner tension was 'towards God alone'. Through worship and prayer he entered into a relationship with the God who had wished to reveal himself to man, and who was to be the God of each man: the being of whom each can and must say 'my God'. He entrusted and surrendered himself to him alone:

Deus meus: it is essentially Christian and beatifying to be able to add '*meus*' to 'God' . . . the '*meus*' not of possession but of pan-dependence.

To accustom oneself to being *alone* with God *alone*; while finding all things and all beings in Ω, we attain it in *isolation*.

In absolute, elementary truth, only God can help us, can reach the core of our being, can constantly and vitally be interested in us, heal us and save us from death – and that, in fact, means that, for all the people and friends who may surround us, each one of us is *alone* as he confronts God.[75]

To the outside world, he had this testimony to offer: 'The joy of worshipping pervades the joys of being and loving – it enlarges and consolidates them, never diminishes them (Curie, Termier, were admirable friends, fathers, and marriage partners) – it includes and brings with it, in its fullness, a wonderful peace.'[76]

Coming from such a man these are words that may well arouse and sustain the meditative reflection of the believer: and they may well, too, provide substance for thought for every theologian and every philosopher who calls himself a Christian.

CHAPTER 4

Jesus Christ

*

Père Teilhard's realism was founded on a 'sense of being', a 'faith in being', a 'zest for being', a 'preference for being', a 'feeling that being is infinitely richer and more refreshing than our logic', which gave his thought both solidity and vigour.[1] At the same time he recognized 'the definitive plenitude of the smallest *fact*, grasped in its total, concrete reality', failure to appreciate which robs the first theories of their weight and strength.[2]

Just as Teilhard's God was the God of Jesus Christ, so his realism pervaded the whole of his Christian faith.

Père Teilhard had done his theological studies at the time of the modernist crisis. He had read Tyrrell, and Loisy, and many other writers of the period. And yet, it has been said, he always remained 'completely a stranger to modernism'.[3] A stranger he remained, it is true, but a well-informed stranger. Even though he did not devote much time himself to the detail of exegetical problems, it would be a mistake to believe that he was ignorant of them. He gave a great deal of thought to the fact of Christ; he saw how it stood up to the erosion of criticism and, in addition, judging the tree by its fruits, he was confirmed in his certainty by observation of the historical phenomenon it produced. For anyone who can appreciate its power and newness, he believed, such a phenomenon inevitably applies at its source, the reality, both historical and supernatural, of its founder. It is impossible to escape the conclusion: *Christus mole sua stat*.[4] Père Teilhard, accordingly, had no patience with the historical short-sightedness, or with the half-baked mysticism which in his view characterized the modernism of his time. He would undoubtedly have been no less severe on a certain neo-modernism, often more superficial and more pretentious, that is becoming prevalent today.

'The Catholic', he wrote, 'is the man who is sure of the existence of Jesus Christ-God, for a number of reasons and in spite of many stumbling-blocks.'[5] The modernist, on the other hand, 'volatilizes Christ, dissociates him from the world'. In 1919 Teilhard noted that, for his own part, he was, 'with the help of God, fundamentally different'. 'I try to concentrate the world in Christ. And the difference is not only verbal. I believe (definitely, I hope) that if our Lord (Jesus Christ) has not a personal and objective reality, then the whole Christian current disappears'.[6] Again, on 12 December 1920, we find: 'The essential point in Christian evolutionism (what distinguishes it *essentially* from every apparently similar modernist conception) is this idea that our Lord is not (not only) a fruit of man's immanent evolution, but the meeting of participated being, as it ascends, with the *unparticipated* being to which it returns.'

He understood perfectly how the modernists attempted to justify their position; he even recognized that the modernist movement, at the beginning, sprang from a real need, a deep-seated and legitimate aspiration, which he himself shared and which represented something of the profoundest value in his own life: that need took the form of a search for a God who was at once greater and nearer. However, as a result of the direction it soon adopted, the movement had become destructive of its own ideal, and had made necessary the reaction marked by the encyclical *Pascendi*. For his own part, as we have seen, Teilhard rejected 'all illegitimate evolution of dogma'. He refused to allow it to be more or less 'rationalized'. That, he said, would be 'to impoverish it and make it commonplace'.[7] In December 1919, Maurice Blondel had been able to tell him, through Père Auguste Valensin, of the 'profound joy' he felt at their agreement on this point. Because 'our world has ex-

panded through the social and natural sciences' both saw
clearly that 'one cannot remain true to Catholicism and be
content with a mediocre explanation, a limited outlook'; both
were 'aware of the options at hand: either to fall back into a
murderous symbolism, or go forward towards a realism which
is self-consistent throughout, towards a total reality which puts
the metaphysics of Christianity in accord with the mystical
theology lived by the saints and even by the faithful following';
and both, from their knowledge of the problem, had chosen
the second course.[8] Again in 1940, meditating one day on the
verse from the first epistle of St John: '*Omnis spiritus qui solvit
Jesum, ex Deo non est; et hic est Antichristus*', Père Teilhard was
to make the apostle's warning his own: 'Allowing Christ to
disappear, that is the mistake'; but, he rightly pointed out, not
allowing Christ to disappear is not enough: 'we must consolidate Christ, enrich him, develop and exalt him'; 'we must
jointly demonstrate the "transcendence" and the "universality"
of Christ Jesus'.[9] And not many years later, in 1950, he agreed
joyfully with what a young friend wrote to him: 'Preventing
dogma from evaporating in symbolism: *excellent!*'[10] His wish
for a 'rejuvenated' Christianity was the wish more perfectly to
find again 'the perennial Christ'.

The whole of Père Teilhard's quest in the religious field was
one carried out *in faith*, in order to obtain a better 'understanding of faith'. There was in it no contesting of principle.
At the very moment when he was beginning to follow up, with
uncompromising sincerity, some relatively new line of whose
boldness he was well aware, he used to say to himself: 'This is
extremely tricky, and calls for much humility and obedience in
my attitude to dogma'.[11] The whole of his religious thought,
organized as a function of his faith, was founded on the
historicity of Christ, on what he called, again, 'the palpable and
verifiable truth of the gospel event'.[12] By that he did not mean
some unspecified historicity, but precisely the reality of the
Incarnation, in other words the reality of the divinity of the

Jesus Christ of history.[13] God, who created the world, is incarnate in it and thereby has 'truly inserted himself into the cosmos';[14] he descended into nature to superanimate it and draw it back to himself. In short, 'the transcendent made itself partially immanent'.[15] Thus in Jesus Christ we contemplate 'this mysterious drama: the Master of the world, leading, like an element of the world, not only an elemental life, but (in addition to this and because of it) leading the total life of the universe, which he has shouldered and assimilated by experiencing it himself'.[16]

Some minds are perplexed by, or rebel against, the contrast they observe between the cosmic extension of the attributes recognized by Christian faith as belonging to its Lord, and the humble and rapid passage through history by Jesus of Nazareth. Nevertheless, 'the fact that Christ emerged into the field of human experience for but a moment, two thousand years ago, does not prevent him from being the axis and the peak of universal maturity'.[17] Teilhard, however, would not be Teilhard if he were satisfied with an answer whose trend is still negative. His own special way of thinking called for a more positive expression:

> The more one thinks about the underlying laws of evolution, the stronger one's conviction that the universal Christ could not, at the end of time, appear at the summit of the world if he had not first been introduced into it, during its development, through the process of birth, in the form of an element[18] . . . In virtue of the very characteristics which at first would appear to over-emphasize his singularity, an historically incarnate God is, on the contrary, the only God who can satisfy not only the inflexible laws of a universe in which nothing appears except by process of birth but also the irrepressible aspirations of our minds.[19]

What is more, all the finest speculations of religious philosophy and all the grandest mystical considerations would be barren and have no real effectiveness if they were not firmly rooted in the historical reality of Christ. All that is developed in them has no value for the Christian 'except in so far as the light in which everything seems to him to be bathed radiates from an *historical centre*, and is transmitted along an *exact axis solidly based in tradition*'. This first demand of Christian faith is expressed by Père Teilhard in very strong terms:

> The immense enchantment of the divine milieu owes all its value in the long run to the human-divine contact which was revealed at the Epiphany of Jesus. If you suppress the historical reality of Christ, the divine omnipresence which intoxicates us becomes, like all the other dreams of metaphysics, uncertain, vague, conventional – lacking the decisive experimental verification by which to impose itself on our minds, and without the moral authority to assimilate our lives into it. Thenceforward, however dazzling the expansions which we shall try in a moment to discern in the resurrected Christ, their beauty and their stuff of reality will always remain inseparable from the tangible and verifiable truth of the Gospel event. The mystical Christ, the universal Christ of St Paul, has neither meaning nor value in our eyes except as an expansion of the Christ who was born of Mary and who died on the cross ... However far we may be drawn into the divine spaces opened up to us by Christian mysticism, we never depart from the Jesus of the Gospels.[20]

It is true that Père Teilhard has great reservations about the often uncritical way in which 'pious writers have tried to describe the psychology of the Man-Jesus' – who, indeed, would blame him for that? At the same time he notes the effect of his divinity on his very humanity. In his individual consciousness, Christ was not only perfect man, ideal man – he included in himself total man:[21]

> Let us try to gather together in one single ocean the whole mass of passions, of anticipations, of fears, of sufferings, of

happiness, of which each man represents one drop. It was into this vast sea that Christ plunged, so as to absorb it, through all his pores, in his entire person. It was this storm-tossed sea that he diverted into his mighty heart, there to make its waves and tides subject to the rhythm of his own life. . . . Therein lies the unfathomable secret of his agony, and the incomparable virtue, too, of his death on the Cross.[22]

Teilhard's realism, accordingly, is both historic and dogmatic. It is the realism of the Incarnation. It is the foundation of all Teilhard's Christology, as it is of the Pauline Christology from which Teilhard's draws its inspiration. Without his realism, his Christology would be no more than a theory; but because he has it, Teilhard can in all truthfulness say in his prayer, following Bérulle, Pascal and so many others, 'Jesus, . . . the centre towards which all things are moving'.[23]

This realism is at the same time spiritual and interior. 'Without Jesus Christ, centre of consistence, I crumble away within – everything outside me crumbles away – everything becomes a screen through which my action and influence cannot pass. The one essential thing: to be united with Our Lord.'[24] Love of God's creation took the form, we know, of a love of evolution; but, he makes it clear, 'without the historical and transhistorical Jesus, evolution loses all its warmth of real life'. He notes, among those things which are concrete facts, the '*vitality*' of Jesus; he believes that nothing can take the place for modern man of this life-blood which comes from Jesus and which his mysterious presence keeps circulating in the world. Jesus Christ is unique. 'Neither Goethe nor Nietzsche ever "saved" or consoled anyone'; 'We cannot be in communion with Plato or any other wise man, but we can indeed with Our Lord.'[25] Such words should not be interpreted in a commonplace or superficial sense. Just as Pierre Teilhard refused to allow dogmas to evaporate, so he refused to water down the spirituality which flows from them. He reproaches those who see in Jesus only 'a friend' or a 'perfect man', and those, too, who hope to find in him only an example or a moral support. 'Our Lord God', he answers, 'is all-devouring'.[26]

Parallel with this, moreover, is the breadth and fundamental importance assumed in Teilhard by the doctrine of the cosmic Christ or universal Christ. Its development into the idea of a 'Christogenesis' is too well known to call for fresh exposition. There is little doubt that the working out of this idea called for a great boldness on his part: but did it not call for 'unheard-of boldness' centuries ago on the part of St Paul or St John to assert that the whole world was created by Christ, by this Jesus 'born of woman', and that all things subsist only in him?[27] Teilhard read and reread the passages in which this boldness asserts itself, and would have none of their value lost. He tried, by carrying them further, even to the point of rashness, in his own writings, to 'give a real content' to expressions 'that we have retained without sufficiently "realizing" their primary significance'.[28] Without disguising from himself the novelty of his enterprise, he felt that it was not taking him beyond the limits of our common faith, and that was why he could speak (though without thereby attributing his theories to all believers) of 'the Christogenesis which every Christian reveres'.[29] It would be a complete misrepresentation of his teaching to fail to see it as at all times completely dependent on the divine revelation effected in Christ, on the personal and historical reality of Christ, and as aimed at expressing the full development of the mystery of his incarnation, death and resurrection. This last, he tells us, 'marks Christ's effective assumption of his functions as universal centre':

After being baptised into the world, he has risen up from it. After sinking down to the depths of the earth, he has reached up to the heavens. 'Descendit et ascendit ut impleret omnia' (Eph. 4: 10). When, presented with a universe whose physical and spiritual immensity are seen to be even more bewildering, we are terrified by the constantly increasing weight of energy and glory we have to attribute to the son of Mary if we are to be justified in continuing to worship him, it is then that we should turn our thoughts to the Resurrection.[30]

Teilhard's teaching on 'the extensions of the eucharist' (itself only one aspect of what we have just been discussing) is equally familiar. It is the occasion of a remarkable analogy. 'From the cosmic element into which he has entered, the Word is active to master and assimilate to himself all that still remains.'[31] And again: 'The centre of Christ's personal energy is really situated in the Host. . . . The Host is like a blazing hearth from which flames spread their radiance.'[32] Need we, finally, recall the specially important position he attributes to the mystery of the Cross? On Good Friday, 1955, two days before his own death, he was again to write: 'The crucified God is the most powerful spiritual generator that man has known in history.'[33]

There are some today who seem to be afraid of being thought intellectually childish or sentimental if they admit to loving Jesus Christ. Père Teilhard's intelligence, which was certainly no less adult than theirs, was less apprehensive or less sophisticated. He would have thought it absurd (as his own remarks on modernist exegesis bear out) to use the word myth in connexion with the being who produced, and continues to produce, so unparalleled a revolution not only in history but in the human heart. The only effect on him of the harassing attacks of the unbelief he met on all sides was to encourage his dream of an 'ever-greater' Christ. The formulas of the Church's faith opened up for him a road that had no ending. Un-hesitatingly and unswervingly he affirmed his own faith in the person of Christ and his passionate devotion to it. He once expressed this faith and devotion in a cry in which we can hear the dual echo of the suffering inseparable from the darkness in which our earthly condition confines us, and the depth of the adoration in which the believer is engulfed: 'Lord, I cannot do without you – but who, tell me, who are you?'[34]

Among today's Christians two converse temptations have been noted. Some, it has been said, would be inclined to accept 'Jesus' without 'Christ', and others 'Christ' without 'Jesus'. The former might thereby succumb to an evangelical moralism without any doctrinal substance, whereas the latter might well lose themselves in the structures of a gnosis that is Christian only in name, or as Père André Manaranche says again, 'in an atheism with Christian symbolism'.[35] In either direction, such dissociations are fatal – just as was the distinction recently drawn between a 'Jesus of history' and a 'Christ of faith'. Père Teilhard did not yield to either temptation. He did not sacrifice anything either of Jesus or Christ.

This is not to say that he carried out to perfection the ideal synthesis. He sometimes develops the theme of the universal Christ so fully that it seems to overshadow or obliterate Christ's life on earth. This unbalanced treatment (for we cannot but regard it as such) is due, I believe, to three convergent causes: the very character of his writings, the natural bent of his mind, which inclined more to the future than to the past, and finally an apologetic concern which caused him to make allowances (over-generously, perhaps) for certain difficulties in believing felt by those whom he wished to reach. A passage in his 'Introduction à la vie chrétienne', dating from 1944, sums up his position in this matter. It modifies, while at the same time confirming, a number of the passages already quoted in this chapter. Its aim is to help his reader to overcome his unwillingness to locate in time and space the mysterious Being who is endowed with cosmic attributes:

In concrete fact and historically, it is undeniable that the living, mastering, notion of the universal Christ appeared and grew greater in Christian consciousness from a starting-point in the Man-Jesus, recognized and worshipped as God. Even today, to suppress the historicity of Christ (that is, the divinity of the Christ of history) would mean the immediate evaporation into the unreal of all the mystical energy accumulated during the last two thousand years in the Christian phylum. Christ born of the Virgin, and Christ risen from the dead: the two are one inseparable whole. Confronted with this *factual* situation, a legitimate and 'tranquillizing' attitude for the modern believer would appear to be to say this: 'With every reservation about the often uncritical way in which pious writers have tried to describe the psychology of the Man-Jesus, I believe in the divinity of the child of Bethlehem *because, in the degree to which*, and *in the form in which*, it is historically and biologically included in the reality of the Universal-Christ to whom my faith and my worship are more directly addressed.' It is a confident and reasonable position, which respects and accepts all the implications of what is certain fact, and at the same time leaves all the room and freedom required for future advances in humano-Christian thought.[36]

Such a point of view is undoubtedly one-sided. One can see in it an effect of the fascination exerted by the sublime figure of the Pantocrator, but at the same time it gives evidence of a certain timidity which in other contexts was more fully overcome. It should be noted, however, that even if Pierre Teilhard considers Christ more readily or more habitually in his cosmic function than in his 'Palestinian humanity', he always sees in him the same personal being to whom he has given his faith. There would be no difficulty in drawing a picture of his Christ, based on numerous quotations that have a cosmic tenor; but the picture would be completely false if we overlooked all the passages which connect the statements made in the cosmic passages with the person of Jesus, or, as he says himself, to 'the Christ of history', to the 'radiant sun of love', who has risen to light up the world;[37] not to mention that the 'diaphany' which is habitually the object of his contemplation is seen by him as dependent on an earthly 'epiphany' located in time and space.[38] To forget the countless occasions on which he fondly commented on St Paul's words, '*Descendit, ascendit, ut impleret omnia*', and that the Being who was revealed to him 'at the heart of matter' has a name and a face, and that he is Jesus[39] – this would be to bring out only one half of his synthetic 'vision' and would obscure its authentically Christian character: and yet Teilhard expressed it unmistakably, when, for example, he said: 'Christ is loved as a person: he compels recognition as a world.' As his last letter, quoted above, says again, he lived until his last day from the vision of his faith which he summed up in 1918 in the words: 'The universe assumes the form of Christ – but, O mystery! the man we see is Christ crucified.'[40]

If, then, Père Teilhard de Chardin felt called upon to emphasize one aspect of the one Jesus Christ rather than others, he neither destroyed nor imperilled Christ's unity. Thus there is no difficulty in including in the great body of Christian experience his personal vision of the Christ who is 'more real than any other reality in the world, Christ present and growing greater in all things, Christ the final determination and formative principle of the universe'.[41] With equal force he demonstrated how necessary is the Gospel for man's progress and salvation. Without faith, purity and charity, the three fundamental interior attitudes taught by Christ and propagated by his spirit, neither could the divine milieu be constituted nor could the Kingdom of God flourish. Without them, the progress of earthly society could lead ultimately only to inhuman structures.[42]

Thus it was of Christianity in its entirety that Père Teilhard sought to be a witness. He knew very well what was thought by the unbelieving mind of his century. He knew it not only from books but also from the many direct contacts he had at every period of his life (for no one was more open to dialogue than he). Late in life, in *Le Christique*, he was to sum up the essential criticisms he had met: 'It is easy', he said, 'to criticize in the abstract this contradictory medley of primitive anthropomorphism, mythical marvel, and gnostic boldness.'[43] Such criticism failed to shake him. He found, instead, 'an extraordinary final purpose, in itself alone weighty evidence of divinity', in everything the Gospels tell us of Christ and which they could not possibly have invented, just as he did in the extraordinary interwoven series of the two Testaments and in the vast fact whose origin lies in the faith of the first disciples of Christ risen in glory.[44] To the threefold criticism expressed by theorists who have sometimes made themselves incapable of seeing or appreciating living reality, he offers a threefold answer, in which he points out with pride the miraculous and potent association in Christianity of three great characteristics: tangibility, in the experiential order; power of expansion, in the universal order; and thirdly, in the organic order, assimilative power.[45] These, he believed, are solid criteria which confirm him in his faith.

In Teilhard, then, there is no blind fideism. The idea of a personal God active in the world, which he arrived at by an effort of reason,[46] had already led him to envisage the possibility or even the probability of a revelation: 'a presence is never silent'. Looking at it, then, historically,[47] he recognized the authentic signs of this revelation in Jesus Christ. Christ is for him the Revealer and the actual Revelation of God; he is 'the Word' awaited by mankind: 'the spark leaping the gap between God and the universe *through a personal milieu*'.[48] He then turns to a consideration of the fruits of revelation. He sees in Christianity a teaching, a prospect, a force 'of universal transformation'.[49] He rightly appreciates the miracle of Christian purity and Christian charity. They are so many 'rational invitations' to the act of faith.

Certain disorders can make their way into the Christian body which temporarily distort this force of transformation, and thereby slow down and even bring to a halt Christianity's penetrative power. For forty years on end Père Teilhard de Chardin never ceased to deplore what he diagnosed as the chief disease among Christians of his day, a certain loss of the sense of man, and to beg the authorities of his Church to remedy it. Anticipating later policy, it was his way of urging 'openness to the world'. I believe that his diagnosis was correct, but incomplete and one-sided.[50] Firm in his faith, he rejected with equal force 'a compromise between Christianity and the modern world';[51] he was convinced, too, that Christianity still retains all its strength, that it has lost nothing of 'its power to attract'.[52] Here and now, for anyone with sufficient spiritual alertness, 'there is a truly Christian *note* making the whole world vibrate, like a huge gong, in the divine Christ'. This, however, is on the assumption that Christianity still remains in its integrity. If only one of the three elements is lacking in the 'contradictory medley' the unbeliever denounces, in other words if one of the three aspects of Christological dogma should be doubted or obscured by Christ's disciples – if once the realism of one of its three components is weakened – then the flame of Christianity is extinguished.[53]

Let us hope that all Christians today will take to heart this supreme warning Père Teilhard gives them: that they may join him in making their own and giving practical effect to St Paul's words in the Epistle to the Romans: 'I know that nothing in the world is sufficiently violent, or dazzling, nothing is so immeasurably vast, as to detach us from Our Lord or eclipse him, or *make us cease to dwell in him*: neither angels, nor life, nor death, nor height, nor depth, not the abysses of the past, nor what the future holds ($\tau \grave{a} \ \mu \acute{\epsilon} \lambda \lambda o \nu \tau a$) will be able to separate us from the charity of Our Lord' (Romans 8: 38).[54] 'Lord of my childhood and Lord of my end.'[55]

CHAPTER 5

The Church of Christ

*

Many Christians are too ill-informed or lack the intellectual strength to stand up to the attacks of an intemperate criticism, readier to decry than to understand, which uses mass media to launch a fully developed psychological offensive. I am not referring to serious research and inquiry, for these are indispensable to the life of the faith and should be given every assistance. Indeed, we should hope that in the coming years their scope may be still further extended and even more freedom may be allowed to them. Let us hope, too, that they may produce even wider repercussions, for it is in fact the slowness of their progress in a number of fields which partly explains the nature of the present crisis. In any case, there will never be a time when they will have been more necessary or more deserving of encouragement. For us who live in time, it is only 'in hope that all truths lie in the one truth';[1] and if this truth is itself of all time, never has it been so true or, at any rate, never have men been in a better position to appreciate it than in our own time: at a time when in every quarter we find an intellectual energy as undisciplined as it is magnificent, in which there is what I might call a general explosion of partial truths acting as a constant stimulus to further inquiry.[2] Thus, as Karl Rahner wrote recently, if we are to reject, for example, 'a programme of demythologizing such as that described by Bultmann or popularized by Robinson, we can never devote too much thought to the problems which suggested that programme'.[3] Perennial as these are, they are at the same time symptoms of a change in the way men are questioning the world and themselves. Many are working to find the answers;

they know what they are speaking about, and if this were the right place, it would be a pleasure to make their views more widely known.[4] However, I must confine myself to my present subject, disagreeable though some of its aspects may be.

What we have to discuss here is something very different, and we see so many examples of it on all sides that it cannot be ignored. We see so much theorizing accepted uncritically and popularized, its only criterion being its critical content: such a feverish anxiety to welcome anything that seems likely, not to bear intellectual fruit, but to cause intellectual confusion: so many books and articles in which, as an American writer recently said, the reader is offered 'over-simplification and caricature' and revolutionary exaggeration which refuses to bother about professional competence:[5] such an itch to replace study and meditation by propaganda and agitation: such a one-sided eagerness to decry everything, in the doctrine that is taught, in the Christian past, and in the Church of today. And with this goes a neglect, among baptized Christians, of the spiritual conditions necessary for reflection on their faith, a neglect, too, of the elementary conditions governing all worth-while reflection. Pseudo-prophetism and charismatic language is blown up to cover what is simply a cheap surrender. There are many who insist on hiding behind the myth of 'modern man' in order, piece by piece, to break down the whole structure of Christian life. Others carry to childish extremes the conviction they so loudly proclaim of having attained adult status. (I wonder whether they remember what St Paul had to say about 'coming of age in faith'.) We see all sorts of obtuseness outside the Church treated with humble deference, while at the same time there is such contempt for humble believers inside. What an insult all this is to the perennial freshness of the Gospel – and what a complete contrast to the personal behaviour not of some nervous conservative, some intellectual stick-in-the-mud, or some believer untroubled by problems, but of Père Teilhard de Chardin.

We may well think, with Dr John Bennett, that those extravagances enjoy more publicity than influence.[6] There are in fact many signs of a more fruitful activity, effecting a more authentic renewal in both the intellectual order and the order of charity. Yet, should the climate of undisciplined agitation spread, then the process described above by Madeleine Delbrêl would soon produce its final effects, and for many the Church would soon be no more than a façade, itself doomed to ruin. On the other hand, we know too that there is another side to the picture: the confidence placed in the Church of God and steadfastly maintained can successfully defend the faith and allow it to mature; it can too, when necessary, restore its vigour. Whatever the situation, it is equally clear that this confidence is the first condition of all rejuvenation and progress – and here again this is something which Père Teilhard never forgot. It was this that proved the salvation of his own work, and this is perhaps the most important lesson he can teach us, if we are to overcome the present crisis and profit by it.

There is a word which today sums up a whole crop of tendencies which are not confined to the airy fields of speculation – 'secularism'.[7] It is a convenient word, whose meaning can be extended at will. I am not concerned here with its theoretical background, but only with what is often a very different thing – the confused state of mind which it reflects today when the tendencies in question are passively accepted inside Catholicism. For the sake of clarity, we must be careful to distinguish it from 'secularization'. Transferred from what is secondary or provisional to what is essential, 'secularism' is made in the end to embrace the whole field of churchly institution, the whole of worship, the whole object of faith, the whole of life, until there is nothing left – not even prayer – to recall to the Christian the presence and summons of God. Starting from a factual observation, from what one sees by looking at the world today, a sort of mesmeric power leads the mind imperceptibly to believe in an inevitable, irreversible, evolution, and this in turn soon produces the conviction that it is a form of progress which it is one's duty to assist. It is quite possible that at first there was no thought of anything but a process of secularization ('laicizing' is the word that was used earlier). It is a process that was initiated a long time ago now, and in principle its aim was to bring about a clearer distinction between the kingdom of Caesar and the Kingdom of God, and so restore the Church to her own mission by releasing her from supplementary duties forced on her by historical circumstances. 'For the last ten years or so, there has been a great deal said about the process by which the society which was given a sacred character by the "Christian institution" falls into human control.'[8] On the whole this is, no doubt, a matter for congratulation, but only provided we do not forget the converse movement which at the same time seeks through more spiritual channels (not *a priori* excluding institutions) to infuse the virtue of the Gospel into the world. Moreover, there can be no doubt but that, in spite of certain regrettable factors, the 'pluralist' condition of modern society makes such a secularization inevitable. Père Teilhard recognized this as early as 1916. On 22 July he wrote to Père Victor Fontoynont that, when such burning questions as laicizing are being discussed, 'beneath the fanaticism and sectarianism there lie legitimate claims and the perception of an unanswerable logic'. But what we have now is something completely different from that; it is an attempt by Christians to include the Church herself in an all-embracing secularism. In this view, the Church fades away into the world, the religious into profane, eternal into temporal, mystery into completely human speculation. This means betrayal of the Gospel. The Kingdom of God vanishes. The whole world becomes externalized and without depth. Secularism is then simply a new name for a variety of atheistic humanism.[9]

Teilhard's tendency is the exact opposite of this. I am not concerned with the wild talk about the wholly sacred character of the world which we hear from certain 'Teilhardists' who have rightly been criticized for it;[10] for Père Teilhard, on the contrary, wholly accepts the Christian 'de-divinizing' of the world which surrenders it in its entirety to investigation by the human mind and development by technology.[11] He in no way regards the world as sacred in itself; but, with 'the eye of faith' which sees through appearances, he sees it as wholly 'sacralized' by the universal presence of its Creator – just as all the greatest Christian thinkers have seen it. Further, he sees it as 'consecrated' by the presence of the risen Christ, his 'immortalizing and unifying'[12] presence radiating through the eucharist; the world is then for him an anticipation of what the transfigured universe is to be at the parousia of the Lord. Such a concept of the 'consecration of the world' is therefore equally far removed from the secularist theory and from that which attributes to the world, in itself and by itself, a sacred character. It is meaningless without its eschatological outlook and its expectation of salvation.[13]

A number of intelligent writers have already pointed out how modern secularist theories are completely 'at the opposite pole from Teilhard's thought': for example, Père André Manaranche in an article in *Projet*,[14] or Professor E. L. Mascall in his *The Secularization of Christianity*.[15] It is true that Père Teilhard did not advocate an undiscriminating multiplication of prayers and ceremonies – even though he loved the liturgy and the great feasts of the Church were treasured by him, while his fidelity in observing the requirements of his own state of life was regularly beyond reproach.[16] He knew what strength they can give and was only too ready to recognize the help they contribute, at any age, to spiritual renewal. In a confidential note addressed in January 1919 to a very well qualified judge, Père Léonce de Grandmaison, he freely criticized certain introvert ecclesiastical circles 'who are absorbed in the beatification of a servant of God or in the success of some devotion'.[17] Writing in 1926 to Père René d'Ouince, he spoke of 'theological, disciplinary, and ceremonial excrescences' which depart from the central core of the Christian faith;[18] and there are few today who would not agree that he was justified. It is sometimes necessary to clean things up and simplify them in order to restore their correct emphasis on what is essential. One may well believe all this without being in the least degree 'secularist'.[19] It is true, again, that he saw just as clearly as many others, and probably much more clearly, how small a part the Church plays in this immense world; he noted the weakness of her influence at the present time in spite of a missionary effort that is more powerfully organized than ever before. He analysed its causes, and what he saw with such perception – somewhat one-sided though it may have been – he expressed at times with considerable bluntness. He wrote, for example, in an intimate letter to Père Auguste Valensin, dated 7 January 1934: 'Our influence has ceased to be contagious, because we no longer have a conception of the world to contribute. It is a situation that hits you in the face as soon as you step outside church or seminary.'[20] He was alive to the fact that the majority of men around him seemed even to be insulated from every religious problem. He knew how this situation was interpreted by non-believers: 'There have been many systems in which the fact of religion was interpreted as a psychological phenomenon linked with the childhood of humanity. At its greatest at the origins of civilization, it was gradually to decline and give place to more positive theories from which God (a personal and transcendent God above all) was excluded.' Teilhard's answer was: 'This is pure illusion', and he went on to show that, on the contrary, the more man is man, the more compelling will be the need he, and his activity, will experience for some absolute, and the more inevitably, in consequence, will he have to be religious. At certain times man will no doubt ignore this necessity: but he will suffer, if he does so, and he will come back to recognizing it. For faith in God, the absolute term, is 'the sole possible instigator of reflective life'.[21] Teilhard is the last person one could accuse of falling upon 'one or two unhappy people in their weakest moment' and forcing upon them 'a sort of religious coercion'.[22] Even though he does not shrink from admitting the *essential* limitations and wretchedness of man's condition, religion is for him, as it is for every real Christian, much more than a sort of first-aid, and that is why no human fulfilment and no entry into a new age can be the sign for its decline.

Teilhard, however, was familiar with another objection, one that concerned the Christian form of religion. 'Christianity – a remarkable type of religion, it is true; but only one among many, and only for a particular period of time: that is what is said today, more or less explicitly, by a vast number of "intelligent" people.'[23] Not for a moment does he succumb to this philosophical illusion, and at the same time he is equally opposed to any sort of syncretism.[24] Catholic Christianity is for him *the* religion. In this, his dynamic and unified vision of the world worked hand in hand with the absoluteness of his faith. Just as he recognized a sense of cosmic evolution, so also did he recognize a sense of mankind's religious history. This history is one, it is directed towards one end and must unfold around one specially favoured axis. Christianity's place in the world of man, like man's place in the evolution of life, is 'axial and guiding, the spearhead of human psychic energies'.[25] 'Our Lord contributed the centre, the kernel, the axis . . . There is no way out possible for the noosphere apart from the Christian axis.'[26] This axis is the Church founded by Christ, in which he still lives. Teilhard notes again, with his customary objectively phenomenological method: 'At the very heart of the social phenomenon a sort of ultra-socialization is taking place: the process by which the Church is gradually built up, animating by her influence, and gathering together in their most sublimated form, all the spiritual energies of the noosphere: the Church, the reflexively Christified part of the world – the Church, the chief centre of inter-human affinities through

super-charity – the Church, the central axis of universal convergence and the precise meeting point that springs into
existence between the universe and Omega point.'[27]

Another image constantly recurs in Teilhard, that of the
phylum.[28] As a natural scientist and palaeontologist, he
naturally borrows from his own discipline certain analogies
which enable him to think out his faith – though not without
noting that when we move from one order of reality to
another, we must always apply 'corrections for analogy'.[29] A
phylum is a 'living "bundle" ', with a 'dynamic nature', which
possesses 'a certain initial modicum of consistency and richness'
sufficient for clear-cut individualization, and in consequence a
'power and singular law of autonomous development'.[30]
Christianity has the structure of a phylum:

> Historically, starting with the Man Jesus, a phylum of
> religious thought appeared in the human mass, and its
> presence has never ceased to have an ever wider and deeper
> influence on the development of the noosphere.
>
> Considered objectively as a phenomenon, the Christian
> movement, through its rootedness in the past and ceaseless
> developments, exhibits the characteristics of a phylum.[31]

Christianity, then, continues through duration in the same
way as a phylum develops. It is a living organism which,
without losing anything of its substance or orientation, can
undergo extraordinary mutations.[32] In a fine definition which
echoes Bérulle, Teilhard speaks of it as 'a phylum of love in
nature':[33] but the essential point is that this phylum must have
an axis which will maintain the correct direction of its progress
and so ensure its homogeneous development. This axis, as we
have said, is the Church; and the first service she does us is to
keep us in possession of Christ. In a personal note, Teilhard
refers to a conversation with a friend who 'wants to accept
Christ without the Church'; but, Teilhard answers him,
'without the Church we are always under the threat of

liberalism' (he uses the word in Newman's sense, as a pejorative). Only the Church can give us Christ 'in his traditional,
and *fruitful* form'.[34] It is only the Church, too, that can ensure
the growth of the total Christ. It is around her, and in answer
to her magnetic pull, that all the finest fruits of mankind's
religious effort are destined to be gathered, to live and be
sublimated by her – all the finest fruits, too, of man's effort to
progress. 'The Church is phyletically essential to the fulfilment
of the human.'[35] She is 'the axis of universal concentration',
'the very axis upon which the looked-for movement of concentration and convergence can, and must, be effected'.[36]

Incidentally, another 'convergence' should be noted – that
between these passages from Teilhard and some expressions to
be found in the recent conciliar documents; for example, in the
dogmatic constitution *Lumen Gentium*, paragraph 9: '*Populus
ille messianicus, quamvis universos homines actu non comprehendat,
et non semel ut pusillus grex appareat, pro toto tamen genere humano
firmissum est germen unitatis, spei et salutis.*'[37] There is a similar
convergence of both Council and Teilhard with what we read
in such ancient writers as St Irenaeus and the author of the
Epistle to Diognetus. If the 'Messianic people' is always found
to be a 'little flock' – if, through our fault, this little flock seems
to be so ineffective in spreading itself – even so, was the Church
of Christ so numerous and so powerful when St Irenaeus said
that she was summoned to animate the whole of creation,[38] or
when the author of the Epistle to Diognetus described the
Christian community as the soul of the great body constituted
by the world, with the power to maintain it in being?[39] The
boldness of Teilhard's faith is no less than that of these ancient
Fathers or than that which can still be found in the Church
today.[40]

However, if such boldness is not to be fruitlessly Utopian,
one condition is indispensable: in fidelity to her Founder and
Lord, the Church must remain herself, and she must keep her
will to live intact. 'The Church', says Teilhard, 'owed it to

herself to reject all "Confusionism" '; she must necessarily regard herself as the 'very axis', 'the living, organic axis'; her 'emancipating spirit' is 'indissolubly linked with her existence as an organic body'. This is a 'structural necessity'. 'It is abundantly clear that if Christianity is destined, as it claims and feels, to be the religion of tomorrow' it can be so only if it satisfies that demand.[41] Only so will it be possible for the 'unitive properties of the Christian phenomenon' to come into operation; only so can there continually be preserved the 'synthesis of the ancient Creed and the views that have recently emerged in human consciousness'; and only so can there be effected, throughout the centuries, universal integration in Christ through 'segregation', 'convergence', 'transformation', and 'conversion' – Teilhard uses all four words.[42] This, too, is the only way in which the Church can retain her 'unique power of divinization'.[43]

It is apparent that nothing could be further removed from the idea of a 'secular Christianity' which ends in considering nothing but 'service to man' without any relation to God, and so diverts Christian thought and life only to non-religious realities.[44] Such a 'secularism' would lead us, if not to an immediate surrender of our faith, at least to a watering-down and almost a complete dissolution of its substance. It would in any case quickly annihilate its assimilative power. No one in our day has said this more forcibly (in words addressed to the Christians of the Reformed Church) than a writer who is not usually quoted to make this point, Dietrich Bonhoeffer:

'Ye are the light of the world.' Flight into the invisible is a denial of the call. A community of Jesus which seeks to hide itself has ceased to follow him. 'Neither do men light a lamp and put it under a bushel, but on the stand.' . . . The bushel may be the fear of men, or perhaps deliberate conformity to the world for some ulterior motive, a missionary purpose for example, or a sentimental humanitarianism. But the motive may be more sinister than that; it may be 'Reformation theology' which boldly claims the name of *theologia crucis*, and pretends to prefer to Pharisaic ostentation a modest invisibility, which in practice means conformity to the world.[45]

Père Teilhard de Chardin thought the same. For him the Church was not 'a parasitic organism'.[46] Just as Christ is not lost in the universe, and just as personal relationship with God is not lost in concern with mundane tasks,[47] so the Church cannot afford to be lost in the world. To try to make the Church dissolve into the world would be, in addition, in Teilhard's view, to sacrifice man to some 'heartless, faceless super-society'.[48] That is why he is anxious, on the contrary, to bring out the proper role of the 'Christian phenomenon', incarnate in the Catholic Church.[49] He always admired the strong structure of Catholicism – by which, when necessary, he made it clear that he meant Roman Catholicism.[50]

Among the statements to this effect which are to be found in his writings, there is one which is particularly significant. In October 1948, for the first time in his life, he was summoned to Rome for an interview with his superiors. At the time the atmosphere was by no means propitious. Although he had been received with much sympathy, his visit was, in practical terms, to bring him only disappointment. Even so, it was with humour that he noted the human weaknesses, procrastinations and illusions which he thought he could detect in those who control the government of the Church.[51] Nevertheless, in the letters he wrote at the time to his friends, either from Rome itself or shortly after his return to Paris – and I do not mean formal letters – the dominating feeling, which makes him put up with all the rest, is completely different: it is a feeling of profound admiration. From Rome, for example, he wrote to the Abbé Henri Breuil: 'I have been impressed – and heartened – by Christianity's extraordinary, really imperturbable confidence in the unshakeable solidity of its faith and truth. There is a remarkable phenomenon there, unique, in fact, in this world'.[52]

His impressions were crystallized when, for the first time, he entered St Peter's. He does not devote any time to a description of the building or to criticism of the 'orgy of marbles and mouldings'. The feeling that overpowered him, he says, was one of 'the security (that's a better word for it than fixity) of a faith that will not be side-tracked'; and he adds, 'that, I think, will be the "principal experience" I shall take away from my stay here; and that alone would make the journey worth while'.[53] In St Peter's, he writes again, still using the vocabulary he constructed from his own branch of science, 'I really feel how tremendous is the "Christian phenomenon": I mean this unshakeable assurance, unique in the modern world, of being in direct contact with a personal centre of the universe. This, I must say again, is, from a "planetary" and "biological" point of view, a phenomenon of the first order, and unique.' In short, standing in St Peter's, he recognized in the Church, from almost palpably undeniable evidence, 'the Christic pole of the earth'.[54]

CHAPTER 6

Tradition and Obedience

*

For Père Teilhard de Chardin the Church was in practice a continuous tradition, and a living, present, authority. He knew that nothing good can be initiated in the religious field which does not at the appropriate time fit into the continuity of the tradition and which does not ultimately meet with the agreement of the authority. To emphasize this here is not simply to draw attention to the example given by a faithful son of the Church: it is a way of carrying further our exposition of an essential element in his thought.

There is nothing, indeed, to which Père Teilhard clings so firmly as to this twofold conviction, which is completely in line with the most personal elements in his thought. He is continually anxious to relate his ideas to 'the Church's living tradition', to her 'practical teaching', her 'general, practical influence', her 'attitude at once complex and based on experience' as observed throughout the centuries, to 'the wonderful wealth of religious experience' accumulated in her. Those are all expressions he uses. On one occasion, when he was considering a study of the Holy Spirit, he immediately noted that he would have to examine 'its attributes in the Gospel' and what is taught about it by 'the tradition of the Church'.[1] It has been said that 'the lines along which his piety developed conflict at times with those on which his system was built'. That is a statement which cannot be accepted just as it stands. It may perhaps derive from a view of what is called Teilhard's system that is itself over-systematized or too one-sided. In any case, what we are concerned with here is not only 'piety', but rather thought in the full sense of the word. Père Teilhard de Chardin says that he is 'absolutely convinced' that in the treasure preserved and enriched in the care of the Church there 'is infinitely more truth . . . than in all our simplifying philosophies'. It is the practice of the Church, 'the solid platform built by two thousand years of Christian experience', which is for him 'the basic foundation, the firmest, that all the philosophies can do no more than illustrate, with more or less accuracy'.[2]

These are not the opinions, we may be sure, of a timid conservative imagination; but the more Teilhard became conscious of his vocation as an explorer, which kept him 'continually in tension ahead',[3] the more also he felt that if we are to satisfy the needs of a new age we must follow new roads, and the more, in consequence, he realized that the whole of his effort must be contained within the great perennial Christian tradition.[4] When he argued for the doctrine of the 'universal Christ', it was not because he wished to change anything in the teaching handed down by the Apostles nor even, indeed, to add anything to it. Rather, he explained, did he 'hope with all my strength that the elements of truth which are universally believed and professed in the Church about the universal activity and presence of God and of Christ, may at last be considered as a single whole, without any minimizing of their force'.[5] For he was deeply convinced that 'the dogmas and practice of the Church have for a long time been making available to us all that we need to achieve this' and that to do so we have only to go back to 'the soundest currents of Catholic tradition'.[6] We may, of course, question both the correctness of his appreciation and the success of the attempt he urges, but it would be a mistake to regard such statements as rather an empty form of words.[7]

Père Teilhard was waiting, with longing and anticipation, for the coming of some 'new "saint"', who would give the Christians of our time 'the lived formula, show them a practical example of a form of adoration and perfection that they can vaguely conceive but cannot formulate for themselves'.[8] He wondered 'who then, at last, will be the *ideal Christian*, the Christian, at once new and old, who *will solve in his soul the problem of this vital balance, by allowing all the life-sap of the world* to pass into *his effort towards the divine Trinity*'.[9] Yet, as these quotations themselves show, he knew perfectly well that this 'new "saint" ', this 'ideal Christian', will continue in the line followed by Christians and saints of all times, men whose practice even when 'difficult to ground in rational terms . . . should mould our efforts at systematization, and . . . always lie beyond reach'.[10] The same conclusion emerges from his analysis of the 'growth of the divine milieu'[11] as it does from the record of his intimate thoughts. During one of his retreats he was studying the case of St Teresa, for whom, as did his friend Pierre Rousselot, he had a warm admiration, and made a note for his own use: 'St Teresa is made terrifyingly distant from us by her own religious imagery and by her lack (common to her time) of all cosmic concern . . . But she expresses, for that time, an attitude that must be preserved.'[12]

'In fact, and fortunately, I was born into the heart of the Christian "phylum".' That was how Père Teilhard put it in *Le Cœur de la Matière* (1950). He had once written to Père Auguste Valensin, in whom he always confided: 'If I may use a word which can bear an unacceptable meaning, I feel that I am hyper-Catholic.'[13] The word may equally well bear an acceptable meaning. By it he meant in the first place his opposition to the mentality of a certain 'Christian world' too turned-in on itself – too cut off from the world or too assimilated into the world, according to the sense in which one uses either of those expressions – the 'Christian world' which converts into system or sect what was for Teilhard, on the contrary, the great universal axis 'of man's progress and betterment'. We may readily agree that he was sometimes too harsh or that he sometimes interpreted that progress and betterment too much in his own way; but nevertheless his judgment of the principle involved holds good. The closed society which he criticized was an historical phenomenon produced by a number of politico-social causes; when Teilhard was a young man, for too many Catholics it was almost like a ghetto, and it certainly deserved his criticisms. In a somewhat similar sense, he said with equal justification: 'The Catholic position completely includes and synthesizes all that is valuable and attractive in all other bodies of teaching'.[14] This is precisely what Newman meant when he spoke of the plenitude of Catholicism: and that, too, was the position which Père Teilhard shared with his theologian friend Pierre Charles.

There was, however, another sense in which he was justified in calling himself hyper-Catholic. The word can be taken to mean the attitude he habitually adopted towards the Church's authority. If he dedicated his life 'to the service of the universal Christ' it was, he hastened to add, 'in absolute loyalty to the Church'.[15] 'I cannot', he wrote, 'see Christ except as I depict him . . . but I hold more firmly to his integrity than to the colours in which I present him.'[16] Again, 'I am determined to sacrifice everything rather than impair, in myself or in the circle around me, the integrity of Christ'.[17] And, so far as he was concerned, it was the Church which ensured this integrity. When, in 1917, he dreamed of seeing an *Ecclesia quaerens* organized, 'to forestall a schism in the natural life of man and in that of the Church', it was to be 'under the control of the *Ecclesia docens*', with men chosen for their maturity, their competence and their luminous faith.[18] If – as happened more than once – he was doubtful about the conclusions he arrived at, or if he found himself faced with a distressing or even heart-rending decision, he told himself that 'the safety of the Christian organism is more important than my own personal, immediate, success';[19] or again: 'The Church has the right to expect our compliance in some things, because in the current she represents she is the vehicle of more truth than any one of us in his slender individuality.'[20] He asks those close to him to pray to the Lord that he may guard him from all bitterness. Through the declarations of the magisterium whose tenor seems to him harsh, he tries above all to see clearly what the Church is trying to preserve, and he emphasizes this to ease the minds of those around him who are anxious or perturbed. And if the sacrifice sometimes seems hard, whether it be he himself who is concerned or one of his dearest friends with whom he feels he has a community of thought, he simply remarks, putting his trust in the future: 'Time and obedience will bring out what is immortal and essentially Christian in the ideas that have been censured.'[21]

Teilhard could not escape the conviction – in some cases, possibly, one might say the 'illusion' – that, in what was most personal in his thought and in that part of it, accordingly, to which he naturally attached most importance, he was ahead of the main body of the Catholic community; and he must often have had inner thoughts similar to those of Newman which he wrote down in his notebook during the First World War: 'The things that are really useful, Newman says, happen as and when God wills it, at one particular moment and not another: and if you choose the wrong moment to try to do what is the right thing you can find yourself a heretic. It is disheartening to be before one's time, and to be misjudged or stopped the moment one starts to do something.'[22]

No one who feels obliged to express such views can be completely sure of never being out on his own. Père Teilhard, too, felt, sometimes with distress, that he was ahead of his time. In 1917 he was vaguely considering a plan of writing a study on 'Forerunners of Truth':[23] 'their role is fruitful and necessary', but they are 'wiped out like the first wave of the regiment going over the top'. Much later, he was to say in the foreword to one of his confidential memoranda:

My only aim in writing what follows is to make a personal contribution to the common task of Christian consciousness, voicing the demands in which, in my own particular case, the '*fides quaerens intellectum*' is expressed. These are suggestions, not assertions or instructions. For reasons that are part of the very structure of my outlook, I am deeply convinced that religious thought develops only traditionally, collectively, 'phyletically'; and my only wish and hope in these pages is to *sentire* or, more precisely, *prae-sentire cum Ecclesia*.[24]

That second verb, '*prae-sentire*', might cover not merely an illusion but a secret pride. Its equivalent can be found in a number of his letters.[25] As in the case of Newman, if we wish to assess it we must take into account a context that has two sides, intellectual and active. In this case, both would appear to be equally clear. Père Teilhard himself was well aware of the possible ambivalence. His 'phyletism', he pointed out, implied 'adherence to the Church', but what is difficult is the nice problem of 'defining the true sense of the phyletic, and of acting in a way that is really appropriate to the phylum', and he accordingly resolved to 'watch himself' in this matter.[26] That was in 1942. Next year, we find the same, with a new emphasis and more exactly qualified: 'My faith must necessarily involve, at the very outset, the (official) Church and her guiding influence on me.'[27] And the reason for this was that he did not wish, by cutting himself off no matter how slightly from the community of the faithful, to risk 'becoming the *cymbalum tinniens* of which Scripture speaks'.[28] He knew that, like every man, he was fallible. 'How fortunate we are to have the authority of the Church! Left to ourselves, how far might we not drift?'[29] At times the thought occurred to him that his own temperament made the protection of her authority more necessary to him than to others. 'I am so ill-adapted to belonging to an organized body . . . And yet that has been so salutary for me.'[30]

Nor should we now say that he was exaggerating. He was

equally well aware – as the preceding quotations have shown – that the cases of conscience which a Catholic thinker has to face are not always simple; and if the restrictive measures he came up against were not always without serious reasons, they were at times, it is only too clear, dictated by considerations that were not in themselves acceptable. On such occasions, when the question was one in which he was competent, Père Teilhard was able habitually to follow the right line – though not, it is obvious, without being deeply disturbed and having to face crises. In every case, however, the disturbance died down and the crisis was overcome. Writing in 1927 to Léontine Zanta, he described the correct line as follows: 'All that is asked of us is to try, ceaselessly, to climb upwards towards more breadth and more light, without letting go of these two threads: loyalty towards ourselves, and attachment to the Church.'[31] As he was leaving for Rome in 1948, he wrote to his friend Pierre Lamare: 'I am going to Rome, but not to Canossa.'[32] We know that he sent to Rome a short confidential note on polygenism as he had not only the right but the duty to do. He expressed to the competent authority his boldest – one might indeed say his most debatable – views, with the freedom, the 'parrhesia', which, in the lack of self-interest and modesty it entails, is an eminently Christian virtue. For example, in 'The Heart of the Problem' he says:

> For the use of those better placed than I, whose direct or indirect task it is to lead the Church, I wish to show candidly *where*, in my view, the root of the trouble lies, and *how*, by means of a simple readjustment at this particular, clearly localised point, we may hope to procure a rapid and complete rebound in the religious and Christian evolution of Mankind.[33]

On another occasion he confided to a friend:

> Have no fear, I am hoping to succeed in finding the middle

term, which seems to me a sort of loving docility towards the content of truth which exists outside ourselves in the whole body of the Church, combined with a sovereign respect for what is the truth revealed to my own individual mind. I am convinced that the best way of preserving all that is most right in the line I follow and making it bear fruit, is to adhere more closely to the Church, the more her representatives seem to me to stifle the 'Holy Spirit' in her ... Pray to the Lord that he may help me to act, when need be, in conformity with the faith (which is indeed my most precious possession) which he has given me in his omni-action and omni-presence in all the world's forces, for those who love him.[34]

This was written during the first crisis, the most unexpected and severe that he had to undergo in his relations with his superiors.[35] In his personal notes at that time, we read, on 10 June 1925, the simple phrase: 'Cutting oneself off is not Christian.'

I am not claiming, I need hardly repeat, that he was never over-convinced of being right on the grounds that he could 'see' what others were blind to. (Could Teilhard himself always 'see' what others saw?) Everyone must judge this according to his own lights. I am not concerned here to examine any particular one of his theories, but only to deter-mine the basis of his spiritual attitude towards the Church of Christ, to understand it as it emerged from his life and as it is evidenced in his most personal and most obviously sincere writings.

During the terrible summer of 1925, during which the 'tragedy' took place which has been described by Père René d'Ouince and Mgr Bruno de Solages, he again noted, on 28 June: 'If I left the Church, the immense beauty which cap-tivates me would vanish in insubstantial smoke.' Until a more propitious time should come, he obeyed. On the other occasions, too, he was consistently obedient, without knowing, he said, 'where life is taking me'.[36] He knew that no other course is more worthy of the Christian who knows what his obedience means, of the man who has freely pledged himself to the service of Christ in his Church, of the lover of unity. This is a momentous lesson. All the advances of 'coming of age' can in no way change it, nor will they ever do so. They will only serve to bring out more fully its importance. 'A Christian who does not understand the unity of maturity and Christian obedience within the Church is far from being mature. Because the connections between the two are clear only to the really faithful pray-er, and without this prerequisite everything is lost in shallow and dangerous chatter, the concept of maturity has to be used sparingly and carefully. Most of those who continually trot the word out clearly fail to understand the meaning given to it in the Bible.'[37] Père Teilhard's silence might well teach them.

To take another striking example of his obedience – it was during the month of May 1933, in Peking. He had received a letter from his Superior General, forbidding him to accept an invitation to stand for a post in the Institute of Human Palaeontology. This is how he breaks the news to his most intimate friend:

I imagine Père de Bonneville[38] will have shown you the letter I received from Rome a few weeks ago. I really think that it did not upset me, in a vague way, for more than half a day. And then I forgot it. It is, rather, a release for me to know that I do not have to bother about any candidature: the idea of possibly appearing an 'interested party' horrified me and pulled me down – even so I would not have dared, I believe, to reject a post if it had been offered (because in the ordinary course of things it would have been a means of active work). Rome is taking the initiative in rejecting this. All right![39]

On this occasion, as on others, he remained faithful to what he had once written: 'All progress in the Church is made through a common quest in prayer.' On 25 September 1947, in a letter to his Superior General, he once again showed the loyalty of his obedience, basing it on the same reason: 'I am too convinced (and ever more so) that the world cannot be fulfilled without Christ, and that there is no Christ without fidelity to the Church, to have been able to feel the least hesitation on hearing of your decision. I only hope that the Lord will help me faithfully to find the right road in a difficult psychological situation.'[40] Even those who are most hostile to Père Teilhard's thought will, I am sure, have no difficulty in recognizing the nobility and dignity of such words. He was to say the same again to the same Superior on 17 October 1951: 'I can truly say – and this in virtue of the whole structure of my thought – that I now feel more indissolubly bound to the hierarchical Church and to the Christ of the Gospel than ever before in my life.'[41]

He remained true to the line of conduct he had laid down for himself at the very beginning of his intellectual activity, and of which he reminded himself in his diary on 29 June 1925: 'St Peter – "*Modicae fidei*" – Renew my "vow" to the *Body of Our Lord* to develop (effort), to accept (faith), never to let go (the Church).'

I cannot conclude better than by quoting the comments which such a way of life recently drew from an English writer: 'Others who seek, these days, to "bring Christianity up to date" by the jettisoning of established doctrine, and in pursuit of contemporary fashions (temporary only, precisely because they are "contemporary") destroy the foundations of the Christian religion, would benefit by studying carefully the life and works of this Jesuit scientist who was maligned at times by some as the arch-heretic of the age. His acceptance of the restrictions imposed on him . . . represent an object-lesson to us all.'[42]

Abbreviations

*

AE   *Activation of Energy* (Collins, London, and Harcourt, Brace & World, New York, 1970)

AM   *The Appearance of Man* (Collins, London, and Harper & Row, New York, 1965)

CM   *Le Cœur de la Matière* (1950, unpublished)

DM   *The Divine Milieu* (Harper & Brothers, New York, 1960)

FM   *The Future of Man* (Collins, London, and Harper & Row, New York, 1964; Fontana edition, London, 1969)

FTC   *The Faith of Teilhard de Chardin* by Henri de Lubac, s.j. (Burns & Oates, London, 1965)

HE   *Human Energy* (Collins, London, 1969)

HU   *Hymn of the Universe* (Collins, London, and Harper & Brothers, New York, 1965; Fontana edition, London, 1970)

✓ LLZ   *Letters to Léontine Zanta* (Collins, London, and Harper & Row, New York, 1969)

LME   *Let Me Explain* (Collins, London, and Harper & Row, New York, 1970)

LT   *Letters from a Traveller* (Collins, London, and Harper & Brothers, New York, 1962; Fontana edition, London, 1967)

MD   *Le Milieu Divin* (Collins, London, 1960; Fontana edition, London, 1964)

MM   *The Making of a Mind, Letters from a Soldier-Priest* (Collins, London, and Harper & Row, New York, 1965)

MPN   *Man's Place in Nature* (Collins, London, and Harper & Row, New York, 1966)

PM   *The Phenomenon of Man* (Collins, London, and Harper & Brothers, New York, 1959; Fontana edition, London, 1965)

RTC   *The Religion of Teilhard de Chardin* by Henri de Lubac, s.j. (Collins, London, and Desclée, New York, 1967)

SC   *Science and Christ* (Collins, London, and Harper & Row, New York, 1968)

VP   *The Vision of the Past* (Collins, London, and Harper & Row, New York, 1966)

WTW   *Writings in Time of War* (Collins, London, and Harper & Row, New York, 1968)

Écrits   *Écrits du temps de la guerre* (Grasset, Paris, 1965)

Cuénot   *Teilhard de Chardin, A Biographical Study* (Burns & Oates, London, and Helicon Press, Baltimore, 1965). This is an abridged version of *Pierre Teilhard de Chardin: Les grands étapes de son évolution* by Claude Cuénot (Plon, Paris, 1958)

Notes

*

Part One

CHAPTER I

1. 'My first paper of any note' (letter of 15 April 1929, *LLZ*, p. 89).
2. He was then at Fort Mardick, near Dunkirk.
3. This passage is a draft, or perhaps a copy, of a letter to Marguerite Teillard-Chambon. There are no letters in *MM* between 9 April and 18 June 1916.
4. On 22 July he wrote to Père Victor Fontoynont that he was considering a complementary paper to 'Cosmic Life' on 'The Counsel of Virginity'.
5. He had then been for a week with his regiment at Nant-le-Grand (Meuse) after returning from Thiaumont.
6. *WTW*, pp. 85–6.
7. *MM*, p. 178.
8. *WTW*, pp. 98–9, 108, 112. Cf. p. 172: these two virtues are 'practised in renunciation'.
9. *WTW*, p. 135.
10. *WTW*, pp. 170–2.
11. *MM*, p. 195.
12. Finished on 13 August 1917, at Beaulieu-lès-Fontaines.
13. 'Three things, tiny, fugitive: a song, a sunbeam, a glance.'
14. *WTW*, pp. 117–18. Cf. M. Barthélemy-Madaule, *Bergson et Teilhard de Chardin* (Éd. du Seuil, Paris, 1963), p. 80.
15. The experience is again described and reappears in a parallel passage in *DM*, pp. 108–10; *MD*, pp. 119–21; Fontana, pp. 128–30.
16. Cf. André-A. Devaux, *Teilhard et la vocation de la femme* (Éd. universitaires, Brussels, 1964).
17. *CM* (1950): 'A certain "love of the invisible" never ceased to be active in me [note:] more or less aroused and fed by the influence of the Feminine.'
18. *WTW*, pp. 120, 123. Cf. M. Barthélemy-Madaule, op. cit., p. 306: 'In

appearance it is human love that opens the breach through which divine love enters. In fact, according to Teilhard, it is divine love which uses human love to open the breach by which it forces its way into a being.' On this priority of divine initiative, see the conclusion of 'The Mystical Milieu' (*WTW*, pp. 147–9). Cf. ' "Ascent" and "Descent" in the Work of Teilhard de Chardin' in Blondel and Teilhard de Chardin, *Correspondence* (Herder & Herder, New York, 1967), pp. 143–68. See also below, chapter 2, p. 35.

19. Teilhard was then at Mourmelon, in the Marne.

20. 4 November 1917.

21. Not, from their roots or initially, the uniting of pre-existing realities, however slight and fugitive the existence we attribute to them. On this point there is no mistaking Teilhard's view; cf. *RTC*, pp. 195–205. At the same time one cannot say that he succeeded in presenting a satisfactory theory of creation. Cf. below, p. 90.

22. 'The Grand Option' in *FM*, p. 53; Fontana, p. 55. 'Does Mankind Move Biologically upon Itself ', ibid., p. 254; Fontana, p. 265. *HE*, pp. 144–5, 149. 'Centrology' in *AE*, pp. 115–17, etc.

23. *HE*, p. 152.

24. In *Psyché*, Vol. 10, 1955, p. 9. See below, pp. 41–2. Cf. *CM*, note: 'Union (biological union) does not identify. But it differentiates the simple living being. And it personalizes upon itself the Reflective.'

25. We may say that in Teilhard the theory of creative union represents 'the speculative side of a mystical experience' (G. Martelet, Vézelay, September 1967).

26. *WTW*, p. 172. See above, p. 12. Cf. 'Science and Christ' (1921): 'What is the specific effect of purity if it is not the concentration and sublimation of the manifold powers of the soul, the unification of man in himself?' (*SC*, p. 34); 'My Universe' (1924): 'purity, which knits together the fibres of the soul' (*SC*, p. 70).

27. Teilhard was still at Mourmelon.

28. The 'acute problem' of progress in relation to morality, of 'the association of evil and progress', was one of the problems which at that time were acting as the liveliest stimulus to Teilhard's thought.

29. Pp. 191–202.

30. On several occasions, when he is embarking on a new subject, we find him hesitating between an essay in exposition and the development of a symbol.

31. From the earlier entry, 12 January; cf. above, pp. 15–16.

32. Later, speaking from experience, he was to write in a letter: 'I know only one sort of (effective) prudence, the prudence of burning with a

stronger flame.' Père Teilhard, we know, made frequent use of the symbol of fire. To Léontine Zanta, 15 October 1926: '*Per quem omnia semper bona creas, sanctificas, vivificas et praestas nobis . . .* as we say at Mass. What science or philosophy is comparable to the knowledge of that Reality – and above all to the perception of it, even at the most modest and inchoate level! May God give that gift to you and me and preserve it within us. With the possession of that light and that fire one can go everywhere, enlightening oneself and nourishing oneself on everything' (*LLZ*, pp. 72–3). 'The Mystical Milieu': 'It is . . . as fire that I desire you; and it was as fire that I felt your presence, in the intuition of my first contact' (*WTW*, p. 128). *CM* (1950): 'Christ. His heart. A fire: with the power to penetrate all things.' The feast of the Sacred Heart was to him the feast of Fire. One might say of Teilhard what Julien Green says of Surin, whom he loved: 'In Surin we find, as we find in many mystics, a pyromaniac.' (Preface to the *Correspondance* of Jean-Joseph Surin, ed. Michel de Certeau (Desclée de Brouwer, Paris, 1966), p. 20.)

33. *WTW*, p. 59.
34. With this should be compared the end of the 'Hymn to Matter' (Jersey, 8 August 1919): 'Raise me up then, matter, to those heights, through struggle and separation and death; raise me up until, at long last, it becomes possible for me *in perfect chastity to embrace the universe*' (*HU*, p. 70: our italics).
35. As in Hans Urs von Balthasar's interpretation, which agrees with that of Auguste Valensin. See below, chapter 2.
36. We shall be returning to this point in chapter 5; see below, p. 103.
37. It will be remembered that four months earlier he was noting that chastity, understood in the widest sense, is one of the two fundamental virtues of Christian morality ('Creative Union'); see above, pp. 12, 16.
38. *WTW*, p. 222.
39. Cf. Cuénot, p. 109. The author also records a later interview: To an intelligent and trustworthy person who asked him in what state of mind he was before taking his solemn vows, Père Teilhard 'made answer in some such words as these: I am making a vow of poverty; never have I more clearly realized to what extent money can be a powerful means for the service and glorification of God. I am making a vow of chastity; never have I understood so well how a husband and wife complete each other in order better to advance towards God. I am making a vow of obedience; never have I better understood what liberation there is in God's service. Had you not, he was asked, some little anxiety in making your vows? No, he answered, not even momentary misgivings; I

placed my trust in God, certain that he would grant me the grace to do his will in my life as a religious and to be faithful to my vows' (p. 27). This is no doubt an abridged version of the second answer.

40. On this characteristically Teilhardian word, see *Teilhard missionnaire et apologiste* (Éd. 'Prière et Vie', Toulouse, 1966), pp. 103–7.

41. The scholastic tone of this passage should be noted.

42. Cf. 6 March: 'In the Christian scheme the Feminine . . . reaches its term in Christ . . .'; 7 March: 'Feminine=*the unitive side of things*. Its development (progressive, not suppressive) gives "the Virgin", who gives Christ.'

CHAPTER 2

1. This does not justify the conclusion that Père Teilhard regarded original sin as sexual in nature. Everything, in the idiom of the poem, is symbol. Love is the unitive principle, and everything which runs counter to universal union in God is sin.

2. *WTW*, pp. 105–6: 'The appearance of the immortal soul produced . . . in the world . . . a counter-attack by the shrinking, suffering, guilty, Multitude. . . . This temporary disintegration of life is not ordered towards death but towards . . . the resurrection, of spirit. One thing, however, is needed to re-unite and gather together the unnumbered, scattering flock – a most mighty Shepherd.' The affinity with the Gospel of St John and patristic teaching is apparent (cf. my *Catholicisme*, 4th ed., 1947, pp. 10–21). '*Ubi peccata sunt, ibi est multitudo*', said Origen, *In. Ezech.* hom. 9, n.1 (ed. Baehrens, p. 405). Cf. 2 Macc. 2: 7: 'Jeremias . . . blamed them, saying: the place shall be unknown, till God gather together the congregation of the people, and receive them to mercy.' Cf. 'A Note on Progress' (1920): 'Christ is already revealing himself, in the depths of men's hearts, as the Shepherd (the Animator) of the Universe' (*FM*, p. 23; Fontana, pp. 23–4). 'Le Christ Évoluteur' (1942): '*Primario*, to consummate creation in union with God; and, to that end, *secundario*, to annihilate the evil forces of dispersion' (*Cahiers Pierre Teilhard de Chardin*, 5, p. 25).

3. *DM*, p. 114; *MD*, p. 125; Fontana, p. 134.

4. Mgr. Gérard Philips, in *Maria*, by Hubert du Manoir, Vol. 7 (1964), pp. 365–6.

5. See, for example, Isaac de l'Étoile, *Sermons*, 42, 45, 51 (Migne, P.L., 194, 1832 B, 1841 CD, 1863 A).

6. Bérengaud, *In Apocalypsin*, 12, 3–5. Augustine, Sermon 192, n.2, etc. 'Perichoresis' is Scheeben's word.

7. G. Philips, loc. cit.

8. *L'Épée et le Miroir* (1939), p. 90; there are any number of similar passages. See below, p. 123.

9. *Die ewige Frau* (Kösel-Verlag, Munich, 1934), in particular part 3, 'Die zeitlose Frau'. See below, chapter 6, p. 123.

10. *La femme et sa destinée* (Amiot-Dumont, Paris, 1956), pp. 69, 125–30.

11. Cf. *Paradoxe et mystère de l'Église* (Aubier, Paris, 1967), pp. 103–8, 112–19. Charles Kannengiesser, 'Marie figure de l'Église', in *Christus*, 17, pp. 45–59. In addition to the better known passages from Claudel, there is this line from the poem *Visages radieux* (8 September 1942): 'Woman-Church, God-brimming, high and clear, Our Lady singing her own Magnificat' (*'Notre-Dame, la Femme-Église, à grands cris, pleine de Dieu, érigeant Son propre Magnificat'*). See also his *Mémoires improvisés* (1951), pp. 50–60. Cf. Clement of Alexandria, *Paedagogus*, Bk. I, c.6, 42, I: 'There is but one Virgin to have become a mother, and her I love to call the Church!' (H.-I. Marrou and M. Harl, *Sources chrétiennes*, 70, p. 187).

12. On this point, see below, chapter 6.

13. In *HU*, pp. 68–71; Fontana, pp. 63–6.

14. Cf. Robert Speaight, *Teilhard de Chardin: A Biography* (Collins, London, and Harper & Row, New York, 1967), p. 92.

15. There is a similar reference to the 'universal smile' in *DM*, p. 109; *MD*, p. 120; Fontana, p. 129.

16. Cf. *FM*, p. 34; Fontana, p. 35.

17. These two lines were added at the very end; they are inserted between the lines of the original manuscript.

18. Auguste Valensin, *L'art et la pensée de Platon* (from Vol. I of *Annales du Centre universitaire méditerranéen*), p. 33.

19. 'The science of medicine [said Eryximachus] seems to me to prove that, besides attracting the souls of men to human beauty, Love has many other objects and many other subjects; and that his influence may be traced . . . in every form of existence' (Plato's *Symposium*, tr. Michael Joyce (Dent, London, 1935), p. 30).

20. What Socrates says, literally, is simply: 'All my life I shall pay the power and the might of Love such homage as I can' (op. cit., p. 87).

21. Cf. Xavier Tilliette, 'La femme et la féminité' in *Recherches et débats*, 45 (1963), p. 115. François Chatelet, *Platon* (N.R.F., Paris, 1965), pp. 11–12. Valensin, op. cit., p. 35.

22. M. Barthélemy-Madaule, *Bergson et Teilhard de Chardin* (Éd. du Seuil, Paris, 1963), p. 389.

23. *Écrits*, p. 378.

24. *PM*, p. 264; Fontana, pp. 290–1.

25. Section 29: 'To the psychologist and the moralist love is simply a "passion". To those who, following Plato, look in the very structure of beings for the explanation of its ubiquity, its intensity and its mobility, love appears as the higher and purified form of a universal interior attractive power' (*AE*, p. 119). Love is also 'for Teilhard as for Plato the underlying source of knowledge': Marc Faessler, *Homme réel et phénomène humain*, an essay on the Christological basis of anthropology, as found in the writings of Karl Barth and Pierre Teilhard de Chardin (typed thesis, Department of Protestant Theology, Geneva, 1967), p. 314. The author quotes a note dated 20 July 1946: 'Love is the dynamic basis of knowledge.' Rousselot is apposite in this context.

26. 'My Universe' in *SC*, p. 38.

27. 'The Struggle Against the Multitude' (1917) in *WTW*, p. 96. 'The New Spirit' (1942) in *FM*, p. 85, etc.; Fontana, p. 88

28. 'The Analysis of Life' (1945) in *AE*, p. 132.

29. 'Centrology' (1944) in *AE*, p. 124.

30. *CM* (1950). 'Centrology' in *AE*, pp. 124–6. *SC* (1921), pp. 31, 50. *FM*, pp. 51–2; Fontana, p. 54. *VP*, pp. 159, 160. *PM*, p. 309; Fontana, p. 338.

31. Thus Othmar Schilling, *Geist und Materie in biblischer Sicht* (*Stuttgarter Bibel-Studien*, 25, 1967) is an attempt to reconcile Teilhard's thought with a 'biblical thought' which seems on the one hand to be reducible to Semitism, and on the other to claim the authority of a divine revelation. See in particular p. 65.

32. 'My Universe' (1924) in *SC*, pp. 48–9, 66–7. Cf. *FTC*, pp. 150–68. For Teilhard the word 'soul' is not, as it is for many of our contemporaries, 'the legacy of a meaningless concept' (cf. Pierre Emmanuel, *Le monde est intérieur*, p. 42).

33. *VP*, p. 63. *WTW*, pp. 97–8. Wedding address, 1928 ('Sur le bonheur', 1966, p. 73). See also, for example, *PM*, pp. 195–6, 220, 223, 244, 272–3; Fontana, pp. 175–6, 199–200, 202–3, 221–2, 248. Cf. *FTC*, p. 185; *Teilhard missionnaire et apologiste*, pp. 67–72, etc.

34. *PM*, p. 265; Fontana, p. 291; see below, chapter 5, p. 87.

35. Teilhard's italics.

36. *De operibus Spiritus sancti*, Bk. I, Ch. 7: '*Quaecumque Scriptura nobis de amore Dei vel amante Deo loquitur, tam vera tamque constantia sunt, ut potius haec nostra carnalia de quibus similitudines ducuntur, illius constantis veritatis quaedam quasi umbrae vel transitoriae imagines sint*' (ed. J. Gribomont and E. de Solms, *Sources chrétiennes*, 131, 1967, p. 78).

37. Note dated 14 October 1918. Cf. Auguste Valensin, op. cit., pp. 54–5:

'Plato neglects the person and reduces the essence of love to aesthetic contemplation.' The Christian God of Teilhard, prevenient personal love, is obviously not the same as Plato's Good.

38. In *HU*, pp. 64-5, 70; Fontana, pp. 60, 65. Cf. Diotima in the *Symposium*: 'The man who has thus advanced along the road of love, without ever resisting the force that carried him forward, will suddenly see a thing of astonishing beauty appear; but this time the beauty will be in its very essence . . .'

39. First Paper to Auguste Valensin, in *Correspondence*, p. 32 (12 December 1919).

40. We find the same admiration in Guy Le Fèvre de La Boderie, the sixteenth-century translator of Ficino's commentary on the *Symposium*: 'The many years that have passed have in no way detracted from the excellence of the spiritual fare served at Plato's banquet' (1578). Cf. Raymond Marcel, op. cit., pp. 52, 128-9.

41. Letter to Claude Rivière, 22 January 1943, quoted by Speaight, op. cit., p. 261.

42. Auguste Valensin, 'Platon et la théorie de l'amour', *Études*, April 1954, p. 7. Cf. Blondel-Teilhard *Correspondence*, pp. 46-69.

43. 'Lord of lands and seas, sky-sovereign, Love binds fast this chain of things.' *De Consolatione Philosophiae*, Bk. 2, carmen 8, vv. 13-15, ed. L. Bieler, *Corpus christianorum*, series latina, Vol. 94, 1967, p. 36.

44. *PM*, p. 264; Fontana, p. 291. What is more, Nicolas of Cusa already rejected geocentricism, and taught the plurality of inhabited worlds. There are numerous intellectual affinities between Teilhard and Nicolas.

45. Raymond Marcel, Introduction to Ficino's commentary on the *Symposium* (Les Belles-Lettres, Paris, 1956), pp. 107, 120.

46. c. 1525. French translation by Guy Le Fèvre de La Boderie, 1579. Zorgi quoted Boethius and Denys.

47. *WTW*, pp. 76-7.

48. Cf. *Theologica platonica*, Bk. 4, ch. I (ed. Raymond Marcel (Les Belles-Lettres, Paris, 1964), Vol. I, pp. 144-8).

49. *Oeuvres*, ed. Adam and Tannery, Vol. 10, p. 218: '*Una est in rebus activa vis, amor, charitas, harmonia.*' *Cogitationes privatae*, 1619-21.

50. Cf. Robert Oppenheimer, *Science and the Common Understanding* (O.U.P., London, 1954), pp. 11-12.

51. Henri Lichtenberger, tr. of *Faust*, Vol. I (Aubier, Paris, 1932), Introduction, p. 72.

52. Faust 2, end: 'Das Ewig-Weibliche'.

53. H. Lichtenberger, op. cit., Vol. 3, p. lix.

54. Cf. *Écrits*, p. 442: 'He felt pity for those who take fright at the span of a

century or whose love is bounded by the frontiers of a nation' (English trans. in *HU*, p. 66; Fontana, p. 61).

55. Cf. Auguste Valensin, Textes et documents inédits, pp. 15, 27, 289–97, 358–9. Of these copious notes on Dante left by Père Valensin, only two volumes have been published: *Regards sur Dante* and *Le christianisme de Dante* (Aubier, Paris, 1956 and 1954). From his notebook as a novice: 'From time to time I remember lines from the great poet, and they sing delightfully in my head . . . O Dante! Dante!'

56. *Revue néo-scolastique de Louvain*, Vol. 23, 1921, pp. 121–39.

57. *Paradiso*, 33, 145.

58. *Purgatorio*, 30.

59. 'It is not Dante's habit to offer us imaginary figures': L. Espinasse-Mongenet, *Dante Alighieri, Le Purgatoire*, Vol. 2 (Firmin-Didot, Paris, 1932), p. 216.

60. Cf. Auguste Valensin, *Regards sur Dante*, p. 24: 'Beatrice is now glorified, standing midway between God and him. Being close to God, she is at the source of all real knowledge . . . But (and this is the miracle of *The Divine Comedy*) she is still the miraculous little Florentine who appeared in her red gown in the cloisters of the Portinari palace.'

61. *Herrlichkeit*, Vol. 2.

62. *Le christianisme de Dante*, p. 126.

63. See above, pp. 13, 14.

64. Cf. D. Strémooukyoff, *Vladimir Soloviev et son œuvre messianique* (Les Belles-Lettres, Paris, 1935), pp. 21–5. Maxime Herman, introduction to Solovyev's *Crise de la philosophie occidentale* (Aubier, Paris, 1947), pp. 9–15.

65. Cf. *The Meaning of Love* (Bles, London, 1945), pp. 61–4.

66. Op. cit., pp. 34, 58.

67. Op. cit., pp. 30–64 *passim*. We shall be noting further similarities between Solovyev and Teilhard in the next chapter. Cf. Karl Vladimir Truhlar, *Teilhard und Solowjew, Diertung und religiöse Erfahrung* (Freiburg-München, 1966).

CHAPTER 3

1. On 9 March he had written: '1. *Ab initio creata* . . . 2. *Non desinam* . . . 3. *Omnia bona pariter cum ea.*' On the 15th his plan included only the first two quotations.

2. 'The Rise of the Other' (1942) in *AE*, p. 70. On this, see M. Barthélemy-Madaule, *La personne et le drame humain chez Teilhard de Chardin* (Éd. du

Seuil, Paris, 1967), pp. 110–35. Love is 'centric energy', 'it is that by which the person bears witness to the convergence of the real'.

3. 'Note pour l'évangélisation des temps nouveaux' (1919) in *Écrits*, p. 378. Cf. *HE*, p. 32.
4. 'The Spirit of the Earth' (1931) in *HE*, p. 33.
5. 'Centrology' in *AE*, p. 119.
6. Ibid., p. 119.
7. 'The Spirit of the Earth' in *HE*, pp. 32–4. 'By the love of man and woman, a thread is wound that stretches to the heart of the world' (ibid., p. 78).
8. Cf. *HE*, pp. 32, 145–6; *AE*, pp. 118–20. *PM*, pp. 264–8; Fontana, pp. 290–4.
9. *HE*, p. 149.
10. Stanislas Breton, *La Passion du Christ et les Philosophies* (Edizioni 'Eco', Teramo, Italy, 1954), pp. 43–4; cf. pp. 45–55.
11. Letter of 27 August 1947. *DM*, pp. 78–80; *MD*, pp. 86–8; Fontana, pp. 103–4. 'The Significance . . . of Suffering' (1933) in *HE*, p. 51. 'The Spiritual Energy of Suffering' (1950) in *AE*, p. 248. Cf. Paul Claudel, *Un poète regarde la croix*, p. 240.
12. 'Sketch of a Personalistic Universe' in *HE*, pp. 72, 76. See above, chapter I, p. 15.
13. 2 September 1916.
14. 'Le Christ évoluteur' (1942); *Cahiers*, 5, p. 24. Cf. V. Solovyev, *The Meaning of Love*, pp. 5–29.
15. Cf. Jacques Maritain, *Carnet de Notes* (Desclée de Brouwer, Paris, 1965), p. 308.
16. *PM*, p. 265; Fontana, pp. 291–2. Cf. Emmanuel Mounier to Paulette Leclercq, 20 August 1933: 'It is only the love of God which will not tolerate equal rivalry. These silly lovesick swains who ask the girl to swear that she loves no one but them – as though the love sometimes realized by a man and a woman were not the fulfilment of what our love for every being should be – that is just blindness to the first lesson real love holds, that love multiplies love, that it must be broadcast, lavished around us' (*Oeuvres*, Vol. 4 (Éd. du Seuil, Paris, 1963), p. 536).
17. Cf. 'The Mystical Milieu' (1917): 'It is I [says the Lord] who am the true bond that holds the World together. Without me, even though beings may seem to make contact with one another, they are divided by an abyss' (*WTW*, p. 142).
18. 'Sketch of a Personalistic Universe' in *HE*, pp. 76–7. Cf. note of 1 May 1920: 'Two "lovers" may remain indefinitely in the closest contact with

one another: as they come closer, so does each slowly lose the other . . . only one medium can bring them together, God.'

19. *AE*, pp. 70–1.

20. Other aspects of this will be referred to in chapter 5: see below, pp. 90–5.

21. These are included in *Sur le bonheur* (Éd. du Seuil, Paris, 1966), pp. 65–91.

22. Cf. Solovyev, *The Meaning of Love*, p. 69: 'From the fact that the deepest and intensest manifestation of love is expressed in the mutual relation of two creatures who complete each other, it by no means follows that this mutual relation can separate and isolate itself from all the rest, as nothing is self-sufficient.'

23. To H. de L., Peking, 15 September 1934.

24. To Auguste Valensin, Tientsin, 24 August 1934: 'Moreover, everything is going well – and I am hoping that I shall not drift away from the only axis and the only love that are indispensable.'

25. *LLZ*, p. 111 (Peking, 24 June 1934). The words we have italicized make it quite clear that the substance of this piece was an answer, at least in oral form, to urgent questions and objections from persons who were not disposed to approve of the Church's attitude. It is this, it seems to me, which partly explains the form of the memorandum and the way the argument is expressed.

26. We find the same assertion in Jacques Maritain, *Carnet de Notes*, p. 350.

27. Cf. Solovyev, op. cit., pp. 60–4; pp. 33–4: 'The fulness of . . . [man's ideal] personality' is realized in a 'supreme unity of both [sexes]'.

28. 'Sketch of a Personalistic Universe' (1936) in *HE*, p. 92.

29. Cf. Julien Green, *Vers l'Invisible* (Plon, Paris, 1967), p. 120: 'Spiritual writers of all times have maintained that God has no use for a heart shared between himself and human beings. "But every one of them shared his heart!" exclaimed a friend of mine to whom I had made that remark when I was explaining to him my own misgivings. He quoted St Francis of Sales. I thought, later, of St Ignatius' terrible distress when he heard of the death of St Francis Xavier' (9 June 1959). See also the fine chapter on St Francis of Sales in Henri Bremond's *Sainte Chantal* (Gabalda, Paris, 1912). However exceptional such cases may be, and indeed are, they nevertheless exist. We know, moreover, how perfect was the renunciation to which St Francis of Sales guided Jeanne de Chantal.

30. This sentence has been quoted, in all good faith, as characteristic of Teilhard's thought on the subject. Taken by itself, however, it may well be given, in the minds of some readers, an interpretation which is

clearly ruled out by what follows. It expresses an observation and a value-judgment which are in no way Teilhard's own, and which every Christian owes it to himself to check: material integrity, as such, is of no importance to us.

31. Cf. Nicholas Berdyaev, *The End of Our Time* (Sheed & Ward, London, 1933), p. 118: 'The hopes of Christianity cannot stop at human reproduction, an element too close to the "malignant endlessness" of mere successive generations. A fundamental problem of life is just this of the transfiguration of human sexual relations, of the enlightening of the feminine element, of the turning of generative energy into creative energy: the natural generation of the old Adam must become the spiritual generation of the new Adam. This means finding the mystical meaning of love, of a transfiguring love that looks not to time but to eternity.' Quoted, in part, by Claude Cuénot, op. cit., p. 45, n.1. Solovyev's influence is clearly recognizable here.

32. On the meaning of these words, see chapter 4.

33. *HE*, p. 77.

34. 'The centre of my attraction is imperceptibly shifting towards the pole upon which all the avenues of Spirit converge' (*WTW*, p. 199).

35. *WTW*, p. 64.

36. Cf. Solovyev, op. cit., p. 32: 'Man . . . in his . . . capacities for self-perfecting, possesses infinite potentialities.'

37. See M. Barthélemy-Madaule's comments in *La personne et le drame humain*, pp. 114–16.

38. Loc. cit., p. 115. Cf. Solovyev, op. cit., pp. 73–7.

39. From the same letter, 11 November 1934.

40. We find something similar in Berdyaev, op. cit., pp. 117–18: 'Women will be very much to the fore' in the society of the future. 'Woman is bound more closely than man to the soul of the world and its primary elemental forces, and it is through her that he reaches communion with them.' Women 'as in the gospel, . . . are predestined to be the myrrh-bearers . . . It is the *eternal feminine* that has so great a future in coming history, not the emancipated woman or the epicene creature.' For all the similarity of these passages, the differences between the two writers are very apparent.

41. *HE*, p. 157. 'A Note on Progress' (1920) in *FM*, pp. 15–17; Fontana, pp. 16–18.

42. 'Cosmic Life' (1916) in *WTW*, p. 67. Cf. the conclusion of *MPN*, and *DM*, pp. 121–2; *MD*, pp. 133–4; Fontana, pp. 140–1.

43. It should be remembered that this was written in 1916, not 1967.

44. We meet these again in 1936, in 'Some Reflexions on the Conversion

of the World': 'Detachment does not consist, properly speaking, in contemning and rejecting, but in penetrating and sublimating' (*SC*, p. 123). See below, p. 86, and above, p. 12. Cf. Blondel, 26 February 1886: 'Perfect detachment attaches to all things without forming ties' (*Carnets intimes*, I, p. 80).

45. Blondel–Teilhard *Correspondence*, p. 29. See ibid., p. 72, note (5 April 1919) explaining the *terrena despicere* of the liturgy: 'Disdain for all success or worldly formalities *qua talis* – but profound esteem for the spiritual substance and organism which is evolving through all of terrestrial life, *in Christo Jesu*.' About 1920 Teilhard wrote a short note on the nature of creative transformation.

46. To Père Valensin. Cf. M. de la Taille, 'L'Oraison contemplative', in *Recherches de science religieuse*, Vol. 9, Oct.–Dec. 1919.

47. *Excentré*, i.e. with a centre outside self.

48. 'My Universe' in *SC*, p. 78.

49. *DM*, pp. 42–3; *MD*, pp. 46–7; Fontana, p. 73. Cf. note of 2 July 1919: 'I pray that Christ Jesus may always be *my only*, *my substantial*, *Light*, the light which dispels the darkness and makes me seek after all things – which, *when it vanishes* from within any particular being, that being ceases to mean anything to me.' Again, on 7 October 1920: 'The two ways of approaching things that are both equally beneficial and necessary: (a) it is very important; (b) it is but dust – in this way one is freed from everything and at the same time one retains one's zest for work.'

50. *WTW*, p. 143. Teilhard continues with a valuable section on the universal love of charity, purity and prayer.

51. See above, p. 17.

52. The reference is no doubt to the feminine environment of his childhood, which had a great influence on him. It included his mother, his two sisters, Françoise and Marguerite-Marie, and his cousin Marguerite Teillard-Chambon. On his mother's influence, see Pierre Leroy, s.j., in *LT*, p. 19.

53. *WTW*, p. 170.

54. He puts the objection in extreme terms, in order to counter it more effectively: 'Does not universal experience conclusively prove that spiritual love has always ended in the gutter?' This, however, he does from a different point of view. In this passage he introduces the view of the future we have described above. 'What paralyses life is lack of faith and lack of daring. The difficulty lies not in solving problems but in expressing them. We can now see the real position: it is biologically evident that to gain control of passion in order to make it serve spirit would be a necessary condition of progress . . .'

55. The perfect 'sublimation' which is the subject of his theory, can, we must accept, normally be hoped for only in the man who burns, as Père Teilhard did, with mystical 'fire', and who strengthens his energy by faithful practice of asceticism and prayer. Cf. his note, dated 8 October 1921: 'The only true strength: I must live as an ascetic of the Kosmos. In my attachment to the whole Kosmos, there must be felt an absolute passing through (*trans-ience*) into Omega=not an iota of [illegible], of sticking to things (*viscosité*), of adherence to things themselves.'

56. He may, however, have been at fault in using some expressions in which the two things were not clearly distinguished. Even so, he was completely justified in putting the whole emphasis on the positive character of virtue. Thus, in a fine section of *Le Milieu Divin*, he writes: 'Purity, in the wide sense of the word, is not merely abstaining from wrong (that is only a negative aspect of purity), nor even chastity (which is only a remarkable special instance of it). It is the rectitude and the impulse introduced into our lives by the love of God sought in and above everything' (*DM*, p. 112; *MD*, p. 124; Fontana, pp. 132–3).

57. Cf. Jacques Maritain, *Carnet de Notes*, p. 349, on the religious who takes a vow of chastity: 'He does not, of course, renounce all feminine friendship, however subject it will still necessarily be to strict external vigilance – for that would be damaging to the very progress and refinement of his moral life.'

58. 1942 Retreat, Peking, second day (17 October). Letter of April 1943, etc.

59. *DM*, p. 70 n.; *MD*, pp. 78–9 n.; Fontana, p. 96 n.

60. 'L'Évolution de la Chasteté.'

61. *MM*, pp. 197–8. Earlier, on 2 December 1915, when just back from leave, he wrote about their meeting in Paris: 'Indeed, the Lord is good to give us these happy moments in which our energy is rested and strengthened. If only, don't you think, he will make us understand that he is even better than all that – and that the surest means we have of progressing in a fruitful friendship is to *converge* on him, each from our own side, helping one another, by prayer and effort, to do better.' Cf. note of 2 March 1925: 'I pray, my God, that I may always love you above all things, and that whatever I do may always be done in order that you may spread your radiance (>purify).' 16 May: '*Domine, ne permittas me separari a Te* – and not only that; *Fac me Tibi quam maxime adhaerere.*'

62. It is in this paragraph that we meet an allusion to 'those women whose warmth and charm have flowed into the very life's blood of my dearest concepts'. Père Teilhard's innocent sincerity had no idea of the suspi-

cions such a remark might arouse. In the case of this paper on the evolution of chastity, all he expected, should it be read outside the narrow circle of a few friendly advisers, was that he might be accused of '*naïveté*' or 'foolishness'.

63. Just as Père Teilhard did not work out all the consequences affecting man that derive from his idea of reflection (cf. *RTC*, pp. 212–13), similarly, he failed to develop his idea of person (cf. Marc Faessler, *Homme réel et phénomène humain*, p. 296). On the notion of creative transformation, see M. Barthélemy-Madaule, *Bergson et Teilhard de Chardin*, pp. 45–9, and below, chapter 4, p. 80.

64. To H. de L., Peking, 15 September 1934.

65. It would, however, be unfair to emphasize too strongly the short-comings of an essay which was not only (as is true of others) not revised for publication but was never intended for more than a few readers: to some of these it was addressed in the hope (in some cases justified) that it might help them to understand the Christian point of view; to others, in order to elicit their comments and advice; it was, we should remember, an essay that would never have been read outside this confidential circle, had not the author been so exceptionally well-known. (See above, pp. 48–9.)

66. Cf. a letter, to J.M., dated 24 August 1948, printed by Mlle Jeanne Mortier in her *Avec Teilhard de Chardin*, '*Vues Ardentes*' (Éd. du Seuil, Paris, 1967), pp. 103–4. In this the author applies to the spiritual man what Étienne Gilson says about the artist, and concludes: 'The unitive operation can succeed only if the attraction exercised on the two lovers by God is stronger than their own mutual attraction. In this lies the whole problem of sublimation.'

67. This should not be taken to mean that Père Teilhard worked out any metaphysical or theological system: this was even less his purpose, if one may put it so, in this lyrical composition than it was in any number of other essays. See Père Labourdette's admirable comments in *Le Colloque de Venise*, p. 239.

CHAPTER 4

1. Such misunderstandings are sometimes the crudest of distortions. There are critics, for example, who condemn Teilhard as openly supporting sensualism, pantheism and immoralism. In fact, their condemnation is based on passages which represent the dialectical element in the objection he is examining, and they are too impatient to read on and see what he has to say in reply. A recent example of

this is a booklet described by M.-M. Labourdette, O.P., in the *Revue thomiste* as 'unfortunately of little value'; of its theological criticisms he says, 'one could go on for ever pointing out the misconceptions'.

2. Cf. Blondel-Teilhard *Correspondence*, p. 9; Teilhard, *Lettres d'Hastings et de Paris* (Aubier, Paris, 1965), Introduction, pp. 10–12, etc.

3. Auguste Valensin, *A travers la Métaphysique* (Beauchesne, Paris, 1925); textes et documents inédits, pp. 126–9.

4. This is also the view expressed by Emiliano de Aguirre, s.j., in *Teilhard de Chardin et la pensée catholique* (Éd. du Seuil, Paris, 1965), p. 38.

5. Norbert A. Lutyen, O.P., *Teilhard de Chardin* (Éd. universitaires, Fribourg, 1965), pp. 60–1.

6. Charles (now Cardinal) Journet, 'Note sur Teilhard de Chardin' in *Nova et Vetera* (Fribourg, 1958), p. 385, n.1.

7. Journet, loc. cit.: 'The principle of the univocity of being, which is the source of Teilhard's mistake, is contained in his postulate of the "unity of the stuff of the universe".'

8. 'Hominization' (1923) in *VP*, p. 64.

9. 'The Phenomenon of Man' (1928) in *SC*, p. 90.

10. Or, we may say 'even if they are not univocal'.

11. To Emmanuel Mounier, 2 November 1947 (in *SC*, p. 221). Cf. 'Turmoil or Genesis?' (1948): Christian cosmology is seen to be 'homogeneous' with human cosmology (*FM*, p. 224; Fontana, p. 232).

12. 'The Phenomenon of Man' (1930) in *VP*, p. 170. Cf. 'The Natural Units of Humanity' (1939): 'Far from expanding in a sort of homogeneous network, etc.' (ibid., p. 195).

13. 'Human Energy' (1937) in *HE*, p. 149.

14. *WTW*, p. 120. In these last two passages the sense does not differ essentially from the Teilhardian sense we have already met. It is a question of effecting in a mystical intuition this homogeneity which elsewhere was postulated as a condition of thought.

15. In an unpublished MS. (1921), quoted by Marc Faessler, op. cit., p. 213, three phases of perception are distinguished: homogeneous unity without differentiation; plurality without perspective; higher, heterogeneous unity=differentiation.

16. 'Note on the "Universal Element" of the World' (22 December 1918) in *WTW*, pp. 274, 275. The whole of this note, however, was crossed out by Teilhard; he returned to the subject a little later in 'The Universal Element' (21 February 1919), which is a new criticism of pantheism. In this he explains that fundamentally this universal element is 'the cosmic influence of Christ' rather than 'God's creative action' (ibid., pp. 295, 296).

17. Note of 15 September 1920.

18. To Léontine Zanta, 24 January 1929, in *LLZ*, p. 87.

19. *PM*, pp. 88, 99–100, 106–7, 116, 224; Fontana, pp. 97, 109–10, 118, 128, 246. 'Hominization' (1925) in *VP*, p. 71.

20. Letter of 29 April 1934.

21. Cf. Mgr Bruno de Solages, *Initiation métaphysique* (Privat, 1962), pp. 165–86. Id., *Dialogue sur l'Analogie* (Aubier, Paris, 1946); *Teilhard de Chardin*, p. 77.

22. To Auguste Valensin, 24 August 1934. The resemblance will be noted to Blondel's idea of the universe criticized by Père de Tonquédec in *Immanence* (1912) under the name 'the principle of universal inter-dependence'.

23. 'The Phenomenon of Man' (1928) in *SC*, p. 91.

24. *DM*, p. 103; *MD*, p. 114; Fontana, pp. 124–5.

25. 'Hominization' (1923) in *VP*, p. 60.

26. Cf. *Teilhard missionnaire et apologiste* (1966), pp. 103–7.

27. Cf. *FTC*, pp. 169–77.

28. Ibid., pp. 150–68.

29. *PM*, p. 57, n. 1; Fontana, p. 62, n. 1.

30. *Réflexions sur le bonheur* (Peking, 28 December 1943) (Éd. du Seuil, Paris, 1966), p. 28. Compare with this H. Bergson, 'Consciousness and Life' in *Mind Energy* (Macmillan, London, 1920).

31. 'My Universe' (1924) in *SC*, p. 47; 'The Analysis of Life' (1943) in *AE*, pp. 132, 133, etc. Cf. Émile Rideau, *Teilhard oui ou non?* (Fayard, Paris, 1967), p. 103.

32. *AE*, pp. 33, 132–3. 'A Summary of my Phenomenological View of the World': 'Consciousness presents itself to our experience as the effect or the specific property of this Complexity taken to extremely high values' (*LME*, p. 71).

33. In this connexion Père Smulders appositely quotes St Thomas, *In Librum de Causis*, lectio 15, where he defines spirit as '*quod redeat ad essentiam suam reditione completa*, etc.' – it 'returns to its own essence in a complete return' (*La Vision de Teilhard de Chardin*, 2nd ed., 1965, p. 75).

34. 'Turmoil or Genesis?' (1948) in *FM*, p. 220; Fontana, pp. 228–9. 'Centrology' (1944), Section 13, 'Eu-centrism': 'Thus, by passing through a new critical point, an isosphere of a fundamentally new type is produced: the isosphere of spirit, the noosphere' (*AE*, p. 109).

35. 'Hominization and Speciation' (1952) in *VP*, p. 260. 'The Reflection of Energy' (1952) in *AE*, pp. 324–5, 332. 'The Singularities of the Human Species' in *AM*, p. 265, etc.

36. 'The Analysis of Life' (1945) in *AE*, p. 138.
37. 'The Singularities of the Human Species' (1954) in *AM*, p. 224.
38. Cf. Henri Bergson, *Creative Evolution* (1907; Eng. tr., 1911), *Mind Energy* (1919; Eng. tr., 1920), *The Two Sources of Morality and Religion* (1932; Eng. tr., 1935).
39. Étienne Borne, *Passion de la Vérité* (Fayard, Paris, 1962), p. 230.
40. 'The Reflection of Energy' in *AE*, p. 325, n. 3.
41. In particular by J.-M. Domenach, who believes that Teilhard did violence 'not only to strict scientific usage but to the very function of language' (in *Esprit*, 1963, p. 347); similarly, Père Norbert A. Luyten, o.p. Cf. *Colloque de Venise*, pp. 197–200. Teilhard's use of analogy is one of the points most frequently raised in the *Colloque*; see pp. 143–4, 160–1, 189, 201, 218.
42. 'Centrology', Sections 29 and 30, in *AE*, pp. 118–19, 120. This should be borne in mind if we are to understand any particular statement. Thus in 'The Phenomenon of Spirituality' (*HE*, p. 108) Teilhard says: 'To try everything and force everything in the direction of the greatest consciousness; this, in a universe recognized to be in a state of spiritual transformation, is the general and highest law of morality.' What he has in mind here is 'consciousness-love', as the editors have appreciated, who refer the reader to a later essay in the same volume on 'Human Energy'.
43. Mgr de Solages, *Teilhard de Chardin*, p. 122. Cf. 'The Analysis of Life' (1945) in *AE*, p. 133, on the 'psychic polarization' of each elementary grain of energy. 'The Spirit of the Earth' in *HE*, p. 23. For a discussion of this, see É. Borne, *Passion de la Vérité*, pp. 191–3.
44. Valensin had been working on a thesis on 'Leibniz and Scholasticism' which was interrupted by ill-health.
45. We find, too, in Blondel an analogical concept of thought which has some relation to Teilhard's concept of consciousness: 'Just as un-thought thought is the foundation which is universally imposed, so thought (unthinking though it still be) is present in embryo, is pregnant, in all the differentiations without which the universe would be impenetrable and unliveable, an anti-being and a defiance of all intelligibility' (*La Pensée*, Vol. 1 (P.U.F., Paris), 4th ed., p. 45, n. 1; cf. pp. 3–56). Cf. J. Paliard, *Maurice Blondel ou le dépassement chrétien* (Julliard, Paris, 1950), pp. 140–3.
46. His friend Pierre Charles had done the same in an 'Ontology' (which Teilhard could not stand). In both cases, of course, the imitation was confined to the form adopted.
47. *Colloque de Venise*, pp. 160–1.

48. *Homme réel et phénomène humain*, p. 165.

49. François Marty, s.j., *La Perfection de l'Homme selon St Thomas d'Aquin* (Pontificia Università Gregoriana, Rome, 1962), p. 173 and note. (Analecta Gregoriana, 123.)

50. J.-L. Russell, s.j., *Colloque de Venise*, p. 57; cf. p. 58. See, however, p. 61, what Père Luyten says about distinguishing between the case of 'love' and the case of 'consciousness'. Id.: 'Matière et esprit dans la pensée de Teilhard de Chardin' in *Revue thomiste*, 1967, pp. 226–47. The author of this meticulous study rightly concludes that there are ambiguities. At the same time the textual evidence does not justify the further conclusion that Teilhard reduced spirit 'to a dimension of the material'. A remark of Paul Tillich's in *The Courage To Be* (Nisbet, London, 1952) is apposite in this connexion: 'Concepts like world soul, microcosmos, instinct, the will to power, and so on have been accused of introducing subjectivity into the objective realm of things. But these accusations are mistaken. . . . It is the function of an ontological concept to use some realm of experience to point to characteristics of being-itself which lie above the split between subjectivity and objectivity, and which therefore cannot be expressed literally in terms taken from the subjective or the objective side. . . . They must be understood not literally but analogously' (p. 24).

51. *Colloque de Venise*, p. 150. On the word 'biological' in Teilhard, see Père Smulders' comments in *La vision de Teilhard de Chardin*, 2nd ed., p. 79.

52. 'The Singularities of the Human Species' (1955) in *AM*, p. 239. Cf. *RTC*, p. 191. Mgr de Solages, *Teilhard de Chardin*, pp. 274–7.

53. M. Barthélemy-Madaule in *Science et synthèse* (N.R.F., Paris, 1967), p. 366. 'If you look at all the passages in which the presence of the biological in the social is discussed (a subject which arouses many of the analytically minded), you will find that Teilhard safeguards himself. Any sentence which introduces the biological in connexion with the human always contains a qualifying "from the point of view we are adopting", or again, "as applied to the fundamentally mechanical element", etc.'

54. *Les Deux Sources*, p. 103. Cf. Teilhard, 'Introduction à la vie chrétienne' (1944), on the sacraments: 'In the domain of the life of personal union with God, they operate biologically what they stand for.'

55. 'Hominization' (1925) in *VP*, pp. 71–2; cf. pp. 56–8. Cf. Christian d'Armagnac, *Archives de philosophie*, 1957, p. 25.

56. 'The Phenomenon of Man' (1928) in *SC*, p. 95.

57. 'Zoological Evolution and Invention' (1948) in *VP*, p. 235.

58. *PM*, p. 116; Fontana, p. 128.
59. 'Hominization' (1925) in *VP*, p. 71.
60. 'The Natural Units of Humanity' (1939) in *VP*, p. 213.
61. 'Transformation . . . of the Mechanism of Evolution' (19 November 1951) in *AE*, p. 309.
62. *Comment je vois* (1948), Section 9. Cf. Mgr de Solages, *Teilhard de Chardin*, pp. 277–8. M. Barthélemy-Madaule, *La personne et le drame humain*, p. 32.
63. Émile Rideau, *Teilhard de Chardin: A Guide to His Thought* (Collins, London, 1967), p. 42.
64. The essence of his complaint against spiritualists, psychics, and 'false mysticisms' is that they confuse the planes and mix up the spheres (cf. *MM*, p. 268, 13 December 1918). In this he supports Blondel's criticism of Bergson's view of spirit.
65. Letter of 29 April 1934.
66. 'Mastery of the World and the Kingdom of God' (20 September 1916) in *WTW*, p. 83. Cf. below, p. 84.
67. Teilhard speaks also of 'zones', 'planes', and 'spheres': 'Science and Christ' (1921) in *SC*, p. 23, etc.
68. M. Barthélemy-Madaule, *Bergson et Teilhard de Chardin* (1963), p. 243. *La personne et le drame humain*, p. 27; and in *Esprit*, 1964, pp. 372–3. Cf. Étienne Borne, *Passion de la Vérité*, p. 64.
69. Letter of 29 October 1949.
70. Hominization brings the emergence of 'very ancient and absolutely new characteristics'; 'thought, properly so called, suddenly breaks in, to dominate and transform everything' ('Hominization' in *VP*, p. 64; 'The Reflection of Energy' in *AE*, p. 325).
71. Cf. 'The Atomism of Spirit' in *AE*, pp. 25–6.
72. Cf. 'Man's Place in Nature' (1932) in *VP*, p. 180.
73. *L'Échec* (P.U.F., Paris, 1962), p. 73.
74. *PM*, p. 79; Fontana, p. 87.
75. *PM*, foreword, p. 34; Fontana, p. 38. Cf. 'the appearance in the world of something completely new' (*WTW*, p. 155).
76. Note of 4 March 1920.
77. *PM*, pp. 86, 182–3; Fontana, pp. 95, 202. Cf. to L. Zanta, 24 January 1929 (p. 87).
78. Cf. 'The Spirit of the Earth' (9 March 1931) in *HE*, p. 28.
79. *PM*, p. 171; Fontana, p. 190.
80. Letter (23 June 1936) to H. de L.: 'You will have to emphasize the general changes in the point of view, which can, to put it briefly, be reduced to man's being *rooted* in the universe, and the so pro-

nounced RENEWAL in him of all earlier life, on a new and higher plane.'

81. 'The Singularities of the Human Species' (1954) in *AM*, p. 225.

82. 'What Should we Think of Transformism?' (1930) in *VP*, p. 154.

83. That is why, when Teilhard speaks of 'the metamorphosis of "Matter" ' he is careful to put 'Matter' in quotation marks; the word applies, though in a more complex sense, to 'the stuff of things' (*Le Christique*). Cf. 'Science and Christ' (1921) in *SC*, pp. 33–4.

84. This is what Claude Tresmontant calls 'predominance of subsisting form over informed matter' ('Le problème de l'existence de Dieu' in *La Table ronde*, January 1968, p. 68).

85. *How I Believe* (1934). 'Science and Christ or Analysis and Synthesis' (1921) in *SC*, pp. 21–36. 'Centrology' (1944) in *AE*, p. 124. *Observations sur la synthèse expérimentale de l'esprit* (c. 1920 ?): 'To seek to effect the synthesis of the spiritual without leaving the plane of the nervous system's material arrangements, would be to make the mistake of the physicist who thinks he can indefinitely raise the temperature of water and still keep it liquid.'

86. 'Introduction à la vie chrétienne' (1944). Notes (10 February and 16 July 1916, and 1924). 'The Struggle Against the Multitude' (1917) in *WTW*, pp. 97–8. 'The Reflection of Energy' (1952) in *AE*, pp. 323–4. Cf. Étienne Borne, 'Matière et esprit dans la philosophie de Teilhard' in *Recherches et débats*, 40, 1962, pp. 45–65.

87. See above, chapter 3, p. 63, and below, chapter 5, p. 99.

88. 'Centrology' (1944), Sections 24, 32, in *AE*, pp. 112–13, 124–5.

89. His method consists essentially in studying man as an objective phenomenon, and demonstrating the genesis of spirit, from which are derived his unique characteristics and position. Any reader who finds this difficult to accept has not progressed beyond the first aspect of his thought.

90. For example, in 'The Phenomenon of Spirituality' (1937) in *HE*, pp. 96–7. 'My Universe' (1924): 'It is Spirit that constantly carries matter along and supports it in the ascent towards consciousness' (*SC*, p. 50).

91. 'The Natural Units of Humanity' (1939) in *VP*, p. 213, etc.

92. *PM*, p. 172; Fontana, p. 191. 'The Phenomenon of Man' (1930) in *VP*, p. 166.

93. 'The Phenomenon of Man' (1930) in *VP*, pp. 161–6. *PM*, p. 169; Fontana, p. 190. 'The Human Rebound of Evolution' (1947) in *FM*, p. 205; Fontana, p. 213.

94. 'Hominization' (1925) in *VP*, p. 64. *PM*, Preface, p. 29; Fontana, p. 31; cf. *VP*, p. 101. Cf. below, p. 84.

95. To L. Zanta, 23 August 1929, p. 95. Note of 20 December 1917: 'One might well examine more thoroughly, and give general application to the "theory of breaks in continuity".' *DM*, p. 78; *MD*, p. 86; Fontana, p. 103: 'It is perfectly true that the Cross means . . . in a sense, breaking with [the world].'

96. 'The Singularities of the Human Species' (1954) in *AM*, p. 257. 'Faith in Peace' (1947) in *FM*, pp. 149–54; Fontana, pp. 154–60.

97. Henri Bergson, *Les deux sources de la morale et de la religion* (Alcan, Paris, 1932), pp. 310, 324, 332.

98. Cf. Spinoza, *Tractatus politicus*, ch. 5, n. 4: '*Pax enim non belli privatio, sed virtus est, quae ex animi fortitudine oritur*' – 'for peace is not the absence of war but a virtue whose source is spiritual strength'.

99. To George Barbour, 23 September 1940, in Barbour, *In the Field with Teilhard de Chardin* (Herder and Herder, New York, 1965), p. 111. 'Some Reflections on . . . the Atom Bomb' (1946) in *FM*, pp. 145–7; Fontana, pp. 150–1. 'Faith in Peace', ibid., pp. 150–3; Fontana, pp. 156–9.

100. To M. and S. Bégouën, 20 September 1940, in *LT*, p. 267; Fontana, p. 216. 'Human Energy' in *HE*, p. 136.

101. 'The Atomism of Spirit' (1941) in *AE*, p. 53.

102. 'The Natural Units of Humanity' (1939) in *VP*, p. 213.

103. For references, see *RTC*, pp. 129 ff.

104. 'Reversal' occurs several times in his 1941 Retreat notes (Peking, 26 October–3 November). Cf. *CM*: 'There had been a "reversal" in me of the sense of plenitude.'

105. Retreat notes, Peking, 1941, etc. Ibid., 28 October: 'St Teresa: a typical case of an element undergoing reversal in Ω. Such an interior event is more important biologically than a huge war.' See other passages in Blondel and Teilhard de Chardin, *Correspondence*, pp. 47–8.

106. 'Man's Place in the Universe' (1942) in *VP*, p. 222: 'An impossible dualism'. *CM* (1950), p. 9, etc. Cf. Peking, 28 October, 1941: 'Mystery of the Feminine and (which, when you get to the very bottom, comes to the same thing) of cosmic duality.'

107. 'The Phenomenon of Man' (1930) in *VP*, p. 170.

108. Blondel and Teilhard de Chardin, *Correspondence*, p. 33; cf. p. 84. Note (Strasbourg, 10 January 1919): 'Obviously, the *habitus supernaturalis qua talis* is not natural: but it is transformation, recreation, of natural qualities.' Cf. *DM*, p. 86 n.; *MD*, p. 94 n.; Fontana, p. 110 n. For the application to the soul, see Solages, pp. 286–91.

109. *DM*, p. 109; *MD*, p. 120; Fontana, p. 130.

110. Note of 14 March 1918.

111. 'My Universe' (1924) in *SC*, p. 73.

112. Cf. *PM*, p. 169; Fontana, p. 188. 'The Grand Option' (1939) in *FM*, p. 56; Fontana, p. 58. M. Barthélemy-Madaule speaks of the 'astonishing dialectical fruitfulness of Teilhard's concept of creative transformation' (op. cit., p. 26).

113. In France, the popularity was largely due to Anders Nygren's *Éros et Agapè* (which appeared in French 1944-52; in English 1937-39). He stresses the opposition between the two concepts: 'A dichotomy more provocative than convincing', says A. M. Ramsey in *Recent Developments in Anglican Theology*.

114. Blondel and Teilhard de Chardin, *Correspondence*, p. 47. *DM*, p. 74; *MD*, p. 82; Fontana, pp. 99-100.

115. 'The Spirit of the Earth' (1931) in *HE*, p. 28: 'To control these inherited characteristics at a higher level is the task of morality and the secret of "higher life".'

116. *Correspondence*, p. 29: 'Here again we find the mysterious notion of "transformation" stepping in – linking super-nature and nature as it does spirit and matter.'

117. Note of 19 October 1916. Cf. our essay, *Athéisme et sens de l'homme* (Éd. du Cerf, Paris, 1968), ch. 2.

118. 'Mastery of the World and the Kingdom of God' (20 September 1916) in *WTW*, p. 83. Cf. *DM*, p. 86 n.; *MD*, p. 94 n.; Fontana, p. 110 n.

119. Blondel and Teilhard de Chardin, *Correspondence*, p. 33. To Père Fontoynont, 15 March 1916: 'If we make the mistake of trying to insulate our hearts from love of the universe, are we not in danger of killing it?' Cf. Note of 16 May 1925: 'My vocation, much more even than to preserve what man's effort has won, is *to transfigure the real*.' Cf. Blondel, *Carnets intimes*, I, pp. 269-70.

120. *Correspondence*, pp. 48-9. Cf. *PM*, p. 169; Fontana, p. 188, in connexion with the birth of thought: 'Discontinuity in continuity.'

121. *DM*, p. 78; *MD*, pp. 86-7; Fontana, p. 103.

122. Retreat, Peking, 27 October 1941: 'Transcendence (Reversal) is fo.K of Omega. *Everything holds together*. Christian ascesis is simply an expression of a K. law' (K=cosmic; fo.K=cosmic function).

CHAPTER 5

1. *HE*, p. 33. The whole of this evolution, he wrote later (in 1950) 'is shot through with, animated by, redolent with, a breath of Union – and of the Feminine' (*CM*, Introduction).

2. Note of 14 October 1918.

3. The last of these changes, which takes place outside this world of sense, is 'a total metamorphosis' (*DM*, p. 78; *MD*, p. 86; Fontana, p. 103). Cf. 'Life and the Planets' in *FM*, p. 123; Fontana, p. 127.

4. To Auguste Valensin, 11 November 1934: 'From the point of view I have adopted, chastity is not the suppression but the sublimation of the Feminine.' Cf. 'Some Reflections on Progress': 'To rise above the World, therefore, does not mean to despise or reject it, but to pass through it and sublime it' (*FM*, p. 79; Fontana, p. 82). 'The Heart of the Problem': 'Faith in God, in the very degree in which it assimilates and sublimates within its own spirit the spirit of Faith in the World . . .' (ibid., p. 268; Fontana, p. 281).

5. 'The Priest' in *WTW*, p. 218.

6. Cf. *HE*, pp. 143, 146, 148, 154, etc.

7. *CM* (1950), conclusion.

8. Ibid., p. 28. Cf. *Le Christique* (1955), p. 9.

9. *PM*, pp. 264–5; Fontana, p. 291. In other words, the universe is 'convergent in nature'.

10. 'Centrology', Section 29, 'The function of love', in *AE*, p. 119.

11. *WTW*, p. 143. See above, p. 60.

12. Cf. 'Faith in Man' (1947) in *FM*, p. 192; Fontana, p. 199: 'Everything that rises must converge.' For everything that ascends is 'universalized' as it becomes spiritualized.

13. 'L'Évolution de la Chasteté' (1934).

14. Note of 14 October 1918.

15. Similarly, in *Comment je vois*, Section 4, 'cosmic involution' is conceived as 'being sublimated through synthesis in spirit'.

16. The same essential objection to Freudianism is raised by Jacques Maritain, 'Freudisme et psychanalyse' in *Quatre essais sur l'esprit* (DDB, Paris, 1939), pp. 48–60.

17. Assimilation of spirit with the future: cf. Wedding address 1928 (*Sur le bonheur*, 1966, pp. 72–3), etc.

18. *CM*, p. 17, section on 'The Stuff of the Noosphere': 'And nothing henceforth can divert me from my unalterable conviction that it is in the form of . . . *thought* that the stuff of things gradually concentrates, in the pure state, at the apex of the cosmos, in its most stable form, that is to say in the form which has become the most completely irreversible.'

19. The phrases quoted, and references, may be found in *Images de l'abbé Monchanin* (Aubier, Paris, 1967), pp. 23, 121. See also the Abbé Monchanin's lecture in 1956 to the Alliance Française at Pondicherry, on 'The Crisis of Hope'. In this he quotes from Walter Riese (discussing man in the light of modern neurology): 'Even if Freudianism', says

Monchanin, 'is in some respects a reaction against materialism, a revindication of the psyche, and an attempt to discover the history of each individual's instinct, its underlying inspiration none the less bears the mark of despair. In his old age, Sigmund Freud laid more emphasis on the death instinct than on the sexual instinct, co-extensive with life . . . Freudian time looks not to the future but to the past: the dim and distant past where complexes are formed, and in which they can be resolved, so bringing a cure which restores childhood but opens up no future. "Life is an annunciation", said Von Monakoff; for Freud it is only a reminiscence.'

20. Freud, 7 February 1930. *Correspondance de Sigmund Freud avec le pasteur Pfister* (Gallimard, Paris, 1966), p. 191. Cf. pp. 192, 207.

21. After the passage just quoted from *CM*, Teilhard continues: 'But if this is to be properly understood it calls for certain amplification . . . to be found in the most advanced phase of my interior venture in quest of the heart of things.'

22. Cf. in quite a different context, an exposition on the same lines in J.-Y. Jolif, O.P., *Comprendre l'homme*, Vol. I (Éd. du Cerf, Paris, 1967), pp. 269–70. See also Paul Toinet, *Existence chrétienne et philosophie* (Aubier, Paris, 1965), in particular pp. 42, 65.

23. 'The Psychological Conditions of the Unification of Man' (1948) in *AE*, p. 177. There is, in Teilhard, a sort of equivalence between the categories of spirit, freedom, the future, and the whole.

24. *HE*, p. 129.

25. It presupposes, also, a concept of the human mind more profound than the spiritual empiricism of William James, for example, or Bergson.

26. Cf. *Comment je vois* (1947), Section 28. For a long time Teilhard was in doubt about the way in which the freedom of the creative act should be expressed. He was unwilling to represent it as an 'arbitrary' decision, which led him on one occasion to say that it was not 'absolutely gratuitous' (1917). Here Teilhard is coming round to the view that 'supreme freedom', with no admixture of the arbitrary, is found in love. Nevertheless, there is still some hesitation in his mind. See above, p. 15. On the other hand, in his presentation, in *Comment je vois*, of his doctrine of the convergent universe, Teilhard explains the basis of his doctrine of love.

27. 'The Grand Option' (1939) in *FM*, pp. 54–5; Fontana, p. 57.

28. 'The Rise of the Other' in *AE*, pp. 70–5. Cf. 'The Human Rebound of Evolution' (1947) in *FM*, p. 211; Fontana, pp. 219–20. 'The Grand Option' (1939), ibid., p. 57; Fontana, p. 59.

29. *PM*, p. 267; Fontana, p. 293.

30. 'Sketch of a Personalistic Universe' (1936) in *HE*, p. 78.

31. 'The Atomism of Spirit' (1941) in *AE*, pp. 46–7. 'Sketch of a Personalistic Universe' in *HE*, p. 80. This does not imply, as some have thought, that 'inexorable convergence between individual freedom and collective discipline'.

32. 'The Directions and Conditions of the Future' (1948) in *FM*, pp. 234–5; Fontana, pp. 244–5. 'Human Unanimisation' (1950), ibid., pp. 286–7; Fontana, pp. 300–1. 'A Clarification' (1950) in *AE*, p. 227. *PM*, pp. 267–8; Fontana, pp. 293–4, etc. Cf. Bergson, *Les deux sources*, p. 275: 'A creative energy which would be love.'

33. Ibid. Cf. *HE*, pp. 146–55.

34. *PM*, pp. 295–6; Fontana, pp. 323–4. Cf. *HE* (1937), pp. 150–2, 155–8. *DM*, p. 128; *MD*, p. 140; Fontana, p. 146.

35. Cf. M. Barthélemy-Madaule in *Esprit*, 1964, pp. 381–2. On this necessary relationship, which alone is in line with the Gospel teaching, see Christopher Butler, *The Theology of Vatican II* (Darton, Longman & Todd, London, 1967), conclusion, pp. 188–9.

36. Other writings are directly concerned with the love of charity, among them, to take an example, the 'Introduction à la vie chrétienne' (1944). What emerges above all from the fundamental Christian vision and the structure of dogma is 'the primacy of charity'. Charity consists in 'God's love for the world and each one of its elements' and, in return, in 'the love of the elements for one another and for God'. When the term is reached, there must be unification of all in God, not by fusion, but by 'differentiating synthesis' in a vast network of personal relationships. It is this vision of a final unity that Teilhard sometimes calls 'pantheism of love' or 'Christian pantheism'.

37. He did not mention it, I believe, until his 'Mémoires improvisés' in 1951. There is no reference to it in *Ma Conversion*, which was published in 1913, and which Teilhard probably read. Cf. François Varillon, *Claudel* (DDB, Paris, 1967), pp. 42–3.

38. Cf. Émile Rideau, 'La sexualité selon le Père Teilhard de Chardin' in *Fiches documentaires* (X, Mappus, Lyons), No. 43, May–June 1967, pp. 67–79.

39. Here again we see how important it is not to substitute 'Woman' for 'the Feminine' or identify the two expressions, or see in the latter simply the adjectival form of the former.

40. Our italics.

41. Cf. *WTW*, pp. 194, 197. 'The Spirit of the Earth' in *HE*, p. 34: 'It is fact, that through woman the universe advances towards man. The whole question . . . is that they shall recognize one another.'

42. 'L'Évolution de la Chasteté'.

43. Cf. Pierre Emmanuel, *Le Monde est intérieur* (Éd. du Seuil, Paris, 1967), 'Claudel and Greek Myth' and 'A Female Character in Claudel'; see, in particular, pp. 109–12, 165–7. See also M. Barthélemy-Madaule, *La personne et le drame humain*, pp. 51–5. François Varillon, *Claudel*, p. 82. Jacques Madaule, *Le drame de Paul Claudel*, pp. 139–72, 277–329. Paul Claudel, *L'esprit et l'eau* (*Cinq grandes odes*, pp. 68–74).

44. It is here that the reference to Maurras occurs.

45. 'The Atomism of Spirit' (1941) in *AE*, p. 56. See the passages quoted in chapters 3 and 4.

46. *HU*, p. 64; Fontana, p. 60. See also 'Mon Univers' (14 April 1819) in *Écrits*, pp. 269–79. *DM*, p. 113; *MD*, p. 124; Fontana, pp. 132–3.

47. See above, chapter 4, pp. 81–2.

48. See above, chapter 3, p. 63, and chapter 4, p. 80.

49. Cf. *Phaedrus*, 252b. In the *Phaedrus*, even more than in the *Symposium*, Plato is concerned 'to show one can move from even the most natural sensuality to ideality' (Léon Robin, Introduction to the *Phaedrus* (Les Belles-Lettres, Paris, 1933), p. 140).

50. 14 October 1918. Billeted in Alsace, Teilhard had just been taking advantage of the comparative quiet that followed the Armistice, to reread the *Phaedrus* and the *Symposium*. Reading them, he noted, 'has brought me back to the problem of "passion". There can be no doubt that there are two *real* big problems in the universe: 1. The explanation of the multitude. 2. The meaning of love.'

51. To Léontine Zanta, 22 August 1928 (p. 81).

52. 4 December 1918. Cf. the Abbé Monchanin, *De l'esthétique à la mystique*, 2nd ed. (Castermann, 1967), p. 108: 'Chaste love is directed exclusively towards the spiritual, but from a starting-point in the world of sense. It effects a turning back of the vital into the spiritual, and imposes a direction contrary to the course of nature. It involves the danger of illusions and anomalies, but it can bring about, in its most intense form, the spiritualization of the world of sense.'

53. In *WTW*, p. 134.

54. In *HU*, p. 70; Fontana, p. 65.

55. Émile Rideau, 'La sexualité selon le Père Teilhard de Chardin', loc. cit., p. 79 n.

56. He had put forward this hypothesis as early as 4 May 1916, but on 9 May he was more undecided.

57. Cf. *HE*, p. 130. Cf. p. 77: 'Sublimation. Therefore conservation. But also, and even more, transformation.'

58. To Père Auguste Valensin, 10 January 1926 and 11 November 1934. See below, pp. 105–6.

59. Cf. Note of 29 April 1916 (above, p. 9).

60. 'L'Évolution de la Chasteté'. Letter of 21 August 1919; *MM*, p. 302. Cf. Piet Schoonenberg, 'Le sens de la virginité' in *Christus*, 17, pp. 32–44.

61. While to speak in connexion with Teilhard of 'Hegelian cosmology' would appear to involve a quite arbitrary judgment.

62. 'The Mystical Milieu' in *WTW*, pp. 144–6. Cf. *CM* (1950): 'It was to the actual person of Christ (I can remember this perfectly) that I rebounded from my disappointment with the organic, when, for the first time, I saw a lock of hair burning nastily as I watched it.'

63. *Purgatorio*, XXX, v. 73: '*Guardaci ben: ben son, ben son Beatrice.*'

64. For Teilhard, 'Platonic errors will be, not suppressed, but integrated by "reversal" in the dialectic of agape. It is of this that "Béatrix" is the sign' (M. Barthélemy-Madaule, *La personne et le drame humain*, p. 133).

65. See above, chapter 2, pp. 35–6. From again another point of view (in a criticism of the idea of an initially perfect cosmos) Teilhard could write that one must reject in that 'the final traces of Platonism' (letter quoted by J.-M. Mortier, op. cit., pp. 112–13).

66. In *WTW*, p. 14.

67. 'Does Mankind Move Biologically upon Itself' (1949) in *FM*, p. 257; Fontana, p. 268.

68. 'The Convergence of the Universe' (1951) in *AE*, p. 292.

69. 'The Mystical Milieu' (1917) in *WTW*, p. 118; 'Mon Univers' (1918) in *Écrits*, p. 269.

70. *Comment je vois*, Section 20, note.

71. 'The Psychological Conditions of the Unification of Man' (1948) in *AE*, p. 179. 'Cosmic Life' in *WTW*, p. 68.

72. 'Research, Work and Worship' (1955) in *SC*, p. 215.

73. 'The Moment of Choice' (1939) in *AE*, p. 20.

74. To Père Victor Fontoynont, 15 March 1916.

75. 'My Universe' (1924) in *SC*, p. 44.

76. 'The Eternal Feminine' in *WTW*, p. 198. *DM*, p. 125; *MD*, p. 137; Fontana, p. 144: 'The man with a passionate sense of the divine *milieu*.'

77. 'The Mystical Milieu' in *WTW*, p. 119.

78. 'The Mysticism of Science' (1939) in *HE*, p. 181.

79. *MM* (29 March 1917), p. 190.

80. Wedding address, 14 June 1928, in *Sur le bonheur* (1966), p. 75. Cf. letter to Claude Rivière, 16 April 1943. *DM*, pp. 61–2; *MD*, p. 69; Fontana, p. 89.

81. 'Life and the Planets' (1945) in *FM*, p. 117; Fontana, p. 122.
82. *HE*, p. 148.
83. 'The Struggle Against the Multitude' (1917) in *WTW*, p. 108.
84. *Le Christique* (1955).
85. 'Note sur l'évangélisation' (1919) in *Écrits*, p. 375.
86. 'Cosmic Life' in *WTW*, p. 68.
87. 'Human Energy' (1937) in *HE*, p. 157.
88. 'The Singularities of the Human Species' (1954) in *AM*, p. 267. To Edouard Le Roy, 6 December 1929.
89. 'The Mystical Milieu': 'See, the universe is ablaze!' (*WTW*, p. 129). *DM*, p. 131; *MD*, p. 143; Fontana, p. 149: 'The blazing plenitude of the divine *milieu*.' *CM*, introduction: 'The diaphany of the divine at the heart of a universe ablaze.' 'The Psychological Conditions of the Unification of Man' (1949) in *AE*, p. 179.
90. Note of 27 June 1916.
91. Paul Tillich, *The Courage To Be*.
92. Cf. Hans Urs von Balthasar, 'Relation immédiate avec Dieu' in *Concilium*, 21, p. 41.
93. In particular in their so-called 'Marian' interpretation. See an outstanding example in the twelfth-century commentary of Rupert of Deutz. Cf. our *Méditation sur l'Église*, 2nd ed. (1953), pp. 306–24.
94. There is no explicit reference to Eve in the poem. Nevertheless, on 10 March, Père Teilhard had adumbrated a parallel between Eve and Mary. Shortly before, he had read at least some parts of Péguy's *Eve* – 'a masterpiece of theological art, the grandest portrait any artist has had the courage to draw of woman and the Church at the same time' (Pierre Emmanuel, *Le monde est intérieur*, p. 203). He had been delighted with it. On 1 January 1917, he wrote to his cousin: 'I have a slight grudge against him [Péguy] for having taken the subject of Eve . . . the "natural" mother, whose face, so full of mystery, blends into the distant past, shrouded in symbol and legend. What an admirable personification of the ties so essential and so vital which indissolubly bind our human bundle to nature's laborious and patient advance. If only for having found this central core to his thought, this pillar on which his thought rests, Péguy is a great man. I wish a similar inspiration would come to me' (from Ligny-en-Barrois, *MM*, p. 159). Teilhard had a profound admiration for Péguy. He had copied out some lines of his:

> Car le surnaturel est lui-même charnel,
> Et l'arbre de la grâce est raciné profond
> Et plonge dans le sol, et cherche jusqu'au fond,
> Et l'arbre de la race est lui-même eternel.

('For the supernatural is itself of the flesh, and the tree of grace is rooted deep and reaches down into the soil, and seeks in the depths, and the tree of man's race is itself undying.') Again, a line which also echoes his own thoughts:

> Il allait hériter de tout l'effort humain.

('He was to be the heir to all man's effort.') Although Teilhard could not have read *Clio*, it would appear that in Péguy he recognized someone who had come close to his own theory of 'critical points'. 'There are critical points of eventuation just as there are of temperature, melting points, freezing, boiling, condensation, coagulation and crystallization. In the event there are even those states of superfusion in which there is no precipitation, crystallization or determination except through the introduction of a fragment of the future event' (*Clio*, p. 269).

Just as Père Teilhard said he found in *Eve* 'the mystery of the love of the earthly cradle', so in the *Mystère de la charité de Jeanne d'Arc* he found 'an inspiration very close to that which is at work in me: in *Jeanne d'Arc*, the deep-seated cosmic anxiety: "To what can one cling?" – "The redemption is a failure" – "Charity is impotent" – "Hope, the cosmic virtue which animates the whole of the world's effort"'. And he is grateful to Péguy for having distinguished so clearly 'the world that is damned', which is 'the world of money, in other words an anti-nature world' and 'the world of nature, which has been Christ's fleshly cradle' (29 December 1916). On the other hand, as has been pointed out, Teilhard did not share 'Péguy's humanist and classicist prejudice in favour of Greece and Rome' – although it is true that he once exclaimed: 'What great people the ancients were!' (to the Abbé Gaudefroy).

CHAPTER 6

1. *PM*, pp. 264–5; Fontana, p. 291.
2. *Présence et Prophétie* (Luf, Fribourg, 1942), p. 228.
3. Cf. François Chatelet, *Platon* (N.R.F., Paris, 1965), p. 20. Pierre Emmanuel, *Baudelaire* (DDB, Paris, 1967), p. 115.
4. 'Quelques réflexions . . .' in *Wallstein* (1809), pp. XII–XIII. Cf. Henri Gouhier, *Benjamin Constant* (Desclée de Brouwer, 1967), p. 135.
5. *Le Monde est intérieur*, pp. 280–1.
6. André Feuillet, *Le Christ Sagesse de Dieu d'après les Épîtres pauliniennes* (Gabalda, Paris, 1966), p. 383.

7. Émile Boutroux, *William James* (1911), p. 103 – 24 February 1918.

8. This is, in fact, a misreading of the text. Pascal wrote: 'The one is *in* the other' ('l'un est *en* l'autre') (Brunschvicg, 483).

9. Brunschvicg, 116.

10. Brunschvicg, 72.

11. 'Hominization' (1923), where the reference is to anatomy and morphology: 'because they have operated in a single domain, or with restricted methods, they have disparaged the value of humanity and drained the phenomenon of man of its specific properties' (*VP*, p. 52). 'The Phenomenon of Man' (1930), ibid., p. 166. Cf. Blondel and Teilhard de Chardin, *Correspondence*, pp. 126–7.

12. *Advis necessaire sur la machine arithmétique* (1645), *Oeuvres complètes*, ed. L. Brunschvicg and P. Boutroux, Vol. 1, 1908, p. 305.

13. '... *numquam satis mirata connexio, qua etiam quae remotissima videntur in unum adducat unitatis amatrix natura*', *Oeuvres*, Vol. 3, pp. 266–7.

14. 'The Phenomenon of Man' (1930) in *VP*, p. 166. In pointing out this affinity between Teilhard and Pascal, we are not forgetting the difference in their orientation. This has been forcibly emphasized by Étienne Borne, *De Pascal à Teilhard de Chardin* (G. de Bussac, Clermont-Ferrand, 1962), in particular pp. 57–65.

15. 'The Analysis of Life' (1945) in *AE*, p. 139.

16. 'Sur l'essence du sentiment mystique' (1951). Cf. 'The Struggle Against the Multitude' (1917) in *WTW*, pp. 98–101.

17. As, for example, in *Le Christique* (1955), p. 9.

18. Cf. note of 10 July 1917: 'The fundamental mystical state is a dynamic feeling of omnipresence' – Teilhard made it clear that in such passages he is only trying to describe the root meaning of mysticism. Cf. *WTW*, p. 147 n. He speaks of the man 'who is born' a mystic (*WTW*, p. 119).

19. *Apologia*, ch. 1. It will be remembered that Teilhard was proposing to write an essay which he intended to call 'The Sacrament of the World'.

20. 'A profoundly human concept', writes Père Émile Rideau of Teilhard's analogy, 'which is the essence of knowledge, poetry and religion' (*Teilhard de Chardin: A Guide to his Thought*, p. 42).

21. 'Almost all', because in 'The Spiritual Power of Matter' the character of Elias has only an allegorical role, as in Vigny's symbols: Teilhard points this out himself (*Écrits*, p. 435). Marc Faessler (op. cit., pp. 80–2) has noted and linked together 'five supporting allegories which Teilhard was fond of borrowing from biblical tradition in order to retrace his spiritual journey': Jacob wrestling with the angel, Peter walking on

the waters, the miracle of Cana, Elias in the fiery chariot, and the burning bush.

22. Cf. *FTC*, pp. 56–61.

23. Benson was widely read in France at that time in Catholic circles, and his books were very popular in Teilhard's family.

24. Teilhard gives a summary of it in *DM*, p. 113; *MD*, pp. 124–5; Fontana, pp. 133–4.

25. 16 July 1916, Avocourt.

26. Étienne Borne, op. cit., pp. 79–80, where he compares the three stories with Pascal's Memorial, and so brings out the spiritual experience on which they are based.

27. Cf. 'Human Energy' (1937): 'May the moment come (and it will come) when the masses realize that the true human victories are those over the mysteries of matter and life . . . [then] a decisive hour will strike for man, when the spirit of discovery absorbs the whole vital force contained in the spirit of war. A supreme phase of history, etc.' (*HE*, pp. 135–6). Teilhard had already expressed the same idea in 'My Universe' (1924) in *SC*, pp. 82–3. Cf. 'The Atomism of Spirit' (1941) in *AE*, p. 53, etc. See above, pp. 81–2.

28. See Mgr Robert Coffy's well-chosen comments in *Teilhard de Chardin et le socialisme* (Chronique sociale de France, Lyons, 1966), p. 145.

29. 25 September 1917, *MM*, p. 205.

30. 'In spite of everything', he compares it to a 'loved shore' (*Écrits*, p. 203).

31. Teilhard was to experience a similar feeling later, during his desert expeditions.

32. Cf. *CM* (1950): It was from being plunged into 'the atmosphere of the front', for a long time 'in contact with the immense human masses which confronted one another at that time in the trenches of France, from Ypres to Verdun', that Teilhard discovered 'the organicity of collective magnitudes': what he called 'mega-man, with its own psychic temperature and internal energy'. It was there, too, that he finally developed his sense of the noosphere. This concept of 'mega-man' (which Teilhard borrowed from other writers) is analysed in another aspect in *PM*, pp. 256–7; Fontana, p. 282.

33. As late as May 1966 a survivor of Verdun was speaking on television about the love of comrades living under the incessant threat of death, a love stronger than any other and one 'they have never found again in civilian life' (quoted by Julien Green, in *Vers l'Invisible*, p. 478).

34. 23 September 1917, in *MM*, pp. 203–4. The whole passage should be read.

35. 'Human Energy' (1937) in *HE*, p. 136.

36. 'La Nostalgie du Front', we know, was published in *Études* of 20 November 1917, with this paragraph omitted. With this should be compared the last part of the essay on 'Hominization' (1923) in *VP*, in particular pp. 75–6.

37. Cf. the preface to *MM*, p. 10: 'He saw beyond the horizons of this world so that the field of battle, where death seemed to triumph, was to him the living crucible or mould in which a new world was being fashioned.'

38. In *CM* (1950).

39. Note of 26 January 1918: '. . . the movement has to be *reversed*.'

40. *CM* (1950).

41. Cf. *RTC*, chapter 5, 'Meditation on Death'.

42. See above, pp. 103–4.

43. 'Sketch of a Personalistic Universe' (1936): 'The most incommunicable and therefore the most precious quality of each being is that which makes him one with all the rest. It is consequently by coinciding with all the rest that we shall find the centre of ourselves' (*HE*, p. 65).

44. *Écrits*, p. 91; English translation in *HU*, p. 41; Fontana, p. 39. *WTW*, pp. 209, 250–69, 275.

45. *Le Christique*. Cf. *CM*: 'A universe which is personalized by convergence' – 'a person (the person of Christ) who is universalized by radiation'.

46. Peking, 28 October 1941.

47. 'Mon Univers' in *Écrits*, p. 269.

48. *WTW*, pp. 118–19.

49. Note of 17 December 1918.

50. *Exigences philosophiques du christianisme* (P.U.F., Paris, 1956), p. 185.

51. *Une énigme historique, le 'Vinculum substantiale' d'après Leibniz et l'ébauche d'un réalisme supérieur* (Beauchesne, Paris, 1930), appendix D (extract from letter to Père Valensin), p. 144. Cf. *L'Action* (1893), p. 461; *Lettre sur l'apologétique* (1896, in *Les premiers écrits de Maurice Blondel*, Vol. 2, P.U.F., Paris, 1956), p. 90 n. 1.

52. *Theologie der Geschichte* (Johannes-Verlag, Basle, 1959). With this 'absolute Norm' cf. Blondel's 'measure of all things' in *L'Action*, p. 461.

53. 'Sketch of a Personalistic Universe' (1936) in *HE*, p. 71.

54. *HE* (1937), pp. 143, 147.

55. *CM* (1950), p. 7.

56. M. Barthélemy-Madaule, *La personne et le drame humain*, p. 128.

57. *PM*, 267 and n.; Fontana, p. 293 and n. Cf. *Comment je vois*, Section 20, etc.

58. Note of 17 December 1918: 'Eckhart has the right feeling here, but he misses the point' (Teilhard's comment may have been intended more for Eckhart the younger).

59. *CM* (1950), p. 8.

60. Stanislas Breton, O.P., *La Passion du Christ et les philosophes*, p. 30, n. 1. Hegel, he adds, 'says this so often that there is no need to emphasize the point'.

61. Note of 24 February 1916 (Nieuport).

62. The universal Christ is 'the universal nature of the historic Christ' (letter to Marguerite Teillard-Chambon, 8 November 1953, in *LT*, p. 347; Fontana, p. 290). It is the personal being of Christ 'universalizing itself by radiation' (*CM*, p. 23).

63. Cf. *HE* (1937), pp. 141–5.

64. Note of 8 December 1921.

65. *Die ewige Frau*, pp. 3–7.

66. Pp. 10, 22, 41. The theme of the veil is more fundamental in Gertrud von le Fort than in Teilhard. Cf. Xavier Tilliette, 'Gertrude von Le Fort, histoire et symbole' in *Études*, Vol. 303, 1959, pp. 49–50. The veiled woman is also one of Claudel's themes. When Tête d'Or meets the Princess she is veiled in black, etc. (cf. François Varillon, *Claudel*, DDB, Paris, 1967, p. 80). The Princess is 'the true woman', i.e. 'the Church': Claudel, preface to a new edition of *Tête d'Or*, 1949 (*Oeuvres complètes*, Vol. 6, p. 400); see also *Mémoires improvisés* (Gallimard, Paris, 1951), pp. 59–60.

67. Olier, *Traité des saints Ordres*, part 3, ch. 6.

68. Paul Claudel, *L'Épée et le Miroir* (1939), pp. 43, 73, 217.

69. *De nativitate B.M.V.*, Sermo 5 (*Opera*, Vol. 9, p. 715), etc. Cf. *Méditation sur l'Église*, ch. 9.

70. See below, pp. 126–7.

71. Cf. Note of 8 March 1918: 'The mystery (and the attraction) of the Feminine *increases with* chastity. . . . The Feminine: the Virgin'.

72. Cf. *CM* (1950), part 2, note: 'My irresistible need to universalize what I love.'

73. Retreats, Peking, 26 October 1944, 24 October 1945.

74. 'Le Christ universel' (1920).

75. Retreat, Tientsin, 30 November 1939.

76. This (Ephesians 4: 8–10) is the Pauline text which Teilhard quotes, or alludes to, most frequently.

77. To Père Pierre Leroy, 8 August 1950. All that he was apprehensive of was the wording in which the definition might be expressed.

78. To Maryse Choisy, 1955 (*Psyché*, 10, 1955, p. 8). We may note the

contrast with the line taken by Auguste Comte, or by Louis Ménard, in *Rêveries d'un païen mystique*, p. 516: 'The apotheosis of mankind would never be complete, if the Feminine had no part in it.'

79. To Léontine Zanta, Obok, 24 January 1929: 'Once again, the great animating Power, to which it is so good to entrust ourselves, seems – in a motherly way – to have brought the inner and outer forces of the world into harmony around me' (p. 86).

80. Pierre-Jean de Menasce, o.p., *Permanence et transformation de la mission* (Éd. du Cerf, Paris, 1967), p. 45.

81. In any case one should not examine too critically the language of a letter in which Teilhard, as he so often did, was obviously adapting himself to his correspondent.

82. On the Annunciation, see above, chapter 2, p. 28. To Teilhard, as to Dante, the mystery of the Annunciation seems to have been 'particularly dear' (cf. Auguste Valensin, *Le christianisme de Dante*, p. 131).

83. *DM*, p. 120; *MD*, p. 132; Fontana, p. 140. In his 'Note pour l'évangélisation des temps nouveaux', what he calls 'the Gospel of human effort' constitutes only a first phase. To make up 'the complete cycle of the interior life', he distinguishes in it three phases, the third of which gives access to 'the higher forms of activity, represented by purity, contemplation, death *in God*' (*Écrits*, p. 380).

84. 'The Mystical Milieu' in *WTW*, p. 144. In this, and other similar passages we may, I think, detect the influence of Père Jean-Nicolas Grou (1731–1803), a spiritual writer still widely read by Jesuits in the earlier part of this century. Cf. *L'Intérieur de Jésus et de Marie*, part 2, ch. 40; 'Mary was motionless; she did not speak; even her breathing was hardly audible. Prayer was being born so silently in the secrecy of her heart that her mind was hardly conscious of it' (2nd ed., ed. Auguste Hamon, p. 530).

85. *DM*, pp. 112–13; *MD*, pp. 124–5; Fontana, pp. 133–4. In *La Face humaine*, p. 111, Pierre Emmanuel writes: 'Whether expressed in crude or moderate terms the modern Utopia assumes that belief in the necessity of the interior life for the reality and permanence of the world is simply "an attitude of mind", an introversion that may well hinder the progress which evolution forces on us.' Teilhard's doctrine of 'progress' and 'evolution' is obviously completely different from this 'modern Utopia' so rightly criticized by Pierre Emmanuel.

86. *MM*, p. 149 (letter of 5 December 1916): 'To be active in such a way and such a degree, our Lady must have been brought into existence in the very heart of grace, – for no later justification, no matter how immediate, could replace this constitutive, inborn, perfection of the

purity that watched over the birth of her soul. It is thus that I see the Immaculate Conception.' Cf. Paul Claudel, *L'Épée et le Miroir* (1939), pp. 201, 202: 'Her glory is in her purity, she gives only what she receives', she is 'one who looks on God.'

87. 'The Spiritual Energy of Suffering' (1950) in *AE*, p. 249.

88. To Père André Ravier, New York, 24 October 1954.

89. Cf. Robert Speaight, op. cit., p. 313. At his last meeting with Massignon, in New York in January 1954, he was still delighted by his conversation.

90. See *FTC*, pp. 62–3. Letters of 3 and 11 October 1918 in *MM*, pp. 243–7.

91. 'Cosmic Life' in *WTW*, p. 59. Cf. François Courel, in *Christus*, Vol. 19, p. 198. M. A. Enard, *L'Évangile avec Marie* (Éd. du Cerf, Paris, 1968). It is in connexion with the rosary that Cardinal Garrone makes a very Teilhardian comment: 'There are more things in the practice of the Church than in all our philosophy', *Que faut-il croire?* (Desclée, Paris, 1967), p. 152. See below, pp. 190–1.

92. 8 September 1916, in *MM*, p. 123. Cf. Bérulle, *Vie de Jésus*, ch. 6: Mary 'is in the Church what the dawn is in the heavens', or the first three pages of Claudel's *L'Épée et le Miroir*.

93. Note of 7 March 1918. Retreat, Peking, 26 October 1944. Cf. 'Cosmic Life': 'Jesus... You do more than simply stand apart from things as their Master, you are more than the incommunicable splendour of the universe; you are, too, the dominating influence that penetrates us, holds us, and draws us' (*WTW*, pp. 51–2). 'Lord Jesus... I love you as the source, the activating and life-giving ambience, the term and consummation, of the world' (ibid., p. 70).

94. Note of 17 July 1916.

95. Karl Rahner, *Theological Investigations*, Vol. 3 (Darton, Longman & Todd, London, 1967), p. 44.

96. *Paradiso*, c. 32.

97. Notes of 7 and 8 March 1918.

98. *WTW*, pp. 201–2. See above, pp. 22–4: 'I shall still be at hand, lost in the sun I have drawn to myself' – an evident allusion to the Incarnation.

Part Two

CHAPTER I

1. Vatican 2, Constitution *Gaudium et Spes* (beginning).
2. Lesslie Newbigin, *Honest Religion for Secular Man* (SCM Press, London, 1966), p. 12.
3. Paul VI, closing address to Vatican 2, 7 December 1965.
4. 'A Note on Progress' (1920) in *FM*, p. 19; Fontana, p. 20.
5. *MPN*, p. 103.
6. Note of 17 July 1916.
7. Cf. 'The Struggle Against the Multitude' (1917) in *WTW*, pp. 98–102. 'Sur l'essence du sentiment mystique' (1951).
8. 'The Discovery of the Past' (1935) in *VP*, p. 191. 'The Spirit of the Earth' (1931) in *HE*, p. 38. *LLZ*, pp. 114–15 (26 January 1936).
9. *HE*, pp. 48–9.
10. See, for example, 'The End of the Species' (1952) in *FM*, p. 303; Fontana, p. 317. 'The Planetisation of Mankind' (1945), ibid., p. 138; Fontana, pp. 143–4.
11. *CM* (1950) in *HU*, p. 138. We find the same horror at the thought of an intra-cosmic 'immortality' in Solovyev, op. cit., pp. 50 f.
12. 'The Zest for Living' (1950) in *AE*, p. 238. Cf. *FTC*, pp. 150–68: 'Polyvalence of the Cosmos'.
13. 'Hominization and Speciation' (1952) in *VP*, p. 267, etc. Cf. André Manaranche, 'L'éthique sociale chrétienne' in *Projet*, 1967, p. 1162: 'With the death knell sounding for the ideologies that have tried to burke the problem of death, our contemporaries would soon lose the zest for life and enterprise if the world were to appear to them as no more than an inexorable process of disintegration.' Teilhard was constantly making this very point.
14. *HE*, p. 51. Cf. 'The Priest' (1918) in *WTW*, p. 209, etc. Already in 'Cosmic Life' Teilhard had stressed the part played by suffering and had even concluded: 'It is the very life-blood of evolution'. *WTW*, p. 43. *DM*, pp. 120–1; *MD*, p. 132; Fontana, p. 140.
15. 'Outline of a Dialectic of Spirit' in *AE*, p. 151.
16. Cf. Dietrich Bonhoeffer, *Letters and Papers from Prison*, 2nd ed. (SCM Press, London, 1956): 'The optimism that is will for the future should never be despised ... it is health and vitality, and the sick man has no business to impugn it' (pp. 38–9; Fontana, pp. 146–7).

17. The phrase is J.-M. Domenach's.
18. *Athéisme et sens total de l'homme* (Ed. du Cerf, 'Foi vivante', Paris, 1968).
19. *RTC. FTC.* Maurice Blondel and P. Teilhard de Chardin, *Correspondence* (Herder and Herder, New York, 1967). *Teilhard missionnaire et apologiste* (Éd. 'Prière et Vie', Toulouse, 1966). *Images de l'abbé Monchanin*, with appendix on Monchanin and Teilhard (Aubier, Paris, 1967). See also Mgr de Solages, *Teilhard de Chardin, témoignage et étude sur le développement de sa pensée* (Privat, Toulouse, 1967).
20. Note of 18 March 1919.

CHAPTER 2

1. 'Hominization' (1923) in *VP*, p. 76.
2. 'The Salvation of Mankind' in *SC*, p. 128.
3. Some Reflections on Progress' in *FM*, p. 77; Fontana, p. 80.
4. 'Faith in Man' in *FM*, p. 187; Fontana, p. 194.
5. Pierre Emmanuel, *Le monde est intérieur* (Éd. du Seuil, Paris, 1967), pp. 235, 247–9.
6. Cardinal G.-M. Garrone, *Que faut-il faire?* (Desclée, Paris, 1967), pp. 5, 24.
7. Cf. A. Dupront, 'L'Église et le monde' in *Irenikon*, 1967, p. 182.
8. Dom (now Bishop) Christopher Butler, o.s.b.
9. See also *Situation et tâches présentes de la théologie* (Éd. du Cerf, Paris, 1967), pp. 57–68.
10. Two of the many examples are the November 1967 issue of *Choisir*, and *Esprit's* inquiry, 'The New World and the Word of God'.
11. See in particular the brief of 22 February 1967.
12. Cf. Pierre Ganne, reply to *Esprit's* inquiry, pp. 408–9.
13. Cf. André Manaranche, *Cahiers d'action religieuse et sociale*, 1 October 1967, pp. 525–30.
14. 'Éléments permanents et changeants du message chrétien d'après le Concile' in *Rome nous interpelle*, Vol. 2 (Delachaux et Niestlé, Neufchâtel, 1967), p. 155.
15. Letter to the Duke of Norfolk (1874) (*Certain Difficulties* (Longmans, Green, London, 1910), p. 176), and address (2 October 1873) at the opening of St Bernard's Seminary, Olton (*Catholic Sermons* (Burns & Oates, London, 1957), p. 121). Cf. Louis Cognet, *Newman ou la recherche de la vérité* (Desclée, Paris, 1967), pp. 288, 292.
16. *The Peasant of the Garonne* (Chapman, London, 1968), pp. 5–6. Maritain is not exaggerating when, in connexion with certain extremists who

invoke 'the spirit of the Council' or 'the spirit of John XXIII', he uses the word 'falsehood'.

17. 'Hominization' (1923) in *VP*, p. 78. Cf. 'Cosmic Life' in *WTW*, p. 67, etc.

18. Newman, *Sermons preached before the University of Oxford*, 15, n. 6.

19. 'The interior life is not a pejorative expression, synonymous with self-centredness and the opposite of the whole life, of life as it is given to us: it is the total being in which the interior envelops the exterior, in which the invisible saturates the visible' (Pierre Emmanuel, *Le monde est intérieur*, p. 276).

20. Cf. T. J. J. Altizer, *The Gospel of Christian Atheism* (Collins, London, 1967). The author, a Protestant, believes that Catholicism is the most favourable ground for the acceptance and propagation of his 'Gospel', and is finding ready listeners among Catholics. See below, p. 250.

21. 'If the Church ceased to proclaim Christ to and against all, she would no longer be herself, and all the openness to the world which we welcome with such joy would be in vain: what would we have to say that is so new, if it were not precisely that God has become incarnate and dwells among us?', P. Vallet, letter to seminarists, December 1967, p. 3.

22. I shall not discuss this corollary here, as I have already done so in the second part of *Athéisme et le sens total de l'homme*.

23. *Nous autres, gens de la rue*, missionary papers edited by Jacques Loew (Éd. du Seuil, Paris, 1966), p. 29.

24. Lecture, December 1965. Quoted by René Laurentin, *Bilan du Concile*, pp. 362–3.

25. 'The Priest' (1918) in *WTW*, p. 219. 'The Mass on the World': 'Let others, fulfilling a function more august than mine, proclaim your splendours as pure Spirit; as for me, dominated as I am by a vocation which springs from the inmost fibres of my being, I have no desire, I have no ability, to proclaim anything except the innumerable prolongations of your incarnate Being in the world of matter' (in *HU*, pp. 36–7). Cf. letter to X, Tientsin, 26 October 1923: 'I believe that the greatest satisfaction there is, is to be "busy inside", especially (for it all comes back to this) in the quest for the characteristics of God as they are destined to be seen by each one of us, individually' (in *Christus*, 54, p. 244). First Paper to Auguste Valensin: 'There is an infinity of vocations' (p. 35). Note of 23 December 1917: 'St John seems to me a patron of my vocation'. *MD*, p. 131; Fontana, p. 139, on the star of the Magi: 'That star leads each man differently, by a different path, in accord with his vocation.'

26. Cf. Émile Rideau, *Teilhard oui ou non?* (Fayard, Paris, 1967), pp. 39–40, 122. 'Cosmic Life' on 'the problem implicit in life: in any Christian heart there is an inevitable conflict between the divine faith that sustains his hopes as an individual and the earthly passion that is the driving force behind all human effort' (*WTW*, p. 17). 'I have been too conscious of the thrill of universality in my soul to accept a bliss that leaves me in isolation. Do not the promises of Christianity mean the end of cosmic hopes?' (pp. 46–7). Cf. p. 54.

CHAPTER 3

1. Letter of 20 July 1922.
2. 'The Moment of Choice' (Christmas 1939) in *AE*, p. 14.
3. Section 5.1: 'The present intellectual upheaval and the transformation of living conditions are part of an overall change', etc.
4. 'Le Christ évoluteur' (1942), conclusion, in *Cahiers Pierre Teilhard de Chardin*, 5, pp. 26–7.
5. 'Christologie et Évolution' (Tientsin, Christmas 1933), the end, in *Comment je crois* (*Oeuvres X*). See below, pp. 193–4.
6. A passage in *PM* has echoes of both Newman and Blondel: 'One after the other all the fields of human knowledge have been shaken and carried away by the same under-water current in the direction of the study of some *development*' (p. 219; Fontana, p. 241).
7. To Léontine Zanta, 7 February 1930 (p. 101).
8. Père Teilhard would never accept an evolution that was not homogeneous, and rejected all 'illegitimate evolution of dogma' (1929). (This does not, of course, guarantee that all the applications of his principle will be successful.) Bernard Towers, *Teilhard de Chardin* (The Carey Kingsgate Press, London, 1966), pp. 7, 8: 'He was not a "revolutionary" but rather an "evolutionary". That is, his thinking represents a genuine "development of doctrine", wholly within the Christian tradition . . . He was never a relativist where knowledge and thinking were concerned.'
9. To Marguerite Teillard-Chambon, 18 October 1940 (*LT*, p. 269; Fontana, pp. 217–18). A companion passage will be found in 'Mastery of the World and the Kingdom of God' in *WTW*, p. 85.
10. To the Vicar-General of the Society of Jesus, 1940.
11. Retreat (28 October 1941). He adds: 'More simply, a loving-lovable God.'
12. *PM*, pp. 292–3; Fontana, p. 320.

13. 'La Route de l'Ouest.' 'A Clarification: Reflections on Two Converse Forms of Spirit' (1950) in *AE*, pp. 215-27. 'Christianity in the World' in *SC*, pp. 105-6. However, it would not be unfair to say that he was a little over-hasty in dismissing what he calls 'an outworn orientalism'.

14. M. Barthélemy-Madaule, *Bergson et Teilhard de Chardin* (Éd. du Seuil, Paris, 1963), p. 352. Id., *La personne et le drame humain chez Teilhard de Chardin* (Éd. du Seuil, Paris, 1967). One can hardly believe one's eyes when one reads in a serious review that for Teilhard 'men are destined to become a super-organism, a Great Being, impersonal and universal, who is Omega point' (E. Ménard in the *Revue des sciences religieuses*, 1967, p. 227).

15. 'Centrology' (1944), Section 20, in *AE*, p. 112. Cf. *Teilhard missionnaire*, pp. 80-1.

16. *MPN*, p. 121.

17. 'From Cosmos to Cosmogenesis' in *AE*, pp. 262-3, etc. Other references in *FTC*, pp. 22-4.

18. Letter of 9 April 1916, in *MM*, p. 98.

19. 'Introduction à la vie chrétienne' (1944). This revelation will be 'God reflecting himself personally on the organized sum of thinking monads to guarantee an assured success and fix precise laws for their hesitant activities. God bent over the now intelligent mirror of earth to impress on it the first marks of his beauty' ('The Spirit of the Earth' in *HE*, p. 47).

20. To X, Paris, 6 November 1927 (*Christus*, 54, p. 257).

21. *DM*, p. 91; *MD*, p. 102; Fontana, p. 114. Cf. *HE* (1937): 'The totality of a sphere is just as present in its centre, which takes the form of a point, as spread over its whole surface; in fact it really lies only in that point' (p. 143).

22. 'Cosmic Life' in *WTW*, pp. 15, 48.

23. 'La Grande Monade' in *Écrits*, p. 242: 'Raising their eyes to scan the whole face of their world, human beings will see themselves encircled', etc. Many similar passages could be quoted.

24. Ibid., pp. 247-8.

25. Various references in my *Sur les chemins de Dieu*, chapters 4 and 5, and in particular pp. 303-4. Cf. Teilhard, 'Cosmic Life': 'The deeper I descend into myself, the more I find God at the heart of my being' (*WTW*, p. 61).

26. 'On the Possible Bases of Universal Human Creed' (1941) in *FM*, p. 80; Fontana, p. 83. 'Creative Union' in *WTW*, pp. 159, 162. *MD*, p. 15; Fontana, p. 47: 'Without mixture, without confusion, the true God, the Christian God, will, under your gaze, invade the universe . . . He will penetrate it as a ray of light does a crystal . . .' Cf. *RTC*, pp. 181-2.

27. To Léontine Zanta, 24 June 1934 (p. 110).

28. 'Sketch of a Personalistic Universe' (1936) in *HE*, p. 91.

29. *HE* (1937), p. 143.

30. To H. de L., Tientsin, 15 August 1936.

31. 'Man's Place in the Universe' (1942) in *VP*, p. 231.

32. 'Sketch of a Personalistic Universe' in *HE*, p. 67. On Teilhard's distinction between the two contrasting meanings of the word pantheism, see *RTC*, pp. 152 ff.

33. *PM*, p. 35; Fontana, p. 40. Cf. letter of 29 April 1934.

34. *HE* (1937), pp. 158-9. 'The Future of Man Seen by a Palaeontologist' (1941): 'The more I consider the fundamental question of the future of the earth, the more it appears to me that the generative principle of its unification is finally to be sought, not in the sole contemplation of a single Truth or in the sole desire for a single Thing, but in the common attraction exercised by a single *Being*' (*FM*, p. 75; Fontana, p. 78). *PM*, p. 267; Fontana, p. 294: 'The discoveries of the last hundred years, with their unitary perspectives, have brought a new and decisive impetus to our sense of the world, to our sense of the earth, and to our human sense. . . . But this impetus will only end by plunging us back into super-matter unless it leads us towards someone.'

35. Maurice Blondel, 'De l'assimilation', chapter 7, in *Exigences philosophiques du christianisme* (P.U.F., Paris, 1950), p. 245.

36. 'Sketch of a Personalistic Universe' (1936) in *HE*, pp. 64-5, 100-5. 'Human Energy' (1937) in *HE*, pp. 144ff. 'Centrology' (1941), Section 28, in *AE*, pp. 117-18. 'Cosmic Life': '. . . rejecting all the illusions of a narrow individualism'.

37. V. Solovyev, *The Meaning of Love*. For Solovyev, it is 'false existence' – not so for Teilhard.

38. Romain Rolland, to G. Mille, 16 September 1887 (*Cahiers R. Rolland*, 17, p. 24).

39. *PM*, p. 263; Fontana, p. 289. Cf. Solovyev, op. cit.

40. 'Centrology', Sections 20, 22, in *AE*, pp. 111-12. 'Sketch of a Personalistic Universe' in *HE*, p. 81. 'Human Energy' in *HE*, p. 131.

41. 'The Stuff of the Universe' (1953) in *AE*, p. 382. To Léontine Zanta, 26 January 1936, p. 114. To Maryse Choisy (1955). Maritain similarly uses the phrase 'the Emperor of this world' in criticizing this concept. (Quoted by Henry Bars in *Spiritus*, 32, 1967, p. 432.)

42. 'Sketch of a Personalistic Universe' in *HE*, p. 91.

43. Similarly, Alan Richardson, for example, in a vigorous reaction against a concept of God which makes him an anonymous, characterless, faceless being, has no hesitation, even so, in criticizing certain anthropo-

morphic notions of the Almighty 'as our grandfather in heaven' (*Religion in Contemporary Debate* (SCM, London, 1966), p. 112).

44. He was not tempted, as others have been, to imitate the approach whose ambitious aim is 'to rise above the ultimate value of love and transcend the transcendence of the personal God' but which in reality 'allows itself to be unresistingly carried along by a pre-Christian and pre-personal spiritual current' (Jacques-Albert Cuttat, introduction to R. C. Zachner, *Inde, Israël, Islam* (DDB, Paris, 1965), p. 17).

45. Karl Rahner, *Vivre et croire aujourd'hui* (DDB, Paris, 1967), p. 77.

46. Auguste Valensin, textes et documents inédits (Aubier, Paris, 1961), pp. 409-10.

47. 'Réflexions sur le bonheur' (1943), summarizing an objection put forward by W. B. Steele: 'Man can be fully happy only if he merges his interests and hopes in those of mankind'; but, 'if he is to be able to give himself completely, he must be able to love. But how can one love a collective, impersonal, reality – monstrous in some respects – such as the world or even mankind?' It is, says Teilhard, a 'terribly, cruelly just' objection. *Cahiers*, 2, pp. 68-9.

48. Ibid. Cf. 'Some Reflections on Progress' (1941) in *FM*, pp. 75-6; Fontana, pp. 78-9.

49. See, for example, *PM*, p. 269; Fontana, p. 296: 'Love ... dies in contact with the impersonal and the anonymous.' 'The Human Rebound of Evolution' in *FM*, p. 207; Fontana, p. 215. 'Centrology', Section 29, in *AE*, pp. 119-20. 'The Atomism of Spirit', ibid., p. 47. 'The Salvation of Mankind' in *SC*, pp. 148-9. 'The Heart of the Problem' in *FM*, pp. 264-5; Fontana, pp. 276-7. 'Human Unanimisation', ibid., pp. 286-7; Fontana, pp. 300-1. 'Introduction à la vie chrétienne', p. 6 in *Oeuvres*, Vol. X. *Trois choses que je vois*, p. 11. *HE*, pp. 151-2. *Le Christique*, p. 13. *Comment je vois*, Section 20, etc.

50. *HE*, 6 August 1937, pp. 151-2. Cf. 'Sketch of a Personalistic Universe', ibid., p. 81, etc.

51. Similarly Hans Urs von Balthasar speaks of an 'infinitely determined form'.

52. 'Introduction à la vie chrétienne.'

53. Discourse 28, n. 4 (Migne, PG, 36, 29). Cf. *Sur les chemins de Dieu* (Aubier, Paris, 1966 ed.), pp. 165, 167-8.

54. 'If you have understood, it is not God; so vast is he, that when found he must still be sought; if your search is ended, it is not God': Sermon 52, n. 16 (Migne, PL, 38, 360). Sermon 53, ch. 11, n. 12 (col. 370); *De civitate Dei*, Bk. 12, ch. 18 (PL, 41, 368), etc.

55. *Proslogion*, chs. 2, 15.

56. *Contra Gentiles*, Bk. 1, ch. 5. Cf. *De veritate*, Q. 2, art. 1, *ad nonum*.

57. 'To take possession of me, my God, you who are more remote than all and deeper than all, you take to yourself and unite together the immensity of the world and the intimate depths of myself' ('The Priest' (1918) in *WTW*, p. 215). Cf. St Bernard, on the Song of Songs, sermon 4, n. 4: 'The being who exists in himself is not remote from any creature, for he is the life of every creature ... but he is at the same time that which is most present and most comprehensible.'

58. *DM*, p. 70 n.; *MD*, 79 n.; Fontana, p. 96 n.

59. To Marguerite Teillard-Chambon, 11 July 1951: 'All this is directed towards the search for "the ever-greater God", for ultimately it is only the pull towards Him that is sending me on this new – perhaps my last? – adventure' (*LT*, p. 305; Fontana, p. 251).

60. *CM* (1950), 'Prayer to the Ever-greater Christ', English translation in *LME*, pp. 160–1.

61. *DM*, pp. 119–20, 90; *MD*, pp. 131, 100–1; Fontana, pp. 193, 113: *DM*, p. 15; *MD*, p. 15; Fontana, p. 47: 'Very near and very distant at one and the same time.' Cf. 'Forma Christi', on revelation (*WTW*, pp. 255–6). Blondel, *L'Action* (1893), p. 352.

62. Pierre Colin, 'Le théisme actuel et les preuves de l'existence de Dieu' in *L'existence de Dieu* (Casterman, Paris, 1961), p. 142.

63. 'There can be no affirmation of similarity between creator and creature without affirmation of greater dissimilarity' (Fourth Lateran Council, ch. 2).

64. See in particular 'Science and Christ or Analysis and Synthesis' in *SC*, pp. 21–36. 'My Universe', ibid., p. 50. 'The Analysis of Life' in *AE*, pp. 131–2. *RTC*, ch. 15, 'A Reversal of Method'.

65. 'Sketch of a Personalistic Universe' in *HE*, p. 71. Teilhard accordingly sought to re-establish 'the traditional conceptions of a god exerting intellectual influence on immortal monads distinct from him ... no longer sentimental and instinctive but closely linked to contemporary evolutionary ideas (provided that man is not excluded from them)' ('The Spirit of the Earth', ibid., p. 46).

66. To Père Leroy. In Cuénot, p. 244. Cf. Henri Bouillard, *Connaissance de Dieu* ('Foi vivante', Aubier, Paris, 1962), p. 141: 'When God asks us to apply our concepts and words to him, he does not turn us adrift in the vague world of metaphor.'

67. *WTW*, pp. 47–8. Cf. *HE*, pp. 147–8: 'Omega, in which all things converge, is reciprocally that from which all things radiate. Impossible to place it as a point at the peak of the universe without at the same time diffusing its presence within each smallest advance of evolution.' Cf.

Cornelio Fabro in *La Table ronde*, January 1968, pp. 43–4: St Thomas considers that 'God is immanent in the world with a force and intensity that exceed all the demands of theological or philosophical subjectivism. . . . Immanence and transcendence, like concave and convex, are two phases that originate in, and merge into, one another'.

68. New York, 3 August 1952. Cf. *FTC*, pp. 20–8.

69. As in *DM*, pp. 16, 89; *MD*, pp. 16, 99; Fontana, pp. 47, 112. *CM* (1950), p. 9, etc.

70. To Léontine Zanta, 14 December 1929 (p. 96): 'In the great pacifying intensity of the divine Omnipresence.' 'The Mystical Milieu' in *WTW*, p. 121. *DM*, pp. 100, 109, 111; *MD*, pp. 111, 120, 122; Fontana, pp. 122, 130, 131.

71. Among other passages: 'Réflexions sur le bonheur' (1943) in *Cahiers*, 2, p. 63. (Such expressions are not popular with some of our modern purists, who, to be logical, should remain silent.)

72. Quoted by Cuénot, p. 391.

73. 9 May 1940, in *LT*, p. 264; Fontana, p. 213. Tientsin, 14 December 1939: 'The essential thing in life: not to see but to *give reality to*.'

74. 26 July 1923, in *LT*, p. 83; Fontana, p. 44. Again, on 26 May 1950, he wrote to a sick friend: 'This enforced retreat will steep you again in God. And that is the one thing necessary.'

75. Note of 26 January 1940. Retreats, 26 October 1941 and 23 October 1945. For Teilhard, who makes use of analogy and does not allow himself to be misled by a completely negative criticism, God is not only Father: as M. André-A. Devaux has remarked, one might almost say that in his goodness he is mother. Cf. letter to L. Zanta, 24 January 1929: 'Once again, the great animating Power, to which it is so good to entrust ourselves, seems – in a motherly way – to have brought the inner and outer forces of the world into harmony around me' (p. 86). Here again we find his thought close to that of his friend Auguste Valensin.

76. 'Réflexions sur le bonheur' (1943). 'The Mysticism of Science' (1939) in *HE*, p. 181. 'The Natural Units of Humanity' (1939) in *VP*, p. 215: If mankind is to face its problems it must become 'a centre of love and adoration'.

CHAPTER 4

1. See *Teilhard missionnaire et apologiste*, pp. 97–8. Also 'The Singularities of the Human Species' in *AM*, p. 262. 'The Grand Option' in *FM*, p. 45; Fontana, p. 47. *Comment je vois. LLZ*, 15 October 1926, 24

January 1929, 24 June 1934 (pp. 72, 87, 110). Letter of 7 January 1934. Cf. letter of 10 June 1917: 'The realism by which mysticism lives' (*MM*, p. 195). *DM*, p. 108; *MD*, p. 119; Fontana, p. 129. We are not attributing to these expressions, as used here, the full significance which Teilhard often gave them.

2. 'La Puissance spirituelle de la Matière' in *Écrits*, p. 442; Eng. trans. in *HU*, p. 66; Fontana, p. 61.

3. Georges Crespy, *La pensée théologique de Teilhard de Chardin* (Éd. universitaires, 1961), p. 168.

4. Peking, 25 and 26 October 1943.

5. Letter of 4 July 1915, in *MM*, p. 59.

6. Note of 9 June 1919. Cf. letters to Pierre Lamare, 23 April and 26 December 1929 (in Speaight, op. cit., p. 162): 'I feel myself at the antipodes of Modernism, etc.' To J.-M., 4 September 1950: 'Fundamentally, there is a basic agreement even between integralists and us, on a fundamental principle that I would call "the law of the maximum Christ". The orthodox believer is the man who gives Christ a maximum of historical reality, greatness and consistence. We shall know in the end, sure enough, who is going to win the cup in that competition.' Quoted by J.-M. Mortier in *Avec Teilhard de Chardin*, '*Vues Ardentes*' (Éd. du Seuil, Paris, 1967), p. 126.

7. 'Le Sens humain' (1929). To Père Auguste Valensin, 14 May 1922.

8. Maurice Blondel and Teilhard de Chardin, *Correspondence* (Herder and Herder, New York, 1965), p. 23.

9. 9 May 1940, quoting 1 John 4: 3 ('and every spirit which does not confess Jesus is not of God. This is the spirit of antichrist'). Here we see the 'integralism' which Teilhard maintains against both 'integrism' and modernism.

10. To Georges Soulages, 29 September 1950. Cf. note of 1 May 1916: 'One cannot be a Christian without believing absolutely and *definitely* in *all* the dogmas. The least reservation or extension or comprehension makes everything vanish.' Cf. Newman, *Apologia* (Sheed & Ward, London, 1946, p. 32): 'From the age of fifteen, dogma has been the fundamental principle of my religion: I know of no other religion . . . religion, as a mere sentiment, is to me a dream and a mockery.'

11. Note of 26 December 1917.

12. *DM*, pp. 94–5, 106; *MD*, pp. 104–5, 117; Fontana, pp. 116–17, 127, etc.

13. 'The Divinity of the Historic Christ' is one of the sub-headings of his 'Introduction à la vie chrétienne' (1944). Cf. *CM* (1950), p. 30.

14. Note of 14 July 1920.

15. 'Outline of a Dialectic of Spirit' (1946) in *AE*, pp. 148–9. 'What Should we Think of Transformism?' in *VP*, pp. 159–60, etc.

16. *DM*, pp. 77–8; *MD*, p. 86; Fontana, p. 103.

17. 'Christologie et Evolution' (1933) in *Comment je Crois* (*Oeuvres* X), pp. 106–7; *HE*, pp. 91–2.

18. 'Christianisme et Evolution' (1945) in *Comment je Crois* (*Oeuvres* X), p. 211. Cf. 'Cosmic Life' (1916) in *WTW*, p. 49.

19. *CM* (1950). Cf. 'My Universe' (1924): 'The smallness of Christ in the cradle . . . [is] in the first place the application of a law of birth and, following on from that, the sign of Christ's definitively taking possession of the world' (*SC*, pp. 60–1).

20. *DM*, pp. 94–5; *MD*, pp. 104–5; Fontana, p. 117. It is always the 'historical unfolding of the Incarnation' that matters: 'Social Heredity and Progress' (1938) in *FM*, p. 33; Fontana, p. 35.

21. Or as the Abbé Monchanin said, following the Fathers of the Church: 'He assumed the whole man of every man, that so he might save all' (*Hommage à Mahatma Gandhi*, 20 February 1948).

22. 'My Universe' (1924) in *SC*, p. 62. Cf. 'The Mysticism of Science' in *HE*, p. 178. 'Cosmic Life' in *WTW*, p. 67. Note, Good Friday, 21 April 1916: 'In Jesus Christ, man suffers, and mankind, and the world.' Cf. Blondel, to the Abbé Wehrlé, 11 July 1904, on Christ's 'stigmatizing sympathy' (*Lettres philosophiques*, Aubier, Paris, 1961, p. 232). Péguy, *Clio*: 'Over all echoes the full reverberation of all – in the person, too, of Jesus' (*Deuxième Élégie*, XXX, p. 431). Joseph Moingt, s.j., *Universalité de Jésus-Christ*: 'In the particular reality of his humanity, Christ assumed the truthful, effective and universal representation of the whole of human truth, etc.' (*Revue de théologie et de philosophie*, Lausanne, 1967, p. 221).

23. 'Cosmic Life', in fine (*WTW*, p. 70). Cf. Pascal: 'Jesus Christ is the object of all things and the centre towards which all things tend'. Bérulle, *Discours de l'état et des grandeurs de Jésus*, 2: *La Vie de Jésus*, 1, 21. Cf. *FTC*, pp. 36–8. The similarity with Bérulle has been noted by Mlle Jeanne Mortier, op. cit., pp. 13–19.

24. Tientsin, 27 November 1939.

25. Peking, 21 October 1945. Note of 1 June 1925.

26. Personal note, undated.

27. Karl Barth, *Church Dogmatics*, 3, 1.

28. Joseph Maréchal, s.j., quoted by É. Rideau, *Teilhard de Chardin: A Guide to His Thought* (Collins, London, 1967), p. 533.

29. *Le Christique* (1955).

30. 'My Universe' (1924) in *SC*, p. 64.

31. 'The Priest' (1917) in *WTW*, p. 207. This invites comparison with M. Blondel, *Une énigme historique*, pp. 103–6: 'Transubstantiation . . . is therefore seen by us as the prelude, hidden under the veil of mystery, to the final assimilation and supreme incorporation in the incarnate Word of all that exists, etc.', with the more exact qualifications given in the notes.

32. 'My Universe' (1924) in *SC*, p. 65.

33. To Père André Ravier.

34. A cry that cuts across centuries and differences of mentality and reminds one of certain passages in St Mark's Gospel. Cf. St Bernard, second sermon on the Annunciation, n. 1: '*Abyssus sane imperscrutabilis, incarnationis dominicae sacramentum; abyssus impenetrabilis. Verbum caro factum est, et habitavit in nobis* (John 1: 14). *Quis enim investiget, quis attingat, quis apprehendat? Puteus altus est, et in quo hauriam non est mihi.*' ('An unfathomable abyss indeed is the mystery of the Lord's incarnation; an impenetrable abyss. The Word became flesh and dwelt among us (John 1: 14). For who may search it out, take hold of it, understand it? It is a deep well, nor have I wherewith to drain it'.) Migne, PL, 183, col. 390c.

35. *Cahiers d'action religieuse et sociale*, 1 October 1967.

36. *Comment je crois*, p. 187.

37. 'Forma Christi' (1918) in *WTW*, p. 253.

38. Similarly, 'the radiation of the Christic light in the universal mechanism of the world' is 'the second phase' of a process in which 'the Transfiguration of the Gospels' is the first. Retreat, Peking, 28 October 1943.

39. 'The Mystical Milieu' (1917) in *WTW*, pp. 144–7. Cf. *RTC*, pp. 60–8.

40. 'The Priest' (1918) in *WTW*, pp. 208, 213. *CM* (1950). 'Cosmic Life' in *WTW*, pp. 65–8.

41. 'Note on the "Universal Element" of the World' (1918) in *WTW*, p. 275.

42. See above, pp. 92–4.

43. *Le Christique* (1955). One is reminded of 'the treasury of absurd anecdotes' that the Catholic religion seemed to the young Claudel, and of the collection of 'infantile nonsense' the young Augustine of Tagaste saw in it before his eyes were opened by the preaching of St Ambrose in Milan (*Confessions*, Bk. 6, ch. 4, n. 5).

44. Retreat notes, meditating on the Nativity – note of 20 January 1925.

45. *Le Christique*. A threefold characteristic, resulting from the threefold reality of the Incarnation, the Resurrection, and the cosmic power of the incarnate and risen Christ – the threefold and single reality of Christ, distorted, as he has just said, by the mind of the unbeliever.

46. Cf. *Teilhard missionnaire et apologiste*, ch. 2, 'From the World to God and to Christ'.
47. *How I believe*. Cf. *FTC*, pp. 185-203.
48. 'Outline of a Dialectic of Spirit' (1946) in *AE*, p. 147.
49. 'The Mysticism of Science' (1939) in *HE*, p. 178.
50. This point is developed in *RTC*, p. 235.
51. 'Some Reflexions on the Conversion of the World' (9 October 1936) in *SC*, p. 123.
52. 'The Heart of the Problem' (1949): 'Nor is it because Christianity has lost anything of its power to attract: on the contrary, everything I am about to say goes to prove its extraordinary power of adaptability and mastery' (*FM*, p. 260; Fontana, p. 272).
53. *Le Christique*, January 1955.
54. 31 October 1920.
55. *Le Christique*. Anything can be used as an argument or made to mean what one pleases. An ardent advocate of Godless theology finds support in Père Teilhard's 'revolutionary thought'. This, he believes, already comes close to atheism, for no other reason than that it is 'Christo-centric'. The fact is that for this writer the Incarnation of the Word is equivalent to God's self-negation, to his self-annihilation, to an end of all transcendence, so that the Christian has to cease even using the name of God. In a more general way, the same writer holds that Catholicism is the form of Christian faith best adapted to propagating his new 'gospel'. Thomas J. J. Altizer, 'Catholic Philosophy and the Death of God' in *Cross-Currents*, 17, 1967.

CHAPTER 5

1. René Le Trocquer, p.s.s., 'La formation de l'intelligence du prêtre de demain' in *Bulletin du comité des études de Saint-Sulpice*, 51, 1967, pp. 71-84. This article describes the present intellectual situation and the programme it entails for the philosophical training of future priests.
2. Cf. a similar sentiment in Étienne Borne, *Passion de la Vérité* (1962). I have so often drawn attention to this law of intellectual life that I have no need to emphasize it further.
3. 'Les Tâches actuelles de la théologie' in *Recherches et Débats*, 51 (1965).
4. As I write, two examples (out of many more) catch my eye. Articles such as Bernard J. F. Lonergan's 'The Dehellenization of Dogma' in *Theological Studies*, June 1967, and Édouard Pousset's 'Remettre sa foi en question ?' in *Études*, September 1967, open up avenues of inquiry in

their treatment, as profoundly thought out as it is faithfully Christian, of points that touch the heart of today's situation.

5. Cf. Lonergan, op. cit., p. 347: 'Catholic theology today has a tremendous task before it . . . But that task is not helped, rather it is gravely impeded, by wild statements on misconceptions or suggesting unbelief.' Harsh though it is, I cannot but quote the remark of a well qualified observer in which he admits that he sometimes wonders whether those who so lightly publicize theories obviously contrary to the faith 'would not be both more logical and more honest if they frankly jettisoned a religion which will never be compatible with annihilation of spiritual being': Pierre-Henri Simon in *Choisir*, October 1967. 'It would be better', says Père Louis Bouyer also, 'to leave Christianity alone, rather than try to convert it into its own contradiction' (*Notre Foi*, Beauchesne, Paris, 1967).

6. Cf. *Theologians at Work* by Patrick Granfield (Collier-Macmillan, London, 1967), p. 197, speaking of the widely publicized 'Death of God' campaign.

7. See the analysis and critical discussion in Lesslie Newbigin, op. cit. For a short history of the word 'secular', cf. Ronald Gregor Smith, *Secular Christianity* (Collins, London, 1966). See also René Marlé's treatment in 'Le Christianisme à l'épreuve de la sécularisation' in *Études*, January 1968. A Lutheran theologian has recently warned us against a false *aggiornamento* which accommodates itself to the spirit of the time, and against a 'conversion of the world' which ends up in 'absorption by the world' (Hermann Dietzfelbinger, in *Rome nous interpelle*, Vol. 2, 1967, p. 181).

8. Mgr Charles Moeller, 'Sur la théologie de l'incroyance' in *Concilium*, 23, 1967, p. 37. This process was the subject of Karl Rahner's lecture in Toronto, August 1967.

9. Cf. E. L. Mascall, speaking at the Toronto Theological Congress, August 1967, on secularism as practically synonymous with humanism, when used as it is used today – wrongly, he believes, and deceptively.

10. Cf. Hans Urs von Balthasar, *Who is a Christian?* (Burns & Oates, London, 1968), pp. 122–3.

11. Cf. Joseph Ratzinger, 'L'athéisme' in *La Table ronde*, January 1968, p. 51.

12. *Le Christique* (1955). *DM*, p. 124; *MD*, p. 136; Fontana, p. 143, etc.

13. Cf. Pierre Smulders, *La vision de Teilhard de Chardin*, 2nd ed., 1965, p. 272.

14. 'Foi d'aujourd'hui et distinctions d'hier' (*Projet*, 16, June 1967, p. 655).

15. (Darton, Longman & Todd, London, 1965), pp. 44, 140–3.

16. See, for example, the really extraordinary adventure described by George Barbour in *In the Field with Teilhard de Chardin* (Herder and Herder, New York, 1965), pp. 104–5.

17. 'Note pour l'évangélisation des temps nouveaux' in *Écrits*, p. 372.

18. Quoted by Robert Speaight in *Teilhard de Chardin*, p. 150.

19. As Fénelon, for example, in his *Lettre à Louis XIV*: 'Will God be satisfied with a devotion which consists in gilding a chapel, saying a rosary, listening to church music, being ready to take scandal, or hunt out some Jansenist? Not only have we to put an end to the war abroad but we have also to give bread to the masses who are dying at home . . . to reform the luxury which is corroding the nation's whole moral behaviour, etc.' (*Oeuvres*, Paris ed., Vol. 7, p. 323).

20. Cf. 'Some Reflexions on the Conversion of the World' (1936) in *SC*, p. 125.

21. 'The Spirit of the Earth' (in the Pacific, 9 March 1931), Section 6, 'The Arising of God' in *HE*, p. 44. Cf. 'Christianity in the World' (1933) in *SC*, pp. 99–100.

22. Dietrich Bonhoeffer, quoted by John A. T. Robinson, *Honest to God* (SCM Press, London, 1963), p. 38. Precisely what the author means by that phrase is more than I would care to try to determine here. Cf. Cornelio Fabro, 'La fin de la religion selon D. Bonhoeffer' in *La Table ronde*, 1968, pp. 33–44.

23. *Le Christique* (1955), p. 5.

24. In particular, he vigorously rejected Toynbee's prophecy that there would be in the future a conflation of the great religions.

25. *Le Christique*.

26. Note of 11 January 1919 (Strasbourg). Letter to the Abbé Gaudefroy, 16 June 1929. Cf. *PM*, p. 142; Fontana, p. 157, on 'a precise orientation and a privileged axis' in evolution; pp. 164, etc.; Fontana, pp. 182, etc., on a 'definite axis of evolution'.

27. *Comment je vois*, Section 24. Cf. note of 13 December 1918: 'The Church is, for me, the axial *current* of life. I feel that this conviction can withstand every doubt and every scandal.' And on 12 March 1920: 'It is the Church alone which provides Omega!' 'Turmoil or Genesis: Is there in the Universe a Main Axis of Evolution?' in *FM*, p. 223; Fontana, p. 231. Cf. also Jean Guitton, *Dialogues avec Paul VI* (Fayard, Paris, 1967), p. 164: '*The Pope*: There is only one Church, the axis of convergence.'

28. It is applied to man in his first essay, 'Cosmic Life' in *WTW*, p. 26.

29. For nothing, as Teilhard says in *Comment je vois*, 'is more false and sterilizing' than the 'alleged uniformity of the laws and forms of

evolution at all levels'; and this is true even within the same order of things (as, for example, within geology). Cf. *HE*, p. 158.

30. *PM*, pp. 114–15; Fontana, pp. 126–8.

31. 'Outline of a Dialectic of Spirit' (1946) in *AE*, p. 147. *PM*, p. 298; Fontana, p. 326.

32. Phylum: 'A highly natural zoological unit' ('The Singularities of the Human Species' in *AM*, p. 218). Cf. 'The Transformist Paradox' (1925): 'Understood in the beginning principally as a need for change, evolution has become principally a law of birth' (*VP*, p. 101).

33. Cf. 'Introduction à la vie chrétienne' (1944) in *Comment je crois*, p. 199. Cf. 'Human Energy' in *HE*, p. 158.

34. Note of 4 November 1916. Cf. letter to Père Auguste Valensin, 31 December 1926: 'I find myself in the position of being unable to breathe apart from Our Lord – and of realizing that without the revelation of history and tradition Our Lord vanishes.'

35. Letter of 16 August 1951. 'Turmoil or Genesis?' (1947): 'The Church is neither an Epi- nor a Para-phenomenon in the growth of the Human Social Organism, but constitutes the very Axis (or Nucleus) about which it Forms' (*FM*, p. 223; Fontana, p. 231).

36. 'The Zest for Living' in *AE*, p. 241 n. Note of 9 July 1921: 'The Church is an axis – but around her there is much of great value, still held in abeyance, which must be given life and be sublimated *by her*.' Cf. *Paradoxe et mystère de l'Église* (Aubier, Paris, 1967), chapter 4: 'Les religions humaines d'après les Pères', in particular pp. 143–6.

37. Chapter 2, 'Constitutions, Decrees, Declarations' (1966): 'Although that Messianic people does not in actual fact include all men (and that not simply in order that it may be seen to be a little flock), yet it is the surest seed for the whole human race of unity, hope and salvation.' Cf. chapter 1, note 1: '*Cum autem Ecclesia sit in Christo veluti sacramentum et signum et instrumentum intimae cum Deo unionis totiusque generis humani unitatis*, etc.' ('Since the Church is in Christ as it were the sacrament and sign and instrument of intimate union with God and of the unity of the whole human race . . .') The Church is, in history, the crucible in which universal reconciliation is first forged.

38. *Adversus Haereses*, Bk. 3, ch. 24, n. 1 (Éd. F. Sagnard, SC, p. 398).

39. Ep. to Diognetus, ch. 6 (Éd. H.-I. Marrou, SC, 33, pp. 65–7).

40. The only difference is the dynamic point of view of the modern texts, which was not, and indeed could not be, explicit in the older writers.

41. 'The Zest for Living' in *AE*, p. 241. 'Introduction à la vie chrétienne' in *Comment je crois*, p. 197. Note of 4 November 1916. Or, to take another metaphor, that of the phylum, 'concentrated in Roman

Catholicism there must necessarily be a phyletic structure and infallibility' (Introduction, pp. 2–3). 'Ecumenism' (1946) in *SC*, p. 197.

42. Or through 'turning back', 'in a reflex movement'. 'Some Reflexions
on the Conversion of the World' (1936) in *SC*, p. 123. 'The Heart of the
Problem' (1949) in *FM*, p. 268; Fontana, p. 281.

43. Cf. *Teilhard missionnaire et apologiste*, pp. 49–50. *Paradoxe et mystère de
l'Église* (Aubier, Paris, 1967), pp. 143–6. To Léontine Zanta, 14 December 1929 (p. 98). Cf. Baron von Hügel, quoted by Jean Steinmann,
Friedrich von Hügel (Paris, 1962), pp. 491, 492: 'Nothing that is deliberately lacking in visible unity can or should serve as a goal . . . In one
single Church, through one Christ alone, we must seek, even more
fully and firmly, the infinitely rich unity of God alone.'

44. At the very moment when Teilhard is preaching the 'duty of state' and
urging enthusiasm in temporal tasks, he is at pains to remind us of the
ever present necessity of prayer and the sacramental life. Cf. *DM*, p. 35;
MD, pp. 38–9; Fontana, p. 66.

45. *The Cost of Discipleship* (SCM Press, London, 1959), pp. 106–7. See
also Charles Moeller and Paul Ricœur in *Concilium*, 23 (1967), p. 43.

46. 'Outline of a Dialectic of Spirit' (1946) in *AE*, p. 149.

47. 'Some Reflexions on the Conversion of the World' in *SC*, p. 123. See
Christopher F. Mooney, s.j.'s analysis in 'Teilhard de Chardin and
Christian Spirituality' in *Thought* (Fordham, New York), 42 (1967),
pp. 383–402.

48. 'The Salvation of Mankind' (1936) in *SC*, p. 148.

49. *Comment je vois*, Section 37. *Le Christique*, p. 7.

50. 'Introduction à la vie chrétienne' (1944) in *Comment je crois*, p. 197.

51. 'As one sees it at the present time, this centre of focus of spiritualization
is completely out of touch with the changing human world that
surrounds it. All around Rome there is, not an iron curtain, but a cot-
ton-wool curtain which muffles all sound of men's discussion and all
expression of human aspiration.' What a change from those days!

52. 28 October 1948, in *LT*, p. 302; Fontana, p. 248.

53. To J. T. de C., Rome, 19 October 1948, ibid., p. 300; Fontana, p. 246.

54. To H. de L., Paris, 9 November 1948. I can still remember the great
impression made on me when I read this letter. There is a similar letter
to Père Pierre Leroy, dated 15 October, on 'the paradoxical and
humbling assurance of representing the earthly extremity of an arc
springing out between man and what is beyond man' (in Speaight, op.
cit., p. 283). Cf. 'Introduction à la vie chrétienne' on 'The Infallibility
of the Church', which crystallizes in that of the Pope, 'formulating or
expressing not his own ideas but the thought of the Church'. Another

form of present-day secularism is activism, which discounts contemplation and all interiority. Here again Teilhard offers us the exact opposite. See above, pp. 126–7.

CHAPTER 6

1. Note of 4 June 1919.
2. *DM*, p. 15; *MD*, p. 15; Fontana, p. 47. Second Paper to Auguste Valensin, 29 December 1919, in *Correspondence*, p. 52. Letter of 21 August 1919 in *MM*, p. 302.
3. *RTC*, pp. 224–5.
4. Both in every aspect of culture and in the field of religion, if he resolutely looked to the future and hoped it would bring a richer harvest, it was because their roots were to extend further and deeper – what a contrast with the rootless concentration on the present which some modern thinkers advocate!
5. 'Mon Univers' (1918) in *Écrits*, p. 279.
6. 'Forma Christi', introduction, in *WTW*, p. 250. In his note on original sin (1920) the charge he made against theologians whom he considered over-conservative in their biblical literalism, was that 'they surrendered the substance of dogma and tradition for an empty shell'. And on 24 March 1921 he wrote: 'We should note how often exegesis, in trying to preserve the letter, sacrifices or kills the spirit': with this he contrasted the older, more liberal and more profound, exegesis of the Cappadocian Fathers.
7. For a fundamental discussion, see *Teilhard missionnaire et apologiste* (1966), part 1.
8. Letter of 25 August 1947, in Cuénot, p. 403.
9. 'Mastery of the World and the Kingdom of God' in *WTW*, p. 88.
10. Second Paper to Auguste Valensin, op. cit., p. 52. Cf. note of 4 October 1921: 'St Francis. *Renovatur facies Ecclesiae!*'
11. *DM*, p. 114; *MD*, p. 125; Fontana, p. 134.
12. Retreat, Peking, 28 October 1941.
13. Letter of 29 June 1926.
14. 20 March 1916.
15. Letter of 22 September 1954, in Cuénot, p. 366.
16. Heading to 'Christologie et Évolution' (1933).
17. To Père H. de L., 8 October 1933.
18. To Père Victor Fontoynont, 26 July 1917.
19. Note of June 1925.
20. Note of 10 January 1920.

21. To Père Auguste Valensin, 11 August 1920, in connexion with the treatment by Rome of Père Rousselot's (d. 1915) teaching, which involved his two friends Valensin and Charles, and, indirectly, himself. Paul VI, we know, recently quoted (giving the exact reference) Rousselot's *Les Yeux de la foi*.

22. Copied out on 17 July 1916 from Paul Thureau-Dangin's *Newman catholique*, p. 64. From p. 99 he also copied this saying, which can be paralleled in Blondel: 'The Church must be ready for converts, just as much as converts must be ready for her.'

23. Note of 15 August 1917.

24. 'Christianisme et Évolution' (1945) in *Comment je crois*, pp. 203–4.

25. For example in a letter to Père Gorce, 4 October 1950. Cf. *Teilhard missionnaire et apologiste*, pp. 42–3.

26. Retreat, Peking, 20 October 1942.

27. Retreat, Peking, 20 October 1943.

28. To Père Auguste Valensin, 2 April 1930 and 26 February 1933. Cf. Retreat, 30 August 1948: 'Grant, Jesus, that I may not be merely the *cymbalum tinniens*!'

29. To Mgr Bruno de Solages, 1935. Cf. Mgr de Solages, *Teilhard de Chardin*, p. 341. Note of May 1925: 'I believe in the hierarchical Church, mediatrix between God and the world: and this is to me a great source of peace.'

30. Retreat, 2 December 1929.

31. Tientsin, 7 May 1927 (pp. 79–80). On the cases of conscience he had to face at the time and the attitude he adopted, see my introduction to *LLZ*, 'The Trial of Faith', pp. 27–44.

32. 17 September 1948, in Speaight, op. cit., p. 282.

33. In *FM*, pp. 260–1; Fontana, p. 273.

34. Letter of 13 July 1925.

35. It is described by Mgr de Solages, op. cit., chapter 3, 'The Tragedy and its Consequences'.

36. To Max Bégouën, Tientsin, 11 November 1929, in *LT*, p. 161; Fontana, p. 117.

37. Hans Urs von Balthasar, *Who is a Christian?* (Burns & Oates, London, 1968), pp. 90–1.

38. Their Provincial, with his headquarters in Lyons.

39. To Père Valensin, Peking, 4 June 1933. ('All right' in English.)

40. Letter to the Very Revd Fr Janssens, quoted by René d'Ouince, *L'Homme devant Dieu*, Vol. 3 (1963), p. 342. 'Faithfully to wait God's good time', he had written in 1918 (in *MM*). Fidelity, with purity and faith, is one of the three forces which effect 'individual progress in the

divine *milieu*': *DM*, pp. 112–21; *MD*, pp. 123–33; Fontana, pp. 132–40.

41. To the same; quoted by Pierre Leroy, s.j., *Pierre Teilhard de Chardin, tel que je l'ai connu* (Plon, Paris, 1958), pp. 57–8; also in *MD*, Fontana, p. 39.

42. Bernard Towers, *Teilhard de Chardin* (The Carey Kingsgate Press, London, 1966), p. 19. On Teilhard's Catholicism, see *RTC*, pp. 234–8.

Acknowledgements

*

The translator and publishers wish to acknowledge their indebtedness for permission to reproduce copyright material as follows: from *The End of Our Time* by Nicholas Berdyaev, published by Sheed & Ward Ltd., 13 Maiden Lane, London, W.C.2; from *The Cost of Discipleship* by Dietrich Bonhoeffer, published by SCM Press, Ltd., 56–58 Bloomsbury Street, London, W.C.1., and the Macmillan Company, 866 Third Avenue, New York, N.Y. 10022; from *Teilhard de Chardin* by Claude Cuénot, published by Burns & Oates Ltd., 25 Ashley Place, London, S.W.1.; from *Correspondence* by P. Teilhard de Chardin & M. Blondel, published by Herder and Herder, 232 Madison Avenue, New York, N.Y. 10016.

Index

In this volume Père de Lubac begins by studying Teilhard's reflections on 'the eternal Feminine', from the first notes he made on the subject when he was in the trenches in 1916 to the time before he took his vow of chastity. He was then questioning whether he was about to banish 'the Feminine' from his life. On reflection his answer to this was an emphatic 'no'. On the contrary, he believed, as did C. G. Jung, that the feminine element needed to be stressed, for he held that love and attraction played an important part in his vision of evolution, which extended even to the attraction of atoms to each other, and indeed he regarded it as the cement of the universe: 'All the great and pure loves, love of God, of speculative inquiry, of the cosmos, are they not transformations of the fundamental, cosmic (= sexual) love, which the individual diverts towards particular objects?'

Père de Lubac analyses and highlights the main themes of the poem in which Teilhard's thought ranges over the transformation of the feminine principle from its pagan aspect to its sublimation in the person of the Virgin and the entity of the Church. There is nothing abstract or evasive in Teilhard's ideas which present 'the Feminine' (Beatrice in particular who acts as a catalyst to his thought) as a symbol of a world in gestation destined to culminate in Christ.

The second essay 'Teilhard and the Problems of Today' is a study by Père de Lubac of the whole of Teilhard's work considered as an anticipation of, and an answer to, problems which play a large part in Christian life today. It is directed chiefly to showing that half a century ago Teilhard was saying that the Christian faith would have to be expressed in terms of an evolving world and that there was no conflict between the World God (the God of the Ahead) and the Christian God (the God of the Above), the universe itself being absorbed in the pleroma.